WOMEN of
DEVOTION
through the
CENTURIES

WOMEN of DEVOTION
through the
CENTURIES

Cheryl Forbes

Baker Books

A Division of Baker Book House Co
Grand Rapids, Michigan 49516

Published by Baker Books
a division of Baker Book House Company
P.O. Box 6287, Grand Rapids, MI 49516-6287

Printed in the United States of America

Library of Congress Cataloging-in-Publication Data

Forbes, Cheryl.
    Women of devotion through the centuries / Cheryl Forbes.
       p.   cm.
    Includes bibliographical references (p.).
    ISBN 0-8010-6351-5 (paper)
       1. Devotional literature—Women authors—History and criticism. I. Title.
BV4818.F67   2001
242'.082—dc21   00-140125

Unless otherwise indicated, Scripture quotations are from the King James Version of the Bible.

A version of chapter one was published in *Lived Religion in America: Toward a History of Practice*, ed. David D. Hall, Princeton UP, 1997.

The papers of Professor Henry Wilder Foote and Family, bMS575, Andover-Harvard Theological Library of Harvard University, Cambridge, Massachusetts, used by permission.

Information regarding Mrs. Charles E. Cowman used by permission from OMS International (formerly the Oriental Missionary Society) archives, Greenwood, Indiana.

For current information about all releases from Baker Book House, visit our web site:
http://www.bakerbooks.com

We whistle while Rome burns, or we scrub the floor, depending. Don't dare presume there's shame in the lot of a woman who carries on. On the day a committee of men decided to murder the fledgling Congo, what do you suppose Mama Mwanza was doing? Was it different, the day after? Of course not. Was she a fool, then, or the backbone of history? . . . *Conquest* and *liberation* and *democracy* and *divorce* are words that mean squat, basically, when you have hungry children and clothes to get out on the line and it looks like rain. . . . I knew Rome was burning, but I had just enough water to scrub the floor, so I did what I could.

Barbara Kingsolver, The Poisonwood Bible

CONTENTS

PROLOGUE

I have a confession.

I have never been a reader of daily devotionals, that staple genre of hundreds of thousands, if not millions, of readers—mostly women, mostly religious, mostly trying quietly to make sense of their nights and of their days, women like my mother.

I confess that I did not understand the draw, the pull, the staying power of the daily devotional or daybook. I confess that I did not understand the form: the scrapbooklike collection that is the genre, the way it reflects the mind, the reading habits, the organizational skills and patterns, the concerns of the compiler and how close a daybook is to a diary, journal, letter. What was a daily devotional other than a grab bag, a hodgepodge, a printed white elephant, or a church jumble sale? What was a compiler other than a thought thief—certainly well below composer on my authorial scale—weighed and found wanting? I didn't consider devotionals to be repositories, safety deposit boxes, or museums of and for great ideas and glorious language and I didn't consider their compilers as savers or saviors or savorers.

I confess that I knew nothing or next to nothing about the compilers of the most widely read daily devotionals—*Daily Strength for Daily Needs* by Mary Wilder Tileston and *Streams in the Desert* by Mrs. Charles Cowman being the most significant—or even how widely read they were and are. But once I did know, once I had found out something of the publishing history of Cowman's *Streams in the Desert,* which was in print for three-fourths of the twentieth century and remains in print today, and after I had discovered other such devo-

9

tionals that clearly influenced Cowman, like Tileston's even more remarkable *Daily Strength for Daily Needs*, more than a century old, I wondered why it had taken me so long to learn what so many readers obviously already knew.

I wondered why I had never read anything about Mrs. Cowman or Mary Wilder Tileston—or Ellen M. Dyer or Mrs. C. S. DeRose, two more devotional compilers. I wondered why I had heard so little about the women whom they quoted in their devotionals, like Canadian poet Annie Johnson Flint or Lucy Larcom, who wrote *A New England Girlhood* (Houghton Mifflin published her *Life, Letters, and Diary* in 1895), or Charles Dickens's protegé Adelaide Procter. Dickens lives on his own; Procter lives through Tileston.

I had read numerous studies by women scholars that resurrected other nineteenth- and early twentieth-century women writers who were well known and widely read during their lifetime, but I never found any mention of Tileston or Cowman or Flint or Procter. Could it be the form they had chosen for their work—the compiled daybook—or was it the subject—religion—that put critical scholars and historians off? As historian Joan Jacobs Brumberg *(The Body Project)* admitted to me when she heard about my study, "We [the community of feminist scholars in women's studies] know these women are out there, but no one's wanted to touch them. I'm glad you're doing it." Well, I wondered to myself, was my project like working with a leper colony? Would I be contaminated by touching these untouchable women? Even my husband, always my first and most critical reader, wondered why I wanted to immerse myself in daily devotionals and the lives of these largely unknown (because undocumented) women.

I had only one answer: Look at the publishing record.

I could not ignore such books or the women responsible for them even if I was not a (typical) reader. There must be a reason, I concluded, why *Streams in the Desert*, the book that began my search and is the center of it, and its models, is as popular today as it was seventy-five years ago. I wanted to find the reason.

Of course, it was not only the publishing record of these women that interested me. Many, many books have enviable publishing records and much longer print histories than Mrs. Cowman or Mary Wilder Tileston (think of Homer or Plato, for instance). I was fascinated by the type of book; the invisibility of the women who compiled and wrote some of the entries; the link of the devotional daybook to such medieval women as Julian of Norwich or Catherine of Siena; the record of reading that these books represent; the quiet, cultural influence these books have had; and their publishing success, which for at least two of the women accounted for the success of the publishing house itself or at least contributed mightily to it. After I began looking for the women whom Cowman or Tileston compiled—reading many nineteenth-century magazines, for instance—I decided that to study a daily devotional was to study the reading habits and tastes not just of the compilers but of their audiences. If we want insight into the concerns and thinking of middle-class readers, particularly women, we could do no worse and perhaps no better than to study the devotionals they bought the way readers today buy lattés and Danielle Steele or Sarah Ban Breathnach's *Simple Abundance* (which has netted Warner a small fortune) at their local Barnes and Noble.

"But which is your most important reason?" my husband persisted in asking. Then, I had no answer; today, as I write I answer, the genre and the way it seems to erase the women who produce the works, even though devotionals are such an important historical and cultural artifact. But I also answer with more questions: Why is so little known about these women who clearly have influenced thousands and thousands of readers? And why do readers find this form or genre so compelling? What exactly, critically speaking, *is* a daily devotional? Are they all the same? Are the devotionals of Mrs. Cowman identical in thought and spirit (and theology?) to those of Mary Wilder Tileston?

As I began thinking about this project, I began noticing daybooks in every bookstore I entered. I found a daily devotional for parents (no longer in print) and one for women (still going strong). Searching cyberspace bookstores, I discovered that contemporary editors, recognizing a hot genre when they see one, have turned the best-known medieval devotionalist, Julian of Norwich, into a daily devotional writer, and that there has been something of a publishing renaissance of women writers like Teresa of Avila, Catherine of Genoa, Catherine of Siena, Margery Kempe, Hildegard of Bingen. There is even a novel about the latter, written as a journal or daily diary. I realized that all those calendars published each year with inspirational sayings were simply truncated, abbreviated, and disposable forms of the daily devotional, which readers can use year after year—a dateless dated book. Journals, diaries, and even memoirs, I decided, share characteristics with daily devotionals, if only the compulsion of writers to record something of themselves to provide shape to life. There is an orderliness about the daily devotional that appeals to our early twenty-first century sensibilities, to our obsession with time.

Such thoughts led me to another question: Are the secular versions of the daybook different in any way from their religious counterparts? The most significant example of a secular daybook is Breathnach's *Simple Abundance*. And what about contemporary *religious* devotionals, daily or not, like those by Kathleen Norris, whose books have been praised by major reviews in the most major reviewing publication, the *New York Times Book Review*, and chosen by its editors as one of the hundred best of the year.[1]

An odd thing happened midway into this project. A friend I had not seen in more than ten years—a fellow writer and editor who had been supporting herself in part by compiling books for various publishers—called, said she was going to be in my area visiting family, and asked whether she could come for supper. As I showed her through our house, she noticed Tileston's *Daily Strength* on a table in my office. Later at supper, when she asked about the book I was writing, she said, "Oh, that's why you had Tileston's book. I wondered what you were doing with it."

It was my turn to be surprised. "How do you know about Tileston?" (She was the first person to whom I had explained my book who recognized the name.) Evelyn Bence had recently worked on an anthology of a well-known evangelical writer and found references to Tileston. (But who Tileston *was* she did not know.) This is one more bit of evidence of the far-reaching influence of daily devotionals, and these *particular* daily devotionals, which anthologize such notables as Elizabeth Barrett and Robert Browning and John Ruskin, alongside little known writers like Mrs. Julia Ewing or Anna Shipton. How many readers were first introduced to Browning or Jeremy Taylor or Margaret Bottome or St. Ignatius of Loyola through reading devotionals? Then our conversation moved on to Mrs. Cowman, and Evelyn grabbed one of her own recent books, *Spiritual Moments with the Great Hymns* (published, as is Mrs. Cowman, by Zondervan), opened it, and read me a story of her brother and *Streams in the Desert:* "My younger brother connects 'I Heard the Bells' with a bad-dream scenario related in the December 25 entry of *Streams in the Desert,* the dog-eared devotional by Mrs. Charles E. Cowman that reigned over the bathroom of our childhood."[2] I loved the image and suspect that Mrs. Cowman would have as well. For Evelyn the point was that Mrs. Cowman credited the wrong person with the Christmas carol—"but try to tell that to my brother." To him, Mrs. Cowman could not be wrong. It had to be the unnamed pastor featured in her story and not Henry Wadsworth Longfellow, that favorite of Mary Wilder Tileston, whom Mrs. Cowman herself quotes at least once. Evelyn's brother shows the authority *Streams* wields for readers.

I also didn't know that I too come from a line of Cowman readers. My grandmother, who turned twenty the year the Cowmans returned from the mission field, must have been one of the first to buy *Streams in the Desert*, the original copy of which she passed on to my mother, who thinks she gave it to my sister Stephanie. Soon, every time I mentioned my work on women who compiled or wrote devotionals, I heard yet another Cowman story: from a former English professor at Calvin College, Char Otten, who said, "Mrs. Cowman—we grew up on her"; or Norm Coombs, retired history professor from Rochester Institute of Technology, whose mother until her death seldom started a day without Mrs. Cowman.

From Tileston and Cowman, Evelyn and I moved to Christina Rossetti, who is ubiquitous in the devotionals I was studying. "Did you know she wrote a devotional too, called *Time Flies*? I've been looking for it but haven't been able to find it. If you do. . . ." Why hadn't scholars talked about *that* book—subtitled *A Reading Diary*? I wondered whether Mary Wilder Tileston had used it for the numerous Rossetti excerpts found in *Great Souls at Prayer*. Evelyn had learned of Rossetti's devotional from another friend who was writing a biography of the poet and in discussing the biography with other Rossetti scholars found that *they* did not know about the devotional—more surprising coincidences, more evidence of how little the scholarly community knows about this genre. My project, getting bigger and bigger, made me feel like a small child tossing pebbles into a lake and watching one ring grow ever larger and multiply into numerous rings, each seemingly unconnected to the others, yet obviously resulting from them.

All of which still had not answered my husband's questions: "Why should you care about these women and their work? Why should anyone care about this genre? Is it really all that important?"

I undertook this study to find the answers, and it wasn't until I *had* studied Mrs. Cowman and the others that I could confidently say, Yes, these women and their devotionals are important; yes, these women are more than compilers; yes, this genre is subtle, complex, shifting, amorphous, porous—in short, critically interesting.

These women and their books are also interesting historically and culturally. For the most part, though the devotionals were produced during tumultuous times, little if any hint of political and social crises enters their pages. Reading them, one feels insulated, sealed off, Saran-wrapped, or Ziplocked—sterilized (*not* sterile or arid), as if preparing for surgery. But even writing the words, *these women and their books*, and making such general comments belie the richness to be found. I discovered that Mary Wilder Tileston is not Mrs. Charles Cowman; their devotionals may share a form but not necessarily the same messages, despite how we stereotype them. And if they are different, as I hope to demonstrate, in what ways are they different? What distinguishes the work of Cowman from Tileston from DeRose and Dyer or from the women who originated the form, the women mystics of the Middle Ages, or from Rossetti, who continued it? Could we open a page of one and, without knowing its originator, tell whose hand had touched it? Or does that even matter? Did the compilers seek invisibility or was invisibility accidentally thrust on them? For invisibility and self-effacement characterize these women as they do few other published women.

Earlier I asked why daily devotionals and their writer-compilers have been ignored or are ignored today. I might just as well have asked why they were ignored when they were first published, for there is no record in *Poole's Index*, the forerunner to *The Reader's Guide to Periodical Literature*, of reviews, publishing notices, or the like for these books, despite their large sales, frequent reprintings, and (even) numerous editions. As with Christina Rossetti's devotional, silence is the order, the rule, but it is not golden. Nor can all the women anthologized in the devotionals be found in those indices. So where were they published? How did Mrs. Cowman come across Elizabeth Cheney, Ella Conrad Cowherd, Aphra White, or Freda Hanbury Allen?

I undertook this study at first because I was curious and because I was ignorant and because I was fascinated by this little-known aspect of the history of publishing. Then as I read and reread the daily devotionals I've named, I began to admire the work for itself; I began to admire the passionate imaginations and the breadth of reading that characterize these women and result in the intriguing juxtapositions found in their books. In short, my surprise at what I found so heightened my curiosity and shamed my ignorance that I wanted, as much as possible, to tell the stories of these women and to explain the genre to which they devoted themselves. However, I soon realized that the story would be incomplete without some discussion of the key women who originally claimed devotional writing as female territory or without some discussion of the women saved from silence by their inclusion in the devotionals still selling today.

My recognition that the devotional form has not died but merely migrated from religion to numerous self-help categories led me to investigate the "nonreligious" daily devotional, which has sold just as well as its religious counterpart. And we can't assume that our bits-and-sound-bites culture is responsible, since before computers, television broadcast journalism, and the World Wide Web, people hungered for nuggets of wisdom, words quickly eaten and easily digested, with a high return of theological protein for the time invested: energy to start the day, which may explain why daily devotionals continue to sell well and why a devotional writer like Kathleen Norris can make the best-seller lists, even in such a secular, "post-Christian" culture as ours.

Here at the end of this prologue let me provide an overview of what follows and acknowledge several people who have influenced my work.

I begin where the book began for me, with Mrs. Charles E. Cowman; move to Mary Wilder Tileston, Mrs. Cowman's only rival and greatest influence, if we can judge by how worn was her copy of *Daily Strength for Daily Needs;* look at Mrs. Cowman's other favorite devotionals from Mrs. C. S. DeRose and Mary Ellen Dyer; offer a biographical and critical introduction to several women anthologized by those devotional compilers; trace the genre to women mystical writers of the medieval period, like Julian of Norwich and Catherine of Siena; and in the epilogue consider contemporary devotionals—where the genre is today.

Each chapter pursues several strands of inquiry, like braiding hair, and at times results in some very long pigtails, as my sister and I called them growing up. There is the strand of biographical inquiry; the strand of cultural, historical inquiry; the strand of religious or theological inquiry; the strand of critical, interpretive inquiry; the strand of inquiry into genre. Although some strands (as with some chapters) may be more interesting to some readers than to others, I attempt to make all strands accessible to all readers and thereby hope that all readers will find themselves intrigued and surprised (even despite themselves).

My readers, my audience. Since I have been talking about you, making assumptions all the while, I should be more specific about who I think you are. As I wrote and rewrote this book, I had two very immediate readers in mind and in person, friends and colleagues at Hobart and William Smith Colleges—Donna Davenport, who teaches dance, and Beth Franks, who taught education—neither of whom reads devotional books but who nevertheless read this book about devotionals. The three of us have been reading each other's work every month for several years, and their comments have spurred numerous changes. Both wanted more about my search for these women, more of my growing personal connection to these women and their ethos. They wanted more domestic information on the women. The unfolding story of these women became for them a kind of detective story, as it did for me. Finally, they wanted me to reorganize my chapters and the way I presented information within each chapter. They were demanding readers. Jean Coombs also read parts of the manuscript and offered helpful insights, particularly about the chapter on Cowman. And since a primary audience is students, I asked one of mine, Lauren Witt, to read the manuscript and comment. She not only read it three times and raised tough, penetrating questions, but she helped to define this book for me—arguing that it is a devotional "at the same time that it is *about* devotional compilers."

But what about men? Were men interested in women devotional writers? Would they be interested in this study? Although I said at the outset that women were the primary audience for daily devotionals, men have also read (and do read) Mrs. Cowman and Mary Wilder Tileston, Julian of Norwich, and others. Men teach religious and women's studies to male students, who even major in these fields. So I asked my minister, Jim Kerr, to read and comment on the manuscript; he, too, has helped shape it.

Indirectly, the committee on faculty research grants at my institution, Hobart and William Smith Colleges, has also influenced this book by providing funds three years in a row that helped defray the costs of research: thank you.

If there is an implicit, unspoken assumption, despite the overt theme of each devotional I consider in the following pages, despite the differences among them, it is the following: God is found in the unlikeliest of places and is never what we expect when we do find him. This was as true for women writing in the medieval period as it was for women writing in the early twentieth century and as it is for us today. But we need help. We need hints and clues and directions; we need guides—people who, as Jim Kerr says, played hide-and-seek with God before we were born and far better than we do. They took seriously Christ's promise that if we seek, we shall find; if we knock, the right someone will open the door. Just as I found with this study, seeking and knocking always bring rewards. You never know what you'll find.

Mrs. Charles E. (Lettie) Cowman

THE PATHWAY OF FAITH, READING IN THE DESERT

She was our mentor.
Floyd Thatcher

The foot of the ladder is a poor place to sit down.
Tibetan proverb, quoted by Mrs. Cowman
in *Charles E. Cowman, Missionary-Warrior*

He said not thou shalt not be tempted; thou shalt not be afflicted, but
He did say, thou shalt not be overcome.
Julian of Norwich, quoted by Mrs. Cowman
in the foreword to *Handfuls of Purpose*

*I*t was 1918 and two spent missionaries return from Asia to the United States on a steamer. Woodrow Wilson is president. The war had just ended.

By 1923 the postwar years have become the Roaring Twenties, complete with flappers, speakeasies, Prohibition, bootleg liquor, bathtub gin, and Sweet Georgia Brown. Harlem hops, the heartland shudders, and from that heartland—Cincinnati to be specific—emerges a small daily-devotional book called *Streams in the Desert:*

Just the Very Book You Will Want for Christmas

Mrs. Chas. E. Cowman has compiled one of the choicest books of Daily Readings that is on the market (365 pages). They comprise gatherings of years, special things that will help one in their perplexities and trials. It is a book full of heart-throbs and victories. Be sure to send in your order early. Price $1.50 post paid.[1]

Mrs. Chas. E. Cowman, a former missionary to Japan and China, wrote a column for the fundamentalist magazine *God's Revivalist;* in 1922 her column is called "Moments on the Mount," in 1925 "Streams in the Desert," in 1926 (and into the 1940s) "Thoughts for the Quiet Hour." Published by God's Bible School, the magazine is affiliated with the Holiness movement. It was at this school, some sixteen years before *Streams* first appeared, that Oswald Chambers, known for the devotional best-seller *My Utmost for His Highest,* had briefly taught.

In 1923 when Mrs. Cowman in *God's Revivalist and Bible Advocate* advertises her book, which she publishes originally for the "Revivalist family" (as the magazine calls its readers), neither she nor anyone else knows or would predict that one day *Streams* would come to rival *My Utmost* as the best-known *fundamentalist* devotional of the twentieth century. Nor does anyone know that Chambers himself is not responsible for his success; his wife put the book together from her husband's sermons, which is more in keeping with the genre, always largely a female form.

Where does Mrs. Cowman come up with the idea for a daily devotional? from Julian of Norwich, whom she reads? from Christina Rossetti? Or is it from Mary Wilder Tileston's *Daily Strength for Daily Needs*? Mrs. Cowman owns the thirteenth edition published in 1907 by Methuen. On the flyleaf we find the following words written by her husband, Charles Cowman: "To my darling Lettie, January 1917, Tokyo, Japan, From Charlie." Tileston is still alive, still publishing. I wonder whether Mrs. Cowman writes a fan letter to Mary Wilder Tileston.

Why does Charlie give Lettie the Tileston devotional? A New Year's present, perhaps, a belated Christmas present, or an early birthday present. How does he even find the English version in Tokyo? Do they know that they are a year away from leaving Japan for good—that Charlie is already dying? Does he anticipate that soon his wife will need every ounce of daily strength she can muster for her—and his—daily needs, that her real life's work is ahead of her while his is already behind him? If this were happening to me, I would be angry; are they?

The "published," but incorrect, date for the first edition of *Streams in the Desert* is 1925. Rather, this is the date when the Cowmans give birth to Cowman Publications, Inc., by releasing a new edition of two-year-old *Streams*. It's the time of the Scopes "monkey trial," which dominates the dailies, with H. L. Mencken, the most powerful journalist of the day, leading the way. Mencken doesn't want anyone to be hornswoggled by those fundamentalist anti-Darwinians. It works. General bookstores across the country can't keep books on science and evolution in stock. *The Voyage of the Beagle* is once more a best-seller. It would seem to have been a bad year for religious books, yet religious bookstores cannot keep *Streams in the Desert* in stock; it, too, is a best-seller, perhaps a backlash to the Scopes trial and Mencken's unremitting anti-Christian diatribes.

Three years later, soon after her husband dies, Mrs. Cowman publishes his biography, *Charles E. Cowman, Missionary-Warrior*, in which she recounts their years as missionaries and the founding of the Oriental Missionary Society (OMS). Although in 1925 Scopes had dominated the news, although in 1928 the country and the world are a year away from the stock market crash and the Great Depression, Mrs. Cowman's biography presents an insular world, disconnected from the small and great events of the day. Yet she and her husband lived in Japan and China from 1901 to 1917, at the beginning of the new millennium, the start of the turbulent twentieth century. The opening years, like the opening of a Verdi opera, plunge Asia and Europe into a maelstrom from which they have not yet extricated themselves entirely: World War I, the Russo-Japanese war, the industrialization of Japan and its growing role as a world leader, Japan's financial and political interests and involvement in China, and in that country the rise of Sun Yat-sen, Mao Ze-dong, and Chiang Kai-shek.

From Mrs. Cowman we receive no hint of the political cyclones in either country. She never admits—or even appears to have considered—how *unsuccessful* their missionary media blitzes had been in Japan and later in China. To read the biography of her husband outside of the historical context is to receive a skewed view of reality, since according to historian Mikiso Hane by the 1930s there were only about 300,000 Japanese Christians among 70 million people; however, he points out that because many converts came from the educated and upper classes they exerted a proportionately greater influence than their numbers would suggest.[2] The Cowmans did most of their work among the rural and peasant populations. Nevertheless, *Streams* entered the political arena through strange channels.[3]

When Chiang Kai-shek died in 1975, his family put four books in his coffin; one of them is *Streams in the Desert*. How often did Chiang read the devotional? Or Madame Chiang? In the archives of the OMS International (Greenwood, Indiana), I find a letter dated December 3, 1950, from Madame Chiang to Mrs. Cowman, thanking her for sending *Streams*. "For several years I have been reading 'Streams in the Desert,'" writes Madame Chiang, "and have found it a beautiful and inspiring volume." She concludes the letter with these words: "May I just add a word of personal appreciation for your untiring efforts to lead people to Christ and know His Power in changing not only lives of individuals but also the social conscience and consciousness of all mankind"—a strikingly ironic statement considering how little interest Mrs. Cowman showed about social and political movements. A further irony: A few months earlier (September 6, 1950), the Taiwan Provincial Governor K. C. Wu wrote to Mrs. Cowman, "I fully share President and Madame Chiang's view that the Chinese troops should have the spirit of Christianity in order to be staunch fighters against Communism."

These two letters and another from a Japanese official are shuttered in plastic sleeves, while the rest of the Cowman papers live in paper folders. In the box that holds the Chiang letter, someone has saved Mrs. Cowman's silks and handpainted, wooden Japanese sandals.

Although many readers know *Streams in the Desert* and know the name Mrs. Charles E. Cowman, how many readers regardless of age know even the bare facts of Mrs. Cowman's life? All the biographies are out of print, as is Mrs. Cowman's own biography of her husband—a book crucial to understanding who she was, for it is the closest we have to an *auto*biography; in it tantalizing and incongruous facts emerge, some significant information is left out, the language and structure of the text are revealing—all of which require us to ask, What kind of book has Mrs. Cowman written? What kind of story is she telling? These questions are not unlike those to ask of her daily devotionals. But first, a catalogue of some important information:

Charlie and Lettie "meet" when she is three months and he two years old (he was born in 1868, she in 1870); his family had left Illinois for Iowa, settling twenty miles from the Burd home on a farm called "The Cedars." Burd is Lettie's maiden name.

Lettie's father is a prominent farmer, eventually president of Citizens Bank of Afton. The family is wealthy. She grows up on the eight-hundred-acre Burd "estate," as she calls the farm, off the state highway in Thayer, Iowa (Union County). "The large house," writes Mrs. Cowman, "was a landmark for travelers." In marked contrast to her own interests, her father is passionate about politics—a lifelong Democrat.

Lettie studies opera with a Madame Barnhart. Although the future Mrs. Cowman never becomes the professional opera singer she dreamed of when she was a girl, she sings all her life—in churches and always during deputations to raise money for the missionary work.

Charlie and Lettie meet again when she is thirteen, he fifteen, thanks to her mother, who invites him home because "he needs a little bit of mothering" (*Missionary-Warrior*, 43). It is 1883.[4] On their first "date," Charlie takes Lettie to a Madame Barnhart concert at which she performs. Each female singer must have her brother escort her to the concert, held at the village Methodist church, and then down the aisle to the platform. But since "mine were all grown up," writes Cowman, Charlie takes their place; this sentence is the only indication that Lettie was the youngest of eight children.

Charlie drops out of high school to become a telegrapher. He is fifteen. Would he have been one of the first to hear the news about the terrible explosion on an unpronounceable island?

Lettie marries Charlie on June 8, 1889, "and a honeymoon began which increased in joy and love, lasting for thirty-six years" (46). After that day, she seldom uses her own name again in her role as a public persona but is (only?) Mrs. Charles E. Cowman. His story is her story, even after his death and up to her own. They have no children.

Although raised good Methodists, they do not become Christians until they are adults, first Lettie through the testimony of a former opera singer, then Charlie.

On September 25, 1924, Charles E. Cowman dies after being ill and nearly bedridden for six years. After Charlie dies, Lettie runs the OMS, continues her monthly column for *God's Revivalist*, and publishes seven books, including two volumes of *Streams*, her husband's biography, and a devotional for young people, *Mountain Trailways for Youth*. She dies on Easter Sunday, April 17, 1960, in San Pasqual Sanitorium, Pasadena, California, at ninety years of age.[5]

These basic facts may seem easy to list, but the opposite is true because Mrs. Cowman so resolutely avoids providing dates, even for the most significant events of her life, which is odd considering her work as a compiler of *daily* devotionals. But there is a good reason: Mrs. Cowman wants to transcend the everyday reality of a particular life, hers or her husband's, and place their story in the genre of myth, allegory, religious epic.[6] That she succeeds is a tribute to her skill as a writer, even if in succeeding she fails as a historian.

Sensing this, and recognizing the traditional rhetorical etiquette of apology, Mrs. Cowman asks in a series of lovely, rhythmic alliterative phrases:

> What pen can fully compass or adequately portray the story of simple faith and mighty achievement; of faithful and heroic service of the subject of this memoir, the missionary whose life literally burned out, the man whose master-passion was missions?
>
> From the foreword, 8

She also "beg[s] indulgence for many shortcomings of which I am painfully conscious, because of the fact that [the book] has been written in the few leisure hours of an exceedingly active life" (9).

Just in case her readers miss the epic character of the story she is telling—that "story of simple faith and mighty achievement"—she returns more explicitly to this point:

> The book is a simple record of a real life, but it is *a sacred romance*, though the principal actor never dreamed that he was anything but a common man, not the missionary-hero we see him to be. It is not a biography in the truest sense of the word; but a sheaf of memories . . .
>
> Page 9; italics added

Notice her repetition of the word "simple" from the previous description "simple faith," but how simple is this record, given the book's rhetorical sophistication and reliance on numerous texts with which readers would be familiar, as I explain later? Notice the words "sacred romance"; notice her metaphor "principal actor"; notice how the words "common man" reinforce the word "simple"; notice her claim that she has not written a *true* biography. And she is right. We never see the Cowmans uncomfortable, dismayed, angry. She is being disingenuous to claim that her book is a simple rendering of an ordinary life. How real a life can this be? Therefore, it is not a biography. "But"— that all-important conjunction—it is a romance. I would even call it a novel in the tradition of nineteenth-century sentimental novels; she adored adjectives and adverbs, like any good female sentimental novelist; her style, in fact, is strikingly similar to that of such women as Lydia Maria Child and others whom I discuss in chapters 4 and 5.

And why should she not write in the manner of a nineteenth-century novelist? The first diary of her life—dated 1905—records her voluminous reading. She revels in Dickens's description of Little Nell's death from *The Old Curiosity Shop* and in his novel *David Copperfield*, copying a passage about marriage, which clearly informs her own views ("there can be no disparity in marriage like unsuitability of mind and purpose"), just as she clearly finds the description of David's love for his wife moving enough to copy. She reads and copies passages from Thackary's *Vicar of Wakefield*, from Ruskin's *Modern Painters*, from Victor Hugo's *Les Misérables*, from Alfred Lord Tennyson's *Idylls of the King*, from Robert Browning's "Saul." Lettie even marks the dates of her reading (i.e., July 15–16 '09 for Tennyson) and the place of her reading ("'The Scarlet Letter' was finished while at 'The Washington'"). Interspersed with these notes we find references to the religious books that help shape her mind, her character, and her style, for example Henry Van Dyke, or *The Next Great Awakening* by Josiah Strong. How often in later years does she recall reading Helen Keller on optimism? It is odd, given the number of women anthologized in her devotionals, that she mentions reading no other women.

The first entry in her 1905 diary, dated January 5, is a long account of a concert she attended by the great romantic pianist Paderewski. Along with her responses to his performance, she records the program, which included the Prelude and Fugue in A Minor by Liszt, *The Serenade* and *Erlking* by Schubert, and several études by Chopin. Just as no writer so exemplifies the sentimental, Victorian literary tradition as Dickens, so no performer better illustrates the romantic tradition than Paderewski. Lettie noted Paderewski's ability to create the "many different instruments—floods of melody—a whole orchestra. Beautiful left hand melody while right hand executed the most difficult trills or runs—intricate mazes and tortuous windings. The rests were wonderful suspenses, marvellous expectations, glorious climaxes—audience so still could hear a pin drop meanwhile." Always the romantic, she continues in this vein for several more pages.

Lettie is also not above noticing and noting the "elaborate toilets" of the women—"white satin dresses, ruffled, and sweeping the dust from the floor ornamented profusely with ribbon, velvet and lace. Immense cloaks trimmed with feather and plumes, beads and bangles." As I read her account, which she concludes by quoting the Song of Solomon about vanity, I connect it with her own always beautifully turned out appearance, as her photographs show. According to Maria Clark, whose residence in California became the Cowman office (and for a time the office of OMS), Mrs. Cowman understood the importance of clothing to an audience and always dressed to please—"stark white shirtwaists," for instance—no matter how uncomfortable she might have found them during deputations. Presentation counted.

Mrs. Cowman's early diary demonstrates too her not insignificant eye for detail and an uncanny ability to sum up character with a few words of observation. That she was observant, and not just in a literary way, Mrs. Clark reports; Mrs. Cowman loved to play the matchmaker, loved babies, and always remembered anniversaries of births and deaths. No matter where she traveled—and she traveled everywhere, especially after Charles Cowman died (for instance, England, India, Estonia)—she kept the local post offices busy.

Reading her personal correspondence reinforces the dramatic reconstructions that Mrs. Cowman loved. For instance, to Lydia Bemmels, her nurse and confidant, the woman with whom she shared her home, her bank account, and her deepest thoughts, she always wrote in superlatives: "Dearest Darlin" or "Darlint'" or "Precious Old Pal." Her letters contain such phrases as "heart like a feather." Mrs. Cowman dramatizes her friend's needs, that staying away from her "was my big battle for I felt that I just could not let you be alone any longer" (January 23, 1937). A letter written from Tunbridge Wells, Kent, July 21, 1936, describes what sounds like a not untypical morning: "This morning I rested till nearly noon, had my breakfast in bed, enjoyed such a good long sleep just what I needed so much."[7]

Or consider a letter written to Lydia on March 9, 1936, from a Bible college in Wales, part of which is quoted here and part later in this chapter:

> Every day last week I thought I would write you, but God kept me right to Himself in prayer. . . . I know you will see God's hand in holding me here on this side, for it is indeed God's own hand, and no mere imagination of my own. . . .
>
> I know that you will feel the loneliness terribly, and I have suffered keenly over that; nothing has touched me more than to leave you there in that little bungalow alone, but since it is of God for this moment it must be right, so let us not only be submitted to it, but 'In acceptance lieth peace.' Let us accept it as God's will, and delight in it altogether, because it is His will. It is a comfort to me to know that you are there taking care of that precious little spot, and there are so many precious things within those walls. You can have no idea what those desk drawers contain, and the clippings, the books, and the manuscript,—they are just a gold mine, and then the memories within those sacred walls, and Lydia dear, never shall I forget that night in September, just before Charles went to heaven, when you called me to take my last look at him. Do you remember we stood together near the head of the bed, and at the doorway of our little breakfast room? On his face was such a peace, and a reflection of heaven, and I saw him actually laying down his life—it seemed to crumble to earth and that was the last time you let me see him until he was in his casket.

Charles Cowman's Biography

Although much of what she writes privately would never have been written publicly, regarding the character of her husband and his heroism there is little distinction between her private and public discourse. Mrs. Cowman knows how words reveal one's true personality. For instance, shortly after the publication of *Streams* she receives "such an unkind letter from _____ asking for a refund for my book"; she writes this in her diary (January 5, 1924; name deleted by Mrs. Cowman). "As it was only worth .25 cents! I replied kindly and sent it. How character shows up in a few written words!"

And to reveal character, a particular kind of character, greatly concerns Mrs. Cowman. She and her husband are larger than life, *uncommon*, not ordinary: set apart, set aside, sacred, set pieces. I name them both because, as I said above, his story *is* her story. If he is a hero, then she is a heroine; if he is "a spiritual genius," then so is she; the book he began she finishes. "The task," she writes, "has fallen to her who sits in the after-glow of that rarely beautiful life" (*Missionary-Warrior*, 7). How common is a "rarely beautiful life"? we might ask the author. She can't have it both ways, though she tries for more than four hundred pages.

Charlie becomes Christian from *Pilgrim's Progress* or one of the martyrs from *Foxe's Book of Martyrs*. He is a mix of evangelist John Wesley with capitalist Horatio Alger, the poor, uneducated boy of humble, obscure background, who nevertheless rises to prominence, founds a missionary "dynasty," and reads John Ruskin and Ralph Waldo Emerson, Charles Spurgeon, and Phillips Brooks. He spurns fame and suffers for the faith—burns so hot and fierce that he burns himself out, as Mrs. Cowman tells us in the foreword. But their story is also something more. It is a pastoral, a Garden story, from Eden to Gethsemane. Mrs. Cowman frames her book explicitly in these terms. At the beginning we see Charles Cowman in a Garden of Eden, near the end, as he leaves Japan, in a Garden of Gethsemane. And gardens or gardenlike settings recur throughout the story, starting with their early years:

> It was the month of May, and the whole countryside was unspeakably beautiful—the fields, the hedgerows, the farms and the cherry trees in full bloom. Wild flowers draped every bank and knoll with beauty. . . . Droves of cattle were seen lazily chewing their cud beneath the spreading oaks or maples; the meadow was deep in sweet-scented clover; the woods rang with bird song . . . there was romance even in their surroundings.
>
> Pages 30–31

Is this a particular place, or is it not the generic, stylized, common view when we picture the Garden of Eden, almost a Currier and Ives view? Even naming May as the month when Charles Cowman begins his real life has mythic significance as the time of birth, rebirth, and renewal. The Cowmans, we sense after reading this, are types of Adam and Eve; and we are supposed to understand the story in these terms, given the pointed way Mrs. Cowman uses stock images from her readers' cultural storehouse of stories and pictures printed in so many King James Bibles published at the time; the opening sentence of the book prepares us for these connections: "An old Bible, the treasured heirloom of succeeding generations . . ." (15).

The lack of detail and telling specificity is carefully staged here. For an Everyman, an archetype, Mrs. Cowman provides her husband the quintessential Garden and an idyllic life, someone who "loved God's great out-of-doors" (31). Her descriptions of place contain no hint of nature after the fall, any more than her descriptions of their missionary work hint at frustrations or failures. For instance, "trials" are never defined, the resolutions always conveyed in spiritualized language, like the following letter written by Charles Cowman that Mrs. Cowman quotes: "This month has been full of testings . . . but I have had some of the nearest approaches to God that I have ever experienced" (140). The language of Charles Cowman's letter is typical of Mrs. Cowman's own language.

From the beginning, then, Mrs. Cowman refuses to provide detail and such telling specificity that would lift *this* life, *this* story from myth to reality; her language is too self-consciously sentimental for anything but myth. We might be any place in the golden era of America's past, not an Iowa farm with brutal winters and parched summers nor in a time of financial and social instability, with banking panics, worker uprisings, the brutal aftermath of Reconstruction in the South. We are out of time, thrust into timelessness: out of history, into myth. Not that Mrs. Cowman is inventing facts but that she is conveying a large(r) truth: Their lives can only be understood and told within the biblical framework of the two Gardens. Or cynics might say that Mrs. Cowman exhibits a selective memory.

When Mrs. Cowman nearly halfway through the book tells the story of building their mission headquarters in Japan, the Edenic language returns: "[Charles] . . . took a trip to the suburbs of the great city of Tokyo, where they found a field of waving grain. The air was soft and balmy. Mt. Fuji with her snow-crowned summit lay just beyond, and from the slight elevation, miles and miles of country could be seen" (168). Here Eden emerges in an unlikely place, for "suburbs" and "city" violate the convention, thus the description that rescues the site and gives it to the reader as a place similar to those described at the outset: "a field," "soft and balmy" air, grand vistas, majestic mountains.

At the end of the book Mrs. Cowman tells of yet another garden, also in Japan, "one secluded spot where one could withdraw from the crowds and be quite alone . . . —the garden at the rear of my sweet, old home" (427). This time, however, in this garden, the vision is all first person singular:

... there in the far distance I saw Japan's loveliest mountain bathed in a color as soft and dainty as the blossoms that make the springtime a fairyland. Gradually the soft color changed to a deep crimson; rivers of glory wound through meadows of gold; mountains of glory reared themselves to the heavens with their cloud-capped summits tipped with the splendor of the dying day; and there, in the lavish glory of the sunset,— the faint foreshadowing of the glory of the Father's House,—I watched the afterglow, the beautiful, the exquisitely beautiful afterglow.

So Mrs. Cowman conceives of her project, of her life, and of the life she and her husband shared as examples, as types; they are "idealized" spiritual leaders. The romanticized language and the gardens where the most significant moments occur reinforce this. Naturally no hint of world events can enter, for to allow them entrance would shred the gossamer threads of her tale: mortality impinging on immortality. There is, however, one startling reference to contemporary events:

When the steamer brought him to his native country again, it was just at the time when America was at the feet of a great explorer. The one had explored for science, the other for Christ; the one had risked life for curiosity, fame, adventure, the other to win souls to the crucified, risen, ascended, and glorified Saviour of the lost. Thousands upon thousands were doing honor to a man who lived for the world, while, excepting to the few saints even the name of Charles Cowman was unknown! Meanwhile, the noble missionary has verified the promise: "The people who do know their God shall be strong, and do exploits." Yes, exploits worth doing, and exploits infinitely greater than the discovery of continents, for the exploits of God's chosen ambassador will bring glory to Him, and joy to the redeemed through the countless ages of eternity, long after the judgment fires have passed upon this earth.

Page 330

This is a carefully crafted passage, rhetorically balanced, using a series of contrasts in a parallel structure sentence to sentence. For that reason alone it is notable. But notice the detail Mrs. Cowman leaves out, one that frustrates me.

Mrs. Cowman fails to name the "great explorer," an astonishing fact. But the omission reinforces her argument that appearances are deceiving, that Charles Cowman, not the explorer, deserves the recognition of humanity. The explorer is unimportant except as backdrop and contrast with her husband. Millions of Americans may not know her husband's name, much to her chagrin, but heaven does, God does, and who is more important, God or millions of Americans? At the same time, God *does not know* the great explorer, any more than we do. Thus from God's perspective, and so from Mrs. Cowman's, this explorer can have no name, cannot be named. Mrs. Cowman writes, therefore, as if from God's view (or as if her view and God's were identical).

I, however, want to know the explorer's name and story. Checking the historical records and the *New York Times* for 1918, the year the Cowmans returned to the States, a librarian and I discover that only one famous explorer makes the news that year: Sir Ernest Shackleton, who was then the most famous explorer of the Antarctic and had been knighted by King George. He is best known for his Antarctic expedition of 1914 on a 300-ton Norwegian barkentine he named *Endurance*. Setting sail a week after World War I began, August 8, he and his crew were forced to abandon the ship on October 27 because extreme ice packs crushed the ship. For six months in three lifeboats they drifted north until the pack began to break, and they could sail west, eventually reaching Elephant Island, about 600 miles north of the Antarctic peninsula. Shackleton realized that no one would find them in such a remote location, so he and five men sailed one of the boats to South Georgia, 800 miles in the dead of winter across formidable ocean. His success in only sixteen days, and the subsequent rescue of the rest of his men just four months later, still ranks as one of the greatest adventures of all time. His own account, *South*, was published in 1919.

Mrs. Cowman's readers would have been able to recall Shackleton's feat and might well have read his book. I can imagine readers not simply knowing his name but even lionizing him, as Charles Lindbergh would later be lionized or John Glenn. It is hard to conceive of any American, regardless of his religious beliefs, resisting the hoopla surrounding a great hero or explorer, for although he was British, Americans were riveted by the tale, as they had been by those of Arctic explorers Sir John Franklin and Elisha Kent Kane. And how different in principle was Shackleton's exploration from the Cowmans' own?

So why does Mrs. Cowman refuse to name him? By doing so, she keeps time at arm's length in order to argue that only eternity matters. Her silence also offers a subtle rebuke for her readers who might not have known Charles Cowman prior to reading her biography but who might have known Shackleton. At the same time she mitigates what would otherwise be read as crass jealousy, although it lurks between the lines and just below the surface, like a blood blister painfully visible beneath thin, pale skin. The skin is Mrs. Cowman's, the blood blister those foolish Americans who failed to see the truly great man who had returned to live among them. She criticizes the explorer because he risked his life only for fame and adventure and "lived for the world." But did he? How are we to judge her view without the man's name? Were the biography really a novel, critics would argue that Mrs. Cowman is an unreliable narrator; and she is. How else to reconcile her view with Shackleton's own words: "In memories we were rich. . . . We had seen God in his splendors, heard the text that nature renders."

Am I misreading Mrs. Cowman? Consider another, earlier instance. A visitor from a well-known college asks Charles Cowman for his credentials, a strange, even trivial, incident to record, given how many details she ignores, except that it provides Mrs. Cowman the opportunity to chastise the woman (and, implicitly, skeptical readers) for failing to recognize "a new force" that had appeared, "a leader [who] was a decade or two ahead of his time" (141). For the next three paragraphs she argues that "scholar" and "great man" are mutually exclusive, concluding with the astonishing admission that Charles Cowman had been given an honorary college degree, something "he never permitted . . . to become known"; instead he buried the parchment in a desk drawer. However, earlier she claims that Cowman "spent six years in diligent Bible Study," first at Garrett Theological School in Evanston, Illinois, and then at the recently established Moody Bible Institute (86). Yet even in this passage Mrs. Cowman argues that "the supreme qualification for holy service is not intellectual but spiritual" and cites the eminent A. J. Gordon to support her defense (87).

Mrs. Cowman provides so many provocative hints about their own identity, so many inferences to be drawn about their lives. Another example comes immediately preceding the contrast between the explorer and the missionary. Cowman's associates notice "a character mellowed and rounded out by all the work and all the suffering of his life" (329). Here Mrs. Cowman contrasts the original Charles Cowman, who apparently was not mellow or rounded out—edgy? demanding? impatient?—with the new Charles Cowman. Robert Wood, OMS historian, claims that Charles, no less than his wife, saw life as a Greek or Shakespearean tragedy, with himself as principal among the dramatis personae. Every common event becomes uncommon in their lives, more ecstatic, more tragic, more emotional, more "poetic": miraculous. A little earlier we find another comparison: "It was night when the boat lifted anchor and put to sea and his last look at Japan was under the stars in the moonlight. Long he watched the receding shore-line. . . . A farewell tear dropped upon the hand of her who held his" (329). What scene is Mrs. Cowman describing? What comparison is she making?

Two.

As I read, I recall first the last lines from *Paradise Lost*. Adam and Eve leave the Garden in an elegiac frame of mind, in the same way that Charlie leaves Japan—that final, poignant look back at their earthly paradise. Then, thinking of the other Garden, I read, the "Master in the Garden when He was about to be separated from His disciples" (329). Charlie is implicitly likened to Adam and Eve (and she to Milton?) and explicitly compared to Christ. But there is more to the story of Gethsemane than Christ's separation from the disciples, if we can even say that it is the main point. Isn't it, rather, that Christ is about to be betrayed and sacrificed, that Christ has gone from popular local hero, honored by "thousands," to pariah? This comparison serves as a set piece and a setup for the later comparison. The question should not be, then, Who is the famous explorer? but rather, Who is Charles Cowman? and she provides the answer and determines our response: Ah, he is just like Christ; he is a Christ-figure.

There is another small but significant detail worth noting in these passages and throughout the biography. Mrs. Cowman seldom uses her husband's name, generally referring to him instead by the third person singular pronoun. When she does use his name, she always writes "Charles Cowman," both stylistic choices heightening his larger than life, epiclike character. Never does she write "my husband" or "Charlie." Her choice is in keeping with the elevated language and mythic quality for which she is striving: "Charles Cowman being dead, yet speaketh" (425). Still not content with her previous comparisons, she adds a few more: Martin Luther, George Fox, John Wesley, the latter particularly appropriate given the Cowmans' links to his theology through the Holiness movement. From the opening of her book, where the epigraph is a quote from John Oxenham: "Greatheart is dead they say," she has been searching for the right comparison. Wood explains that from then on Mrs. Cowman refers to him as "Greatheart" and dedicates the twentieth anniversary of his death in the September *Missionary Standard* to "Greatheart whom the world has said is dead . . ." (16–17). There is more than a little sense that Mrs. Cowman worshiped Charlie, and it would not have surprised me had I learned that she kept the room where he died as a shrine for the next thirty-six years.

Cowman's Devotional Writing

As Mrs. Cowman ends her story, she veers into the form that she spent the rest of her life perfecting, for the last pages of the biography read almost as if they could have been included in *Streams in the Desert* or one of the other devotionals she wrote over the next three decades. Claiming that "bookmaking is not my calling," she nevertheless publishes seven books, and in the foreword to her last, *Handfuls of Purpose* (1955, retitled *God—After All* in 1971), she briefly provides a publishing history with the reasons why each book came into being. Quoting Julian of Norwich (see the beginning of this chapter), Mrs. Cowman explains that "we are to rise unvanquished after every blow. . . . To preserve the fruits of triumph one must help his fellow-warriors to gain a similar conquest. . . . For this cause *Streams in the Desert* was born" (v). Of course, she is looking back from the perspective of thirty years. But closer to the initial publication is that letter to Lydia Bemmels of March 9, 1933. What does she recommend to her friend? One of her own devotionals, the one that followed *Streams* but shares with it the purpose to help readers like Lydia Bemmels confront disappointments joyfully. If Mrs. Cowman had a particular reader in mind (other than herself, that is), then surely her "precious, precious Lydia" was she.

Next, Mrs. Cowman lists *Consolation* (subsequently retitled *Words of Comfort and Cheer*)—a special ministry, Mrs. Cowman says, for those who mourn. As she writes to Lydia, "take 'Consolation' for Oct. 26, and read it, especially the poem, 'Die to thy root, sweet flower'"; yet what follows is Mrs. Cowman's own experience with the poem and ends with a strange reference to her birthday: ". . . but on March 3rd. I arose and the Lord said, 'Your captivity is at an end this day.' So I tidied up my room, put on a nice fresh frock, and celebrated my birthday all alone with Jesus in my room in the College; not one soul knew about it, and it was one of the most wonderful days of my lifetime." It is as if Mrs. Cowman is seeking to assuage her friend's loneliness through the story of spending her own birthday alone—unnoticed, unmarked. The letter, however, like so much of Mrs. Cowman's life, is a strange blend of bathos and business. But what might disturb a modern reader—or at least what chills me—are the final lines: "And now this long epistle must close. I have had to dictate it, as I do not have the time to personally write with my pen, and you will understand." Am I too cynical in wanting to ask Mrs. Cowman, What about all the time you had on March 3, the day you say you spent all alone, your birthday unmarked?

In 1938 Mrs. Cowman releases *Springs in the Valley* as a companion to *Streams.* When a youth leader asks her for a young people's devotional, she produces *Mountain Trailways for Youth.* Just as she avoids dates in *Missionary-Warrior,* she does so even here, in a publishing "history." (Thus I find it ironic that her publisher would produce *two* calendars using *Streams.*) She writes, "another interim of time passed" before she compiled *Traveling toward Sunrise,* a devotional for those who have written to her "in the eventide of their life," as she herself then was. Finally, 1955: "Long had the year . . . been talked of as a memorial year. Joshua 14:10" (vi). But she fails to quote the verse, not one that readers would have been able to recite from memory; Joshua, like Mrs. Cowman herself, is eighty-five when he writes a brief history of his own work. *Handfuls of Purpose,* she concludes, "crowns my task!" "the answer to the latest surprise requests," but for what, specifically, and from whom, she does not say. She dates her foreword "September 1955," uncharacteristic and significant because she usually ignores dates: The only date that matters to her is September 25, 1924, the day Charlie "fell asleep," as she always refers to his death. Two years later she enters the final phase of her life, a three-year illness, during which she gives her files, papers, writings, and books to Nulah Cramer, who with the help of Marie Taylor puts together a new *Streams in the Desert* (volume two), published in 1966; this, fittingly, becomes Mrs. Cowman's last work, the two volumes of *Streams* the bookends of her life.

Streams in the Desert

Devotionals are, on the surface, homespun, ordinary, and serviceable, something to read with coffee in the morning, something to think about while waiting for the bus or the carpool, while shoving clothes into the washer or pasta into boiling water. Most devotionals use a plain style and do not attempt the learned discourse of systematic theology; Mrs. Cowman's are no exception. Yet this definition of a daily devotional is in marked contrast to the elevated style of *Missionary-Warrior*, with such sentences as "With such a record behind it, such a foundation under it, and such promises before it, this work of faith may hope to stand until the King Himself appears" (408): the carefully balanced, parallel structure and the combination of the noun "faith" with the verb "hope," recalling 1 Corinthians 13.

Perhaps the paradoxical combination of ordinary concerns and exalted language reflects the paradoxes of Mrs. Cowman's own life, habits of mind, and readerly interests. Although she lived and worked in the twentieth century, though she had roots in the literature of spiritual ecstasy and the Protestant Reformation, Mrs. Cowman, as I said, nevertheless was Victorian in her sensibilities and her sentimentalities, nowhere better revealed than in her numerous descriptions of nature that provide a thematic thread for the "sacred romance" of Charles Cowman's life. It is providential irony that she and her husband leave for Japan on February 1, 1901, a few days after Queen Victoria's death on January 22.

Mrs. Cowman's orotund prose rhythms, as the passages already cited indicate, and her unexpected spiritual affinities, as in her own citations of such contrasting texts as Tibetan proverbs, sermons of Jonathan Edwards, *and* sound bites from the late queen, recall the previous century. Mrs. Cowman advocates hard work and sacrifice to gain spirituality, the opposite of the Reformation theology of grace, and in *Streams* she quotes far more often a Victorian, like the broad churchman and Episcopal bishop Phillips Brooks (1835–1893), who advocated making chapel attendance voluntary at Harvard University,[8] than a Puritan. Although we find repeated references to Brooks, we find only an occasional excerpt from *Pilgrim's Progress*, one citation from Richard Hooker,[9] a couple from Jonathan Edwards,[10] and Matthew Henry.[11] Theodore Parker[12] or Ralph Waldo Emerson appear, as does Margaret Sangster, a turn-of-the-century advocate of women's independence and columnist for *Collier's*.[13]

Mrs. Cowman believed and practiced "that old-time religion," though many contemporary conservative Christians would find her ordination to the ministry at odds with a literal interpretation of the

Bible and fundamentalist theology, which Mrs. Cowman espoused, even as she exercised considerable latitude in her own biblical interpretations. In her choice of texts she seems unconcerned about theological purity, as the partial list of authors mentioned above shows. In fact conventional categories of religious history and theology don't apply when it comes to understanding *Streams*. We cannot assume that Mrs. Cowman interprets certain passages or terms the way theologians even of her tradition would do or that she was much concerned about a writer's theological bona fides.

A few years ago Zondervan received a letter about this very issue. The letter writer claimed that someone *must* have altered Mrs. Cowman's text to include the highly suspect Phillips Brooks, who was, insisted the writer, a believer in evolution and on those grounds alone could not be called a Christian. Of course, no one had altered the text. What mattered to Mrs. Cowman, apparently, was the use to which she could put Phillips Brooks, not whether he held evolutionist views. And Phillips Brooks is not the only "suspect" Christian to be found in *Streams*. Readers can also find writers quoted whom no one would find in Camp Christian, not even the broadest and most inclusive camp we might imagine.

Whether or not Mrs. Cowman's readers would admit it, Mrs. Cowman's vision is fraught with contradictions, twists, reversals, paradoxes, and theological conundrums. It is personal and impersonal, triumphant and tragic, hierarchical and egalitarian. Still, it offers a way for readers, women in particular, to make sense of the inescapable, inevitable, essential daily hardships of life. Not in spite of, but because of her contradictions, paradoxes, and indifference to theological niceties, Mrs. Cowman gives readers hope. Moreover, her own practice of reading recorded in *Streams* offers readers a model they can imitate day by day and year after year; that recording makes her a writer of great significance in understanding women's spirituality in twentieth-century America.

To support this, I want to look at a few key meditations that reveal the themes of suffering, despair, and isolation, which concerned Mrs. Cowman; these themes structured her own reading, and so structure *Streams in the Desert*, making the book a primary example of twentieth-century popular piety unmediated by minister or theologian. The themes suggest why Mrs. Cowman has had and continues to have a profound and loyal following. Although we cannot ever know for certain what a reader takes from a text—even when we are the readers—the place to begin to answer why *Streams* has exerted such influence is with the text itself, the text and its creator. And so in searching the text, we will inevitably be searching for Mrs. Cowman herself.

The Title

Mrs. Cowman has chosen a compelling and fitting title for her devotional for several reasons. First, it conjures up images of Old Testament prophets, of John the Baptist, and of Jesus and his forty days in the wilderness. Second, it echoes certain Bible passages, like the one prophesying John's construction job: to make a straight highway in the desert. And third, it is a quote from Isaiah 35:6: "Water will gush forth in the wilderness and streams in the desert."

This passage follows the famous section used by Handel in *Messiah* about deaf ears unstopped, blind eyes opened, and lame limbs leaping like deer. The desert is a metaphor for the sinner whom God redeems, transformed into a land of crocuses, cedar trees, grass and papyrus, and pools of bubbling springs. In short, the desert is no longer a desert once God gets his hands on it, and a sinner is no longer a sinner. But Mrs. Cowman doesn't use the metaphor in this way. Rather, life remains a desert; we are never out of the slough of despond, to use Bunyan's image; we are never out of the desert. Occasionally, however, just as in a real desert, we find a stream to wet the parched throat and wash the dust off feet and hands. God gives us just a little water so that we don't die of thirst in this weary and wicked and inhospitable land. He gives us just a foretaste of what's to come, but never the thing itself. All else must wait until the other side of death. On this view of life hangs Mrs. Cowman's view of the spiritual life, which she echoes in *Missionary-Warrior*, imagining her husband still at work in heaven.

Fourth, Mrs. Cowman's title is compelling because it presents both desert *and* stream, thirst *and* water, barrenness *and* fecundity. It captures the continuum of life, even if Mrs. Cowman's spiritual bent is to lean toward dust rather than loam, such a contrast to her perspective in *Missionary-Warrior*. A stream often disappears, or goes underground, only to reappear hours or miles later; a metaphorical or religious stream behaves no differently.

The Format

Streams follows the conventional devotional format of Bible verse, brief meditation—usually a page or less—followed by a prayer, poem, or short concluding comment. In many ways, the devotional appropriates the form of printed sermons from seventeenth-century America, which also began with a biblical text, followed by a sermon on the text that incorporated numerous references without attribution (or, as David D. Hall puts it in his story of popular religion in seventeenth-century New England, "by patchwork quoting"[14]). Mrs. Cowman's text does not purport to be a full discourse on the Bible verse quoted, even though the meditations have the force of popular hermeneutics, and thus her role is analogous to that of a minister.

Several important assumptions about spiritual life underlie the genre and Mrs. Cowman's work in particular. A believer needs time during the day for meditation, every day of the year. Such meditation should consist of reading a Bible passage, thinking about its meaning and possible personal significance, and praying. Popular religious books aid a believer in the devotional life. This has always been their purpose, and the belief that a true Christian sets aside daily time for Bible reading and meditation goes back at least to the Puritans.

Mrs. Cowman expected her readers to read and reread her devotional year after year after year. She encourages readers, not necessarily by giving them *new* insights, but urging them to do what they already know they ought to do. Thus Mrs. Cowman uses metaphors, stories, and experiences familiar to her readers to offer daily spiritual sustenance—the same sustenance she has received in her own devotional life, for as we know, Mrs. Cowman's texts *are* the texts she herself read and studied. They show the eclectic nature of her reading—everything from Oswald Chambers to Robert Browning. We also find Francis de Sales, Frances Ridley Havergal, Harriet Beecher Stowe, Christina Rossetti, Adelaide Procter, Lucy Larcom, Anna Shipton, Madame Guyon, and, of course, ubiquitous, the Holiness leader and writer Hannah Whitall Smith, all of whom Tileston also read and used.

Streams, then, is pieced and patched together—a hybrid text, an appropriated text—though it is easy for a reader to forget this, so compelling is the force of the person creating the text. The mind of Mrs. Cowman becomes the thread, stitching Bible verse, daily routine, season, and religious attitudes together: her connections, her responses, her readings of women like Mary Wilder Tileston and other late-Victorian devotionalists whom she marked and copied onto scraps of paper, old envelopes, bills—detritus to devotion. This is not only metaphorically so but literally so. An undated book I discover in the OMS archives shows how Mrs. Cowman compiled her devotionals. Each page of the book has a date, an idea, a verse, a poem, sometimes several, which Mrs. Cowman obviously thought would anchor that particular entry, for instance January 14, "*Mr. Moody* etc." And in between the pages she records other thoughts, prayers, citations: for instance on the back of a coupon for a piece of "gorgeous stainless steel flatware" from the "Better Food Market," I read "Streams Apl 7" and the title of a song. On the back of a letter from Peniel Missions, Mrs. Cowman double-underlined the words "ran ahead of God." Mrs. Cowman used a scrap of letter from Don Hillis to record Judges 5:8. Although the book itself is undated, the date on one of the letter scraps, 1956, suggests that she never stopped thinking about devotional compilation, that the habit begun during the six years of her husband's illness stayed with her even until the last years of her own life; the outline found in the book could well have served as the basis for the posthumous *Streams* two.

For a reader who does not have a library, who does not know many religious writers, or who lacks the time to invent meditations, a dated daily devotional fills the gaps—a package deal: Bible, wise thoughts, prayer. Mrs. Cowman even includes an entry devoted to the subject of daily devotions, September 29. Because the entry is interesting from several perspectives, I will return to it later. Here let me point out that in the entry she asserts that a great Christian is never in a "religious hurry" in his devotions but spends much time "in his closet," the reference being to Jesus' metaphor about prayer (Matt. 6:6).

However, doesn't this reject the very notion of a daily devotional, which is something that can be read quickly? This is not the only odd rejection of the genre to be found within the genre itself. We also discover that *Streams*, supposedly putting the Bible at the heart of its discourse, includes only brief Bible passages used problematically. Is *Streams* food for the spiritual life, or is the book a symptom of someone starving spiritually? Is *Streams* an appetizer or the whole meal? Whether Mrs. Cowman intended this, in practice readers use her devotional to fill the need for and requirement of daily meditation without their expending much time or effort—"daily devotions," a ritual emphasized by her fundamentalist religious tradition, which, at the same time, abhorred the idea of ritual in worship.

Mrs. Cowman begins her book with "A Personal Word," which instructs us how to read her text and what to expect from it and from God:

> In the pathway of faith we come to learn that the Lord's thoughts are not our thoughts, nor His ways our ways. Both in the physical and spiritual realm, *great pressure means great power!* [italics in original]. Although circumstances may bring us into the place of death, that need not spell disaster—for if we trust in the Lord and wait patiently, that simply provides the occasion for the display of His almighty power. "Remember his marvelous works that he hath done; his wonders and the judgments of his mouth" (Ps. 105:5).
>
> Page 6

And then the controlling verse from Isaiah follows: ". . . in the wilderness shall waters break out, and streams in the desert." The stream has been present all along, merely invisible. Just so with God, she implies, who doesn't always make sense to us; we must wait and watch and trust, no matter how irrational or barren life may seem. These instructions also apply as we read Mrs. Cowman's own text, which doesn't always seem to make sense. But if we wait, watch, and trust her, Mrs. Cowman will pull the pattern together. The way she works mirrors the way she sees God work.

Mrs. Cowman also claims a kind of spiritual one-upmanship on behalf of her readers. Not only is life hard, but life is hard in order to make us hardier than it. She advises us to embrace hardship when it comes; she even comes close to recommending that we seek hardship. For when judged by the life of the spirit, people with hard lives receive greater benefits and more power than those who slide through life—indeed, they receive the greatest power. This is certainly in keeping with her view in *Missionary-Warrior,* where Mrs. Cowman exalts her husband and his work by the degree to which he suffered. It isn't a big step from accepting hardships to advocating that we seek hardships to increase our patience and fortitude. She offers us the quickest way to increase our spiritual capital. Maria Clark told Robert Wood in 1976 that Mrs. Cowman, largely from material sent to her from well-wishers, compiled the devotional during her husband's six-year illness. (Clark also claims that she herself wrote some of Mrs. Cow-

41

man's columns for *God's Messenger,* because she "knew" what Mrs. Cowman would have chosen.)

Mrs. Cowman captures an ancient Christian theme about the paradoxical relationship between powerlessness and power, which is particularly significant for women who have long been encouraged to embrace powerlessness as the means to ultimate power. Women who are denied worldly power can have something better, spiritual power. Mrs. Cowman's devotional offers a way out for women who feel powerless and trapped by their circumstances. In addition, Mrs. Cowman suggests that she herself understands her readers' feelings of powerlessness, the daily struggle to survive, an irony when we recall her ordination and her years of influence in OMS.

Let's consider, then, the entry for January 1 (in chapter 2 I quote the full entries for Tileston, but the length of this entry—two pages—makes this impractical and the wider availability of *Streams* makes it unnecessary). Mrs. Cowman begins with a quotation from Deuteronomy after which in a rare, direct address to her readers says: "Today, dear friends, we stand upon the verge of the unknown. There lies before us the new year and we are going forth to possess it. Who can tell what we shall find?" (7). Her direct address to us, her dear friends, indicates a relationship, an intimacy, between writer and reader. We could dismiss it as Victorian affectation, as editor James Reimann apparently does in the contemporary version, since he (wrongheadedly) deletes the phrase; or we could regard it as Mrs. Cowman's feeling for and understanding of her audience, a conclusion warranted by her work as a missionary and the numerous deputations, talks, speeches, vocal concerts, and ladies aid meetings she undoubtedly attended and gave. Her voluminous correspondence is further evidence that she knew her readers.

The opening address serves another purpose as well; it puts writer and reader on the same level, sharing the same fears, the same uncertainties, and the same concerns. Mrs. Cowman lays her hand on the arm of her reader—a gesture of concern, warmth, and mutuality. Unlike an authority, a male preacher, for instance, Mrs. Cowman closes the distance between herself and her audience. Her reader never feels preached at or looked down on from some high spiritual point. Mrs. Cowman assumes a relationship with her reader that from the beginning is nonhierarchical, despite her overarching hierarchical view of reality. In Mrs. Cowman we find a woman able to convey contradictions without seeming to contradict. She makes the contradictions fit into a meaningful pattern, which is a large part of her appeal. Her use of Deuteronomy is a case in point.

The verses refer to the Israelites entering and possessing the land of Canaan, a beautiful, lush land, evocative of all that is bountiful in God's creation. By association and analogy, Mrs. Cowman connects Canaan with the unknown new year. But notice what happens. The good land of Canaan, about as un-desertlike as a land could be described, becomes a land of terror, pain, and desolation. Mrs. Cowman turns golden sand into burial mounds, Mediterranean warmth into a land blighted by winds and desolate of tree and fruit. What happened to the woman who could write the following? "It is only when the leaves have left the tree and the bare arms are lifted against the clear winter sky that you can see how every tendril, every twig turns Heavenward and, looking upward through the bleak and bitter blasts, waits to be clothed upon with immortality" or "there before us was a picture. . . . Beautiful Mount Fuji, clothed in its uppermost garments of thick white snow, had caught the most brilliant light, and shone in it like melted gold, with shadows of pure soft grey across it here and there. . . . A deep crimson cloud hung gently over its crest. . . ."[15]

In the first entry of *Streams*, the hills, a word that conjures up images of gentle, rolling, friendly land, which Isaiah couples with valleys, rain, and fecundity, become sinister:

> The land is a land of *hills* and *valleys*. It is not all smooth nor all downhill. If life were all one dead level of dull sameness it would oppress us; we want the hills and the valleys. The hills collect the rain for a hundred fruitful valleys. Ah, so it is with us! It is the hill *difficulty* that drives us to the throne of grace and brings down the shower of blessing; the hills, *the bleak hills of life* that we wonder at and perhaps grumble at, bring down the showers . . . how many would have been killed . . . but for the hill—*stern, hard, rugged, so steep to climb.*
>
> Page 7, all but initial italics added

God's hills are a gracious protection for his people against their foes! The hill described is really a mountain, and the only mountain Mrs. Cowman knew intimately and wrote about repeatedly is Mount Fuji.

But when she writes and compiles *Streams*, she is nursing her dying husband; in the early 1920s all hills look rugged and steep to climb;

all life looks bleak, grey, ash-covered. According to Robert Wood, Lettie Cowman "look[ed] for the tragic in life. . . . *Streams in the Desert* resulted from her heightened sense of pain, melancholia, and pathos. She often made doleful reference to 'those six pain-filled years' of Charles' (sic) illness in their 'missionary bungalow,' that 'wee, sacred spot,' 'the place called desert "whence came Streams.""[16] Only several years after her husband's death as she writes the romance of his life does Mount Fuji and all of nature become soft, golden, pure, warm—benevolent again, malevolent no longer.

How different is the progression in the passage above, again addressed directly to the reader, from what a reader of the biblical text would expect. Despite the joyful, rich, exultant image of Canaan found in Deuteronomy, and despite the joyful opening to her meditation, by the second paragraph any sufferer who enters Mrs. Cowman's thoughts encounters life's troubling hills. The central reader was, of course, Mrs. Cowman herself, for though I have been writing about her other readers, we need to recognize that first and foremost Mrs. Cowman was writing to and for herself, the reason why her presence is so strong, even though she did not write most of the meditations. And, as I said earlier, her great friend and Charlie's nurse, Lydia Bemmels, was her second reader.

Think of Mrs. Cowman caring for a dying man; think of the dull, daily routines she lived through as she compiled her devotional. Imagine her moving from bedroom to kitchen to bedroom to kitchen, reading and writing, marking and cutting—desperate and despairing—while her husband slept during the day. Picture how her circumstances shaped her responses. See her and Lydia crying together, propping each other up, despairing one day and hoping the next, as Charlie had bad days and good days. On January 3, 1924, Mrs. Cowman writes in her diary, "Charles had a very good night and we spent a very busy day," but the next day she confides that "Charlie had such a bad night and was so depressed all day and gave way to tears several times." At other times, Lettie herself "g[ives] way to tears several times" (January 4, 1924).

Of such despair, she never writes in her biography. But of such despair, she writes over and over and over in *Streams*. Her diaries, in fact, resemble the devotional book she published, as she recorded Bible verses, brief devotional comments, and quotations from often uncited writers. For instance, for that same day of January 3, Mrs. Cowman writes, "In the evening in the quiet these words were greatly illuminated 'Abraham believed God.' He really *believed*. Do I really believe?" Her diaries from those years reveal what is never present in *Missionary-Warrior*.

On January 10 she writes, "I have laid my book into God's hand"— *Streams*. She explains "that healing was just as easy as salvation, and to be obtained in the very *same* way, by faith. We must take the place of *believing* and recognize ourself as in it. We need to give God time, and after we definitely *receive*, *rest* and wait *for* God." Not only can we see her dramatic bent in her words but in her underlining and in her sudden and naive statement about healing—a statement she surely can't have believed and yet so obviously wanted to be true.

Juxtapose the diary, then, to Mrs. Cowman's interpretation of the metaphoric hills in the first entry of *Streams*. The hills help break up that "one dead level of dull sameness," even as they provide rain. But soon the hills become difficult, then bleak, then stern, hard, rugged, and steep to climb. They have metamorphosed into a terrifying land, not a land of milk and honey, just as the anxious reader predicted. The good times just had to be too good to last. And after Mrs. Cowman overturns the image of hills, after she moves us on the first day of the year from fecundity to desolation, she adds a coda. These wretched hills are God's "gracious protection." An experience that appears formidable or even heartbreaking can become the source of great comfort, even, one could say, of great pleasure.

Mrs. Cowman calls her reader "anxious one," knowing that just as she is troubled, we are troubled. Outwardly she may have appeared undaunted by her husband's dying, but in *Streams*, January 1, her real feelings come through. So Mrs. Cowman presents a dualistic vision of life, good and bad, joyful and fraught with trials. In short, she offers a vision of life as most of us experience it. The strength of her devotional is that she confronts the desert with more than grim determination—and she confronts it first for herself and then on behalf of her readers. Could she have composed this devotional at any other time in her life? Could she have said, in effect, I know how quickly the storm clouds gather, how easily a quarrel develops, how a split second of bad judgment can wreck a day, a week, even a life; I know what it's like to watch someone die, to be helpless in the face of sorrow. And then what? she asks. Then what? When it all seems so hopeless, so meaningless, so unfair, so random, then what? How do you climb Mount Fuji?

Compare the entry in *Streams* with another entry from her diary, this one dated January 13, 1924:

A lovely Sabbath day of rest and worship. A rest possessed me that I had things settled to fully trust God to deliver us. I am coming out of the long struggle of uncertainty, and it seems that every way I turn the Lord puts some fresh help in my way. I feel that the struggling days have come to an end.

But, of course, they had not. The mountains had merely turned suddenly beautiful as the storm cleared; once the storms returned, the mountains would again become threatening, not comforting.

Just put one foot in front of the other, Mrs. Cowman counsels, and keep climbing. Before you know it, you've reached the top of whatever hill lies in your way. Mrs. Cowman offers hope to the victimized, marginalized, and disenfranchised, though she would never have used those words about herself or the other women she knew. They weren't on the margins; they were in the center of the action, known to be so by the depth of their trouble. God loves those whom he chastises. She *must* believe this; otherwise the mirror of herself and her husband as spiritual giants chosen by God would shatter. And, in fact, such is the struggle her diary reveals—anguish, torture, doubts, confusion: God is not choosing to heal Charlie, but why, Lettie Cowman wants to know, why, considering what a giant her husband is?

To counteract the anguish, we find daily, sometimes hourly, entries that insist "I am all right. God loves me. Things aren't as terrible as I think. I am all right. God loves me. Things aren't. . . ." On February 11 at 7:30 she writes, "I am in the heart of the storm but my small craft sails along as if on an unruffled sea, carried along on the bosom of the sea anchored fast and secure. . . . I told the Lord to deliver us in His moment." (An hour later she records much the same thoughts.) The last sentence is telling, the verb revealing her character. There is in this statement a presumption and a lack of humility couched in the language of graciousness, as if she were granting God permission to do what she wants on his schedule.

The Devotional Life

With this background, let us return to that strange entry in *Streams* for September 29 in which Mrs. Cowman directly confronts the nature of the devotional life, for the entry relates not only to the genre but also to the question of audience. Two themes emerge: solitude and passivity, and the relationship between them.

Mrs. Cowman chooses the latter part of Psalm 109:4 as her text, "I give myself unto prayer," or as the New International Version phrases it, "I am a man of prayer." The complete verse reads, "In return for my friendship they accuse me, but I am a man of prayer." The word *but* makes no sense unless we know what the first three verses say (and the latter half makes no sense without the first half). Someone or some group has been slandering David, who is giving God the details, intending later to catalogue a list of curses that he would like God to bring off—such as causing the man who slandered him to face bankruptcy proceedings and die young, thereby sending his wife and children to the poorhouse. David is not a nice man.

In trying to persuade God, David says, "*but* I am a man of prayer." In other words, "I'm not what people say because I pray." David is his own character witness and defense attorney in a spiritual trial; this is legal language. We need this context to read the entry for September 29. To declare prayer as his persona acts as a rationalization, a reason, a justification, and a defense for the harsh sentence David asks God to hand out. The accompanying meditation, chosen from "The Still Hour," begins with several rhetorical questions, paramount among them, "Who ever knew an eminently holy man who did *not* spend much of his time in prayer?" And then follows a story about George Whitefield and his claims to have spent "whole days and weeks" praying. "It has been said," the passage continues, "that no great work in literature or science was ever wrought by a man who did not love solitude" (301).

The context of David's claim to prayer and the assertion that greatness comes only to men who spend much time alone is "an elemental principle of religion." True spirituality comes from effort, and although the roots of Mrs. Cowman's devotional are buried in the Reformation doctrine of "by faith alone," and although much of her text recommends forbearance, long-suffering, patience—the sacrificial responses of the religious life—in this entry she advocates hard work and striving for a religious life. David may be the stated model, but given what she says about Charles Cowman in her biography, he is the real model. Charles Cowman suffered; he spent much time alone in prayer; he was never given proper recognition; he worked himself *to death*.

47

Let's look more closely at solitude versus community (so implied) and action versus inaction. Although Mrs. Cowman would never have explicitly said that the practice of true religion comes through time alone rather than church attendance, her choice of texts says it for her. The Christian life is a solitary life; time alone (a synonym for time with God) is the sine qua non of a true Christian. The above entry provides one example of this; we find another for October 2: "And he took them, and went aside privately into a desert place" (Luke 9:10). The first lines of the meditation read, "In order to grow in grace, we must be much alone. It is not in society that the soul grows most vigorously. In one single quiet hour of prayer it will often make more progress than in days of company with others. It is in the desert that the dew falls freshest and the air is purest" (304).[17]

David Hall argues that, although popular religion in seventeenth-century New England was an every-person-for-herself religion, "the everyday meaning of religion . . . involved the social experience of withdrawing from one kind of community and uniting with another."[18] By the time Mrs. Cowman writes, the social experience, the community of believers, has shrunk to a community of two—the Christian and God. Practical piety is private; indeed, it *must* be for good Christians who want to become great Christians. She only needed to look at her husband to defend this position; he isolated himself, and he was, so she insists, a great Christian (remember her calling him a spiritual genius). Daily devotions thus become the singular mark of a true Christian, which was not the case in seventeenth-century New England (Hall points out that Puritans thought of daily prayer, Bible reading, and meditation as duties of a Christian, but not the practices that defined people *as* Christians[19]). It is hard to find a meditation in Mrs. Cowman's work that talks about the communal nature of the Christian life, of the church. In the October 2 entry on solitude, we find yet again an irony in the juxtaposition of this meditation with the passage from Luke. Jesus did not go alone but with his disciples, and when the crowds followed him he turned and talked to them.

Another strange thing happens in *Streams:* The theme of isolation merges with that of passivity. A few examples will demonstrate this. First, the entry for April 5 (2 Kings 4:4):

They were to be alone with God, for they were not dealing with the laws of nature, nor human government, nor the church . . . but they must needs be isolated from all creatures. . . . There are times and places where God will form a mysterious wall around us, and cut away all props . . . and shut us up to something divine, which is utterly new and unexpected. . . . Most religious people live in a sort of treadmill life . . . but the souls that God leads out into immediate and special dealings, He shuts in where all they know is that God has hold of them, and is dealing with them, and their expectation is from Him alone.

Page 116

Here someone chosen by God must do nothing, in fact can do nothing. Why? Because he has had the props knocked out from under him, he has had a wall form around him, a gentle prison—the metaphors oxymoronic. What can someone do who has been walled in? I wonder whether Mrs. Cowman, assembling this entry, looks at her own four walls, at the "little bungalow," and thinks of it as a prison.

Each metaphor in the entry suggests the drama of a suffering Christian (the props, the mystery, the new and unexpected), as contrasted to a boring, uneventful life. Mrs. Cowman could see splendor in nothing but the emotional extremes; for a person who reveled in every low and every high—who needed them as plants do water and sunshine—the level plains would have been suffocating. Mrs. Cowman not only expects but pants after God's unexpected, miraculous intervention to make life a drama. She disdains the "treadmill life" of most religious people, such a contrast to her own life. Many of us, though, do live a treadmill existence, and it is as strong and legitimate an image as that of life as broken, trouble-filled, dramatic. Mrs. Cowman prefers stage metaphors and knows that people trapped on a treadmill would prefer life as drama as well. And I suspect that at this time in her life she felt herself to be trapped on a treadmill.

Her diary confirms my suspicions: "I had real faith in God and anointed him [i.e., Charles] in the *name of the Lord.* It is settled forever" (February 1, 1924). How many times she writes similar words. How many times could such healing have been settled? She simply protests her faith too much, repeats such words too often, as if they are an incantation, a hypnotic formula, a mantra. A few days later, she wrote "There was a real intimation from the Holy Spirit that healing was near" (February 3, 1924). For someone of her theological persuasion, of her missionary experience, and of her temperament, she could not admit that her husband would die. And how strange that in the midst of her words to convince herself that Charles would live, she records "ex-president Wilson died this AM. This AM 'under hopeless circumstance he hopefully believed.'"

"Charles is poorly and very tested" one day (January 31, 1924), has "a fair night" or "a pretty fair night" on other days (i.e., January 26). Some days she thinks "the light is becoming brighter and I feel the hour for the birth of the flower is nearing" (January 26) and on other days she cannot see any hope—"attacks all night with agony and crying for sleep" (February 5, 1924). And all the while, she writes of her suffering—always her own suffering—and of her solace in extreme language, like comparing her experience to a "birth travail" (February 5, 1924). Or an early entry from December 23, 1923: "Charles had a very good night, but I was very nervous and worn and battled for sleep and rest. . . . Have been stronger today," as if she is the one dying. Then I read the following: "When I got up there was a quiet in my whole being, every pore, organ, and sense of my physical organism was open to receive from Christ His fullness" (January 31). On that same day Mrs. Cowman records that "God spoke so strangely through a poem in 'Joy and Strength' page 133"—evidence of her reading Mary Wilder Tileston during the days of deepest distress, right before Charlie Cowman's death. And occasionally Mrs. Cowman notes a passage that she wants to include in *Streams* ("Put this with March 18th Streams, December 23, 1923").

Suffering Joyfully

April 7 of *Streams* talks about waiting and watching, April 8 asserts, "In order really to know God, *inward stillness* is absolutely necessary. . . . I composed my body to perfect stillness, and I constrained my troubled spirit into quietness, and looked up and waited; and then I did 'know' that it was God. . . . There is a perfect passivity which is not indolence." These are the themes too that I find on nearly every page of her diary kept during the deathwatch years.

Composed and *constrained*, such problematic verbs here, for *composed* and *constrained* convey a struggle, an unnaturalness, a tight fit. When I read, "I constrained my troubled spirit into quietness," I picture a size fourteen trying to squeeze into a size four; it just can't be done, even though the entry insists it must be done. The verb recalls the April 5 entry about isolation and composure.

Then there is the next oxymoron, "passivity which is not indolence." Ted Leeson in *The Habit of Rivers* provides an apt metaphor for the kind of passivity without indolence that Mrs. Cowman is advocating:

> Where the river runs swiftly over shallow bedrock, a line of standing waves will develop. If they are spaced just right, you can trap the boat [a driftboat] in a trough between two crests. Though the water rolls and wells on all sides, the waveform remains stationary, and the boat sits calmly amid the turbulence in apparent defiance of some law. You occupy a place within a place, holding in the flux, anchored by the water itself.[20]

We are the boat, sitting calmly, occupying "a place within a place," despite the turbulent waters around—and at the same time, the water is the anchor. Just so, in Mrs. Cowman's text God causes the turbulence and is also the anchor that prevents our foundering in the turbulence. And didn't she herself use the metaphor of a boat in one of her diary entries?

In order to practice passivity, stillness, and silence, in order to "wait" for God, a Christian needs to be alone. Solitude becomes the prerequisite for passivity and if, as in the April 5 entry, a believer does not separate herself, then God does it with his "mysterious wall." Or, as the October 7 entry explains with a different metaphor, God immerses a believer "in times of darkness. . . . The sky is overcast with clouds. The clear light of heaven does not shine. . . . One feels as if he were groping his way in darkness. . . . What shall the believer do? . . . The first thing to do is do nothing."

Isolation, passivity, and, over and over, the promise that a Christian's trials come from God and successful isolation and passivity will result in greatness: "Where showers fall most, the grass is greenest" (October 9); "It is by being cast down and not destroyed; it is by being shaken to pieces, and the pieces torn to shreds, that men become men of might" (October 11); "Difficulty is the very atmosphere of miracle—it is a miracle in its first stage" (October 14); "God uses most for His glory those people and things which are most perfectly broken" (October 15); and "An assured part of God's pledged blessing to us is delay and suffering" (October 18). Surely we cannot read these entries as anything other than autobiographical, as anything other than the grand justification she offers herself for her own anguish. At other times, such as the crucial Sep-

51

tember 25 entry, which begins "Why go I mourning?" (Psalm 42:9), she castigates, even torments, herself about her lack of faith. Who of her readers hasn't done the same?

And didn't she do that the day Charlie died? Here is her diary entry:

> At 12:30 just after midnight my precious Charlie fell asleep in Jesus. Slept away so peacefully—My heart is crushed & broken—Life has lost its all for me! . . . It seemed as if my life would go out also & I lay so weak, so helpless! Jesus, dear Jesus! My soul does not have the comfort I expected but I just lean upon God wholly.

Mrs. Cowman offers contrary, problematic views of life and of God not only because her days are in turmoil but also because she snatches consolation wherever she finds it, no matter what the source. *Any* hand in the desert offering water is welcome, which results in the hybrid, patchwork nature of her text—a bricolage. Not only does she cull passages seemingly at random from throughout the Bible (though preferring the Old Testament to the New and sometimes misquoting)—from Isaiah 24:15 to Colossians 2:15 to 2 Kings 6:17 to Habakkuk 2:1—but she also snips sections from the publications of familiar preachers, theologians, and writers. Taken together, they often clash, jarring each other and the reader, creating disconnections and contradictions, creating also a stream of consciousness. Her entries reflect how she reads, how she composes. Restless, exhausted, fearful, she paces through her books and magazines looking for anything to lift her spirit and (en)lighten her soul. As these come to her, so they come to us. What difference does it make that C. H. Spurgeon, George Mueller, and Johnathan [sic] Edwards rest next to John Ruskin, Henry Wadsworth Longfellow, or Francis de Sales?

Consider Harriet Beecher Stowe, for instance. George Marsden comments that "Beecher's church . . . had the attraction of not demanding exact beliefs"[21]and claims that Harriet Beecher Stowe excoriated not only Calvinism "but any teachings that tied eternal salvation to correct theological belief"; instead "the essence of Christianity was moral character. . . ."[22] Had such ideas been suggested to Mrs. Cowman, she would have been horrified (though she was *not* a Calvinist). Yet in her text such quasi-religious, high-toned Victorian moralists sit hard by fundamentalists like A. B. Simpson, George Whitefield, and Andrew Murray. We also find people like Margaret Bottome, Canadian poet Annie Johnson Flint, Ophelia G. Browning, and Katherine Lee Bates, to list only a few of the unfamiliar, long-forgotten women. Or we find entries with initials only, or the words "from a tract," or "selected," which appears repeatedly. Such are the mental scraps out of which Mrs. Cowman pieces her devotional.

Theology is of far less consequence, obviously, than finding hope to overcome the trials and tribulations God sends (not the devil) and to reject despondency, worry, and anxiety (which would be natural feelings for someone whose life was one trial after another tribulation). Mrs. Cowman may have believed that life was a desert but she nevertheless wanted to inspire readers to rejoice in the desert path because it leads to a great destination. She wanted to inspire *herself* to believe this.

The cumulative Christian narrative Mrs. Cowman tells inevitably means contradiction. Because God loves us, he sends us trials and tribulations that through his love and his witnesses he enables us to overcome. The more we suffer, the more we know God loves us because we know that ultimately, as he is the source of our suffering, he is also the source of suffering's surcease. Undoubtedly life is a spiritual desert—or a treadmill—but just as undoubtedly life is infused with miracle, with deliverance. Charles Cowman dies and *Streams in the Desert* is born. Although we cannot *will* miracles into our life, the daily practice of devotions, the daily determination to suffer joyfully, even with anticipation (and to get credit for doing so), ensures that we are prepared to recognize, if not accept, the miracles when they come. As well-tilled but parched soil can soak up rain when it falls, so can we, well tilled through our devotional life, drink in miraculous refreshment.

Suffering Counts

As I said earlier, what holds the whole of *Streams* together is the mind and life of Mrs. Cowman. Once the texts have passed through her hands, it no longer matters who "David" is, a name we find in June 20, or who wrote her late husband's favorite poem, which we find in the August 26 entry, or what kind of person Annie Johnson Flint was. It does not matter what they believed or what the context of their belief was. It only matters that because their words helped Mrs. Cowman receive God's grace, she believes that they will help others as well. Just as she infuses her selections with personal significance, so shall her readers, whether the selections be by Madame Guyon, Harriet Beecher Stowe, or Ralph Waldo Emerson, whose Christian "credentials" some readers might doubt.

Curiously, only when we turn to *Streams in the Desert 2* do we find Mrs. Cowman named not only as compiler but as author of numerous meditations. Comparing the two volumes reveals that the central themes of the original are indeed the themes and concerns of Mrs. Cowman's own life: "Sorrows are too precious to be wasted" (February 26, *Streams in the Desert 2*); "We must know how to put occupation aside. In an inaction which is meditative, the wrinkles of the soul are smoothed away" (March 27); "It takes a real faith to trace the rainbow through the rain" (April 2); "A shattered and broken personality releases the fragrance of Christ" (June 6); and "What should be the attitude of a Christian when placed in a difficult and trying situation—a place of severe testing? . . . A refusal to look *at* the difficult circumstance, but *above* it" (June 9, italics in original). Here is evidence that Mrs. Cowman offers women a way of *being* that focuses on the inner life of the spirit and so transcends—if not provides a way to ignore—the inescapable, inevitable, essential, daily hardships of life. Once we have read Mrs. Cowman's meditations in volume two, we can return to volume one and hear her voice in those meditations that are unnamed, as in this telling entry: "Left alone! . . . If His followers spent more time alone with Him, we should have spiritual giants again. . . . Covet to get alone with God. . . . It must mean more depth and power. . . ." (*Streams in the Desert*, 73). That theme of becoming a spiritual giant or genius haunted her life.

The two volumes consistently narrate the themes of suffering, worry, active passivity, and passive activity—themes expressed most poignantly in the poetry selections from unknown women. Because verse is central—almost every entry including at least a few lines of verse—let us look at an example before we end. In volume one, the entry for March 9 is almost entirely a poem by Miss Mary Butterfield. The final stanza captures all of Mrs. Cowman's most deeply felt themes and favorite metaphors:

> Oh, paradox of Heaven. The load
> We think will crush was sent to lift us
> Up to God! Then, soul of mine,
> Climb up! for naught can e'er be crushed
> Save what is underneath the weight.

How may we climb! By what ascent
Shall we surmount the carping cares
Of Life! Within His word is found
The key which opens His secret stairs;
Alone with Christ, secluded there,
We mount our loads, and rest in Him.

With language reflecting *Little Women* and *Pilgrim's Progress*, Miss Butterfield reinforces the paradoxical narrative Mrs. Cowman has told. God sends us trials, we climb up (recall the metaphor in the first entry) by resting "within His word," to reach our secluded community, "alone with Christ." And Annie Johnson Flint, who must have been Mrs. Cowman's favorite poet, reaches out to all readers, no matter how great or small their problems: "His grace is great enough to meet the great things. . . . His grace is great enough to meet the small things" (February 26). From "crashing waves" to "insect worries" and "squeaking wheels," God covers them all, his private contract with each believing reader.

Mrs. Cowman has remained a perennial best-seller because she pierces readers' sense of isolation and alleviates their burden of daily trials, confusions, and contradictions. In short, she assures them that their suffering *counts* and that their lives have meaning; they are significant to the one who counts the most, to God—a message that women readers especially would find compelling. She knows us; we know her. We're neighbors, friends, back-fence gossips who commiserate with one another as we hang our clothes on the line. We find companionship and identity in her text. We also find a place to belong, a home. Mrs. Cowman conveys community, her book populated by unbelievers and believers, by fence-sitters, sinners, and saints.

Women's lives and work have long gone unrecognized and ultimately unvalued, as Mrs. Cowman knew. She knew too that while most of the women who read *Streams* never expect reward or gratitude, they do expect hardship, sorrow, and sickness and need to know above all else that their pain matters and that, as deep as the pain may be, there is even deeper comfort. As the entry for August 9 says, "Comfort does not come to the lighthearted and merry. We must go down into 'depths' if we would experience this most precious of God's gifts." The more burdensome their life, the more women experience God's gift of comfort. A central way to experience this comfort is through daily devotional reading.

Mourning readers identify with the creator of *Streams in the Desert*. Reader, creator, and text fuse to become, in the words of the June 9 entry, "the eagle that soars in the upper air, [which] does not worry itself as to how it is to cross rivers." Mrs. Cowman knows that women can become eagles; she knows that women can soar above their troubles, as turbulent as they may be. Wasn't she the first example of many? the pilgrim who broke the trail? the first eagle to leave the nest? Helping women find and strengthen their wings defines the role of her devotional literature.

People hunger for meaning, wanting to know where suffering originates, why it comes, how to overcome it. People need to know that someone shares and understands their grief. Mrs. Cowman gives readers what they seek by making readers her intimate friends, her fellow sufferers, her companions on the most important adventure of life—the daily, necessary, spiritual quest for God. *Streams* fulfills the promise of its title by providing every day, year after year, the spiritual water readers need in the desert of life because it first did so for her.

Mary Wilder Tileston

MORE THAN A COMFORT

[My daughter] Mary . . . is more and more of a comfort. I never saw so happy a human being. She enjoys studying and playing, drawing and dancing, society and solitude, stories, history, and <u>hymns</u>, and is singing in her heart if not with her voice all her waking hours. "Everything I do I think is the pleasantest thing while I am doing it," she says. One of her present delights is taking care of her own room, rising early, and doing everything herself.

Mary Wilder White Foote
From letter fragments April 1 to May 27, 1855

*O*n July 3, 1934, Mary Wilder (Foote) Tileston died at the age of ninety-one. *Publishers Weekly* of July 21 noted that Tileston was "author of some of the most famous compilations of inspirational quotations published in this country,"[1] the best known of these, *Daily Strength for Daily Needs.* What a dry entry for such a remarkable and indefatigable compiler—a one-woman publishing industry!

Mary Wilder Tileston was nearly five years old—she was born August 20, 1843—when the first women's rights conference was held in a Seneca Falls, New York, Methodist church.

Tileston was nine the year *Uncle Tom's Cabin,* the singular American publishing event of the century, struck the country like a blow to the solar plexus; and she was eighteen when the South fired on Fort Sumter.

Mary Wilder Tileston was sixteen when the other most important publishing event of the century occurred: the appearance of Charles Darwin's *Origin of Species.*

Tileston lived through the split between the southern and northern Presbyterian churches. She saw the publication of Walt Whitman's "When Lilacs Last in the Dooryard Bloom'd" and was twelve when *Leaves of Grass* came out. She lived through Reconstruction. She witnessed the laborers' riots that swept the Northeast.

When Archduke Franz Ferdinand and his wife were assassinated in Sarajevo, thus leading to World War I, Tileston was seventy-one; the event came to have particular significance for her, as we shall see. When suffragists were demonstrating outside the White House to give women the right to vote, Tileston turned seventy-four, seventy-seven when the Temperance Movement scored its victory with the Eighteenth Amendment to the Constitution, and ninety—a year short of her death—when Americans decided they'd been dry too long.

In 1925, the year of the Scopes trial, Tileston was eighty-two. She lived through the First World War, the Jazz Age, the Harlem Renaissance, the first Hemingway novels, Edith Wharton and Willa Cather, the stock market crash, the Depression, and the election of FDR.

Why catalogue these events? Each in some way influenced Mary Wilder Tileston, each affected her family, each played a part in who Tileston became: the longest- and best-selling of devotional compilers. Let me explain how, commenting on the most significant historical events, and drawing on almost the only primary evidence we have for Tileston's early years: her mother's letters and journals.

Today we consider the first women's rights conference as a monumental gathering, but it apparently went unnoticed (or at least not commented on *directly*) by Tileston's mother, Mary Wilder White Foote. She was more concerned with her growing family, her many illnesses, her theological ruminations and speculations than in certain current events. This lack of interest seems odd for several reasons. First, despite Mary Foote's traditional role as wife and mother, she nevertheless clearly supported women's education, ambitions, and independent careers, as we shall see. Second, her husband, Mary's father, was a newspaperman, the owner and editor of the *Salem (Mass.) Gazette*, who would have covered the meeting. And third, the

Tileston family was deeply concerned with and committed to the abolition of slavery, from which the women's rights movement grew.

The Civil War directly affected Mary and her family. Her uncle Wilder Dwight, who was ten years older than she, became a lieutenant colonel in the Army of the Rebellion, was wounded at Antietam, and died September 19, 1862, only three years before his niece's marriage on September 5, 1865, to John Boies Tileston. Given family sentiment and abolitionist leanings, Wilder Dwight's volunteering for the rebel cause is inexplicable.

Like so many other Americans at the time, the Wilders were influenced by *Uncle Tom's Cabin,* which Mary undoubtedly heard her mother read aloud, a family habit; Harriet Beecher Stowe appears five times in *Daily Strength for Daily Needs* alone. Mary's Aunt Meggie, writing to Mary's mother about *Uncle Tom's Cabin,* exclaims, "It leaves you . . . in a thoroughly Christian frame of mind. . . . it makes you want to pray for oppressed, yes, but moreso for oppressor. It is so much better to be injured than to injure!" (April 8, 1852). How could her nephew join the injuring side?

Aunt Meggie (Margaret Harding White) was reading her sister's copy of the book: "Enjoyed your marks exceedingly. I do not feel as if I had *lived* anything but Uncle Tom, since I read the first chapter." The publisher, John P. Jewett, issued the book on March 20, 1852, two months before the serial ended in the magazine *National Era.* Meggie was reading the book only *two weeks* after publication—*and* after her sister had already read it.

Therefore, though Mary Wilder Foote may have failed to explicitly discuss every major contemporary political or social issue, she was nevertheless a reader of contemporary literature that dealt with such issues. She was also a voluminous letter and journal writer, who commented on what she read, urging her correspondents to read, read, read. Nearly every letter mentions something she and her family are reading together—a history or biography, for instance, that of Sir Thomas F. Bruxton, an associate of Wilberforce; the *Christian Examiner;* Ralph Waldo Emerson; poetry by Longfellow or Whittier. Were she alive today, she would contribute reviews to on-line bookstores. The letters she received also talk of books, her sister Meggie for instance recommending a biography of Margaret Fuller (1810–1850), transcendental writer, editor of the short-lived periodical *Dial,* author of *Woman in the Nineteenth Century,* friend of Emerson, an influence on George Eliot: "We have been absorbed by Mary Fuller the last fortnight. What an exciting Biography!" (March 6, 1852; although she gets the name wrong, the book she refers to is *Memoirs of Margaret Fuller Ossoli*, two volumes, published in 1851. Volume one includes reminiscences by J. F. Clarke and Emerson).

This reference returns us to the Seneca Falls conference and the nascent women's rights movement. Clearly the sisters *were* interested in women's issues and, thus, in the role of women. Mary's mother never considered anything but an active life for her daughter. For instance, when Mary was not quite five, her mother in a letter to her sister Eliza declared that "little Mary is a stronghearted person," and predicted that she "will bear & endure & do a good deal in life" (June 11, 1848). Could this prediction have in any way been influenced by the ferment of Susan B. Anthony and Elizabeth Cady Stanton? by their reading of Margaret Fuller's biography? Could *this* be Mary Foote's political or social commentary on the times? Could Mary Wilder Tileston's energetic publishing record be the result of her mother's unshakable belief that her daughter would influence many, many people? I can hear Mary Foote encouraging her small child to study and play, dance and draw.

Mary Foote's letters reveal a family of readers with a breadth of literary curiosity. But as I said, they didn't just read to themselves; reading was communal, familial, even, I would say, domestic. Sometimes Mary Foote read aloud, sometimes her eldest son Henry (Harry), who was five years older than his sister, sometimes her darling Mary. For a future compiler of devotional books, such an upbringing, such an emphasis on reading and talk about reading, would have been invaluable, if not essential.

When I look at the other historical events Tileston witnessed, when I list them one after the other, I am struck by what tumultuous times Tileston lived through. Given such tumult and change, she and her thousands of readers needed strength daily—would have hungered for the stability of such writers as Longfellow, Whittier, Catherine Adorna, Thoreau, Christina Rossetti, Fénelon, George Eliot (I will say more about Tileston's selections later).

The Devotionals

Tileston's *Daily Strength for Daily Needs*, the book that Mrs. Cowman read until dog-eared, tattered, and spine-broken—finally held together with a rubber band—a gift from her husband, the inspiration and model for Mrs. Cowman's own *Streams in the Desert,* was first published in 1884 when Tileston was fifty-one. *Publishers Weekly* in its stark three-sentence obituary, reports that the book had 402,500 copies in print, excluding the British edition.

The copy I hold, the memorial edition published by Little, Brown the year Tileston died and reprinted as recently as two years ago, gives a partial publishing history on the copyright page: thirty printings totaling more than a half million copies. (This history, of course, does not include editions from all the other publishers who have issued the book.) In 114 years the book has never been out of print and has been available in numerous formats from various publishers. The fore-word to the memorial edition, written August 1934 by then bishop of Massachusetts William Lawrence compares Tileston to "the great inventors of the age," "those who connect mighty physical resources with the needs of men; Mary W. Tileston, by her love of spiritual lit-erature, her skill in selection and her knowledge of the spiritual needs of men and women, has brought them into connection with eternal truth and spiritual resource" (*Daily Strength for Daily Needs,* vi). High praise indeed. Lawrence obviously did not denigrate the work of a compiler.

But if only Lawrence had told us something more about this "quiet, modest little woman whose skill has given new impulse to millions of men and women through this little book." "Quiet" and "modest" hardly do justice to the reticence, even self-effacement, that charac-terizes Tileston. I wonder whether she requested her publishers to say nothing about her, for I cannot imagine a publisher today giving no information about an author, not even where she lives, the name of her husband, and how many children she has, typical information found in most contemporary books. But no such information appears anywhere, on any volume, even the most recent editions, like the gift edition published by Little, Brown. *Daily Strength for Daily Needs* must be one of the least-known best-sellers in American publishing history and Mary Wilder Tileston one of the most anonymous of best-selling "authors," even among readers of religious devotionals.

How could such an industrious woman remain so unknown? Even after months and months of searching the historical records, I still cannot answer the question. I do, however, at least partly understand why her books have touched so many lives: their breadth, scope, intimacy, pacing, unerringly right combinations of texts, a sense of familiarity without losing freshness, beautiful language. And despite their being compilations, the books have a strong sense of voice and of a personality, albeit a self-effacing one, behind the books—a guarantee, a Good Housekeeping seal of approval.

Part of the success of any book lies with the title, and certainly *Daily Strength for Daily Needs* is good, with its repetition and parallel (or symmetrical) structure (it is emblematic of all her titles). It sounds good when you say it aloud. So I wondered where it came from and found in Mary Foote's papers the probable source. Two months before Mary Foote died of typhoid fever, December 24, 1857, when she was forty-seven and Mary only fourteen, she wrote to her sister Eliza that "Day by day the promise rears/Daily Thoughts for daily needs"; these are the first two lines of a short "poem." But would Mary have read this? I asked myself. A draft of her mother's will gave me part of the answer. Mary Wilder Foote bequeathed all her letters, journals, and diaries to her darling; "my journals and scrapbooks for my Mary," ends a draft of her will, and "all my articles of jewelry to be kept for my darling Mary," begins it—thoughts of her darling first and last. Also, given the extensive correspondence between Mary and her Aunt Eliza after her mother's death, it is reasonable to suppose that Mary read or was told about her mother's letter of October 27, 1857. Family members regularly reported on their correspondence or sent to others the letters they had received, rather the way many people today pass around pictures.

I have called Mary Tileston a one-woman publishing industry, and so she was. But even that description fails to do justice to her output. Not until I had a computer printout of several pages in my hands did I begin to appreciate how much Tileston accomplished—or how much Tileston read! *Daily Strength* was *not* Tileston's first, or only, devotional book; she published more than thirty books, "most of them compilations," according to *Publishers Weekly* (the words "most of them" imply that Tileston was not "just" a compiler), by anyone's standards a prolific output. Among her devotionals are *Joy and Strength for the Pilgrim's Day; Prayers, Ancient and Modern;* and *Great Souls at Prayer: Fourteen Centuries of Prayer, Praise and Aspiration.* I found in a used bookstore an edition of the latter, which was published in a large print edition in 1983 by Keats Publishing in arrangement with a British publisher (James Clark, Cambridge). The back jacket flap copy says that it was first published in 1898 and had been reprinted more than fifty times, thus rivaling (or at least keeping pace with) *Daily Strength*. The publisher concludes, "We know little of the life of Mary Tileston, but her devotion to spiritual literature at its best is evident in her books, which have enriched the lives of so many readers"—adult readers, of course.

Tileston also published for children—sought to educate and inspire, or "inspirit," them as she herself wrote. For instance, the year before issuing *Daily Strength for Daily Needs*, she published a collection of nursery verse, *Sugar and Spice and All That's Nice;* by 1928 she had renewed the copyright three times. In 1910 she published a similar volume for six- to thirteen-year-old children, *The Child's Harvest of Verse;* a third children's collection, *The Children's Book of Ballads* (also published for adults as *Classic Heroic Ballads*, Roberts Brothers, 1883) falls between the other two.

Tileston's publications go beyond daily devotional compilations and poetry for children. She published collections of sayings from hymns and ballads; selections from such ancients as Epictetus, Socrates, and Plato (the only library in the country to own a copy of the last refused to lend it); a compilation from seventeenth-century Catholic archbishop François Fénelon (she drew frequently on Catholic mystics, prelates, theologians); and two books of hymns— all of which demonstrate a wide-ranging intellect, a passionate reader, a thoughtful and well-educated woman. Even women with doctorates today would be hard-pressed to cull from their reading enough material for one best-selling anthology, let alone thirty or more, not to mention finding the time to put such an anthology together. What was it her mother said about her? "I never saw so happy a human being. She enjoys studying and playing, drawing and dancing, society and solitude, stories, history, and hymns, and is singing in her heart if not with her voice all her waking hours. 'Everything I do I think is the pleasantest thing while I am doing it,' she says" (cited at the beginning of the chapter). Obviously the twelve-year-old Mary and the middle-aged Mary were of a piece.

Tileston's publishers read like a who's who of publishing history: Little, Brown; Methuen; Grosset and Dunlop; Doubleday; The Atlantic Monthly; John Wilson and Sons; in 1993 even Barnes and Noble published an edition of *Joy and Strength*. Hardly a year went by from 1877 until 1927 when yet another book from Tileston was not published, sometimes more than one a year. And then there are those family memoirs published in 1903, 1918, 1920, and 1927; she may have been reticent about revealing her own life, but she had no such reticence when it came to helping her aunt Eliza prepare a memoir of Eliza's mother, Mary Wilder White, subtitled *A Century Ago in New England.* Mary Wilder White was Tileston's grandmother, the mother her own mother lost early and mourned throughout her life. (I realize how difficult it is to keep the Marys straight, for every generation has a Mary, a female version of the male practice of naming one son after his father: Mary Wilder White, Mary Wilder White Foote, Mary Wilder Foote Tileston, Mary Tileston; fortunately for us Mary Tileston dropped "Foote" from her publishing name.)

Tileston also published a memoir of her own daughter, Amelia Peabody Tileston, who at forty-eight died of pneumonia February 22, 1920, in Belgrade. The memoir is strikingly contemporary. *Amelia Peabody Tileston and Her Canteens for the Serbs* is a collection of letters written by her daughter from 1916 to 1920, the four years she worked with the Serbians in the Balkans. Tileston included a brief history of Serbia and a sketch of her daughter's life, told in such detached and objective language that, if a reader didn't know Amelia Peabody Tileston was her daughter, nothing in the biography would give it away (I will have more to say about this unusual book below).

Let me repeat. Even given that much of her work was compilation, not composition, it is a formidable record when one considers the time-consuming discipline of selecting, organizing, and shaping required to create 365 entries per devotional book: Bible verse, poetry, commentary (sometimes six different sources an entry), each of which must respond to or expand on the others—a fierce, imbricated intertextuality that literary critics have never explored. A good daily devotional, a successful and long-lived one, must not be so predictable that it bores readers; nor can it be so obscure as to be unintelligible. There's a fine line between clichés and sappy truisms and a truth turned ever so slightly as to appear sharp and fresh. Those who have tried to write condolence letters know what I mean; those who have received letters that truly console also understand. Tileston's devotionals speak to readers in strange and familiar ways both to startle and to reassure.

In one regard, Tileston was spared the most onerous and time-consuming task any compiler faces: the permissions letters. During the years in which Tileston was compiling her work, publishers were much more lax regarding permission than they are today; and this was also true, as we know, about Cowman's devotionals. We seldom find lengthy lists of acknowledgments or permissions, Tileston's collections of children's verse being exceptions, and Tileston excerpted many contemporary writers, like George Macdonald or William Dean Howells. Although she may have benefited from not having to do such a daunting task, we regret that no correspondence exists because it might have given us hints or clues about her life. (That she *did* occasionally write for permission we know from a few brief introductions to her books.) However, if the acknowledgments are missing, indexes of prose and poetry selections, along with dates for most of the writers cited, are not (unlike Mrs. Cowman's books).

With this information, I was able to find many of the women writers whom she anthologized (I talk about some of these women, along with women from Mrs. Cowman's books, in chapters 4 and 5). In her prayer collections Tileston provided a subject and an author index, in the preface giving brief historical information, explaining, for instance, that "there are some striking and fervent collects from the Mozarabic Sacramentary, which was in use in Spain before A.D. 700" *(Great Souls at Prayer)*. *Classic Heroic Ballads* includes an appendix of "Historical Notes," some excerpted from people like Macaulay, Sir Walter Scott, or John Greenleaf Whittier, others written (we may assume) by herself. She did her work without the help of a computer, the World Wide Web, or a secretary; and all without duplicating selections from book to book. At the same time, she raised seven children, her first collection coming out when she had a two- and a five-year-old underfoot.

Tileston more than fulfilled her mother's prophecy about doing a good deal in life.

Letters and Journals

As I said, what little we know about Mary Wilder Tileston's childhood comes from the letters Mary Wilder Foote wrote and the journals she kept. And by a strange twist, what little we know about her adulthood comes from the letters of Tileston's daughter, Amelia, and the sketch of her Tileston wrote, as if Tileston exists only in two places: in the reflections of the women to whom she was the closest

65

and in her books. As I have already indicated, in Mary Wilder Foote's letters we find a dream daughter, a nearly perfect child, whose greatest sin appears to have been mussing a dress while playing during a visit to Aunt Meggie's. Never is there a hint, a whiff, a blush of rebellion, disobedience, or willfulness. And if the witness of Tileston's professional life counts for anything, it tells us that Mary Foote did not exaggerate in her praise of her daughter or in her expectations for the *wholesomeness* of her daughter's life. Even so, Mary Foote *was* anxious about her daughter, as we shall see, but her anxieties were the result of an overheated imagination and her own unhappy childhood and not the result of anything Mary herself caused.

To read Mary Foote's letters is like reading Mary Tileston herself. In fact, while studying Mary Foote's letters, I sometimes forgot whose words I was reading; had Tileston's correspondence survived I do not doubt that it would have sounded like her mother's because Tileston's central, immediate, and defining model was her mother. We cannot overestimate the influence of her mother's scrapbooks and journals—intimate, domestic, homely, and richly, farsightedly female—as we learn from the following letter, written to thirty-one-year-old Mary by her aunt Eliza:

Chestnut Hill
Christmas Eve 1874

My dear Mary

On this anniversary, I think fondly of you. Seventeen years have passed away since your dear mother left us, and yet she is as near to us and we to her as she was all those long years ago. You have all her taste & aspirations, &, in this way, remind me of her. How much she would have enjoyed your "Quiet Hours" [her second collection of poetry; on October 4, 1880, she wrote to Henry Wadsworth Longfellow, asking his permission to reprint "Footsteps of Angels" and "The Two Angels" for "a second series of Quiet Hours"].

Indeed, it was just the sort of book she wanted to prepare herself, but was anticipated, I believe, by Miss Guild, and, if I remember right, contributed to her volume what she had begun to collect for her own. This was so characteristic of her. She was thoroughly unselfish from childhood & throughout her life. Her delight was in contributing to the happiness of others. She would have had pure enjoyment in her children had she lived. They have a rich treasure in her memory.

Your Aunt Margaret writes to me from Keene of your "attractive home." I heard of it, too, from Mr. George Bradford. I am thankful that you are so delightfully situated & I am so glad that you live in Concord so associated with my mother, & my grandmother. Sometime perhaps I shall see you there, but it is getting more & more difficult for me to leave home, & I may only visit you through the power of imagination.

I was glad to speak a few words with your husband at Milton, & to see him looking in good health. Give my love to him & the children & believe me ever, dear Mary, with the best wishes of the season, your affectionate

Aunt Eliza

Although I longed to read Mary's reply to her Aunt Eliza's anniversary letter, unfortunately the only reply we have comes in the devotional books she continued to compile.

Yet even without the evidence of Eliza's letter, by studying Mary Foote's journals and diaries, that rich legacy left to her daughter, we would know that Mary Wilder Tileston was imitating her mother. For example, in a scrapbook dated August 31, 1842, Mary Wilder Foote recorded a snippet of a sermon by Rev. R. Moorehead; a segment from "Letters from the Dead to the Living" by Margaret Klopstock; "To a Dying Infant" by Mrs. Southey; an extract "from a letter of Dr. [Isaac] Watts to Madam Sewall on the death of her children Nov. 2, 1728"; "extracts from 'Isobel's Child' by Elizabeth Barrett—an Englishwoman"; and selections from Coleridge. Several poems on the death of children occur, a preoccupation of Mary Foote in this scrapbook, her first daughter having died in infancy, as did the two children who came between Henry and Mary. Some poems are labeled "not to be copied"; others have no such designation. Some of the poetry lacking attribution may well have been Foote's own, for instance, "The Prayer of the Child-Angel," which is labeled and *underlined* "not to be copied." However, it was copied.

A bowdlerized version appeared in an issue of *Littell's Living Age* and then published correctly by another (unidentified) publication: "We are glad to be permitted to print the following exquisite lines— which seem to us almost unrivalled in their thrilling pathos [a tearsheet found in the scrapbook]. . . . This is the first time that the author [unnamed] has ever consented to their publication" (according to this periodical, "a mutilated copy of them appeared in a late No. of Littell's Living Age").

67

Mary's mother gave her daughter much, more than jewelry, more than journals and diaries and correspondence, more, even, than her own name, Mary Wilder (Tileston gave her own firstborn and daughter the name Mary Wilder). In only fourteen years, Mary's mother gave her daughter a sense of purpose, strength, character, a love of learning, inquisitiveness, stability, peace, hope, and love: "Such perfect health as we all enjoy!" wrote Mary Foote to her sister Meggie, "—and as Mary adds 'and so much love'" (September 26, 1852). We may be skeptical about such an idyllic relationship, we may be envious, we may wish that more such families existed today, but it is hard to dismiss the evidence, even for the most cynical. Although we may not know much about Tileston's life directly, we can infer much from Mary Foote's letters to her sisters and friends that describe the day-to-day routines, the birthdays, Christmases, New Year's Day celebrations. We can infer much from the letters Tileston's mother wrote to her; even her father, Caleb, got into the letter-writing act during one of Mary's apparently frequent absences from home—visiting an aunt or an old family friend or away at school. We also learn something of the household from Mary Foote's journals and diaries, which she kept for years, writing entries almost as frequently as she wrote to her sisters and female friends. We learn some of what Mary read, how she spent her days, with whom she played. And we learn from the letters, themselves models of literate writing and deeply imbued with the love of language, how important literate language was to this family of readers and writers. Here, for instance, is a note from Mary's father:

My dear little daughter.-
Your dear mother was interrupted . . . which I am very glad of, as it gives me an opportunity to say one word to my precious darling—to tell her how happy it makes me to think she can be trusted away so far from home, without a single fear that she will be fractious, disagreeable, or troublesome,—or will ever hesitate a moment in complying with the wishes of her kind and loving aunt and uncle.

[June 18, 1852]

The line "without a single fear that she will be fractious, disagreeable, or troublesome" is lovely, even elegant. Imagine such a sentence coming from the mouth of a father on a TV sitcom, our version of a "written" record.

Three days earlier, on June 15, her mother had written, "Your letter gives us a great deal of pleasure my precious little Mary, and I feel as if I knew all about you. . . ." (Apparently Mary had been sent to her Aunt Meggie's house to recover from an illness—her mother notes that people have said that "you look better" or much improved in health.) The requirements of familial correspondence taught Mary early how to write well.

The June 15, 1852, letter is not the only such remark about Mary's ability: "I was delighted to receive your letter yesterday my dearest Mary. It answered all the questions I wanted to ask. That is just the letter people love best to get when they are away from home. You would enjoy seeing how I enjoy the beautiful scenery here . . ." (Keene, her sister Meggie's home, June 14, 1855). On June 11, 1852, Mary Foote wrote, "My dear little daughter, I have just received your letter and am much pleased with it. You have told me just what I wanted to hear," meaning the right sort of news told in detail, told imaginatively. Then follows the normal concerns of a mother about a child visiting relatives—(to paraphrase) I hope you aren't causing your aunt worry or difficulty or trouble. To Carrie E. Frothingham, an old friend and frequent correspondent to whom Mary had gone for a visit, Mary Foote writes, "Mary has delighted to give me every detail—she has actually placed me in your chamber & now I can only sigh to be there" (February 16, 1855); Mary was not quite twelve years old.

Perhaps her facility with words came from her mother or from her own reading or from the reading the family did together. Or perhaps it came from attending to such instructions as the following (included in the June 15, 1852, letter about Mary's torn dress): "I know it makes a great deal of difference to have a <u>chattering bird inside</u> the house when one is not accustomed to it. I miss the one I am used to, but in Aunt Meggie's quiet grown-up house I fear you will be de trop (See if you can look out that phrase in the Dictionary)." Mary no doubt needed a handy dictionary, for not only does her mother write with a sophisticated vocabulary, but Mary reads her father's newspaper: "Dear Father meant to write to you but he is *very busy*. He was much pleased with your letter to him & will save you a paper as you requested." She ends the letter by asking whether Mary remembered to give "those newspapers" to the Misses Perry. Newspapers and books and letters and poems and foreign phrases flying daily between one household and another.

So what did Mary read other than her father's newspaper? "Mary still reads over & over her favorite book. I think Undine touched her feelings more than any of the stories. She <u>comprehended</u> it and it was very interesting to me to hear her unfold its meaning" (February 19, 1854, to her sister Meggie). For her ninth birthday, Mary received a Bible from her grandmother and White's history of Shakespeare from her grandfather. For her thirteenth birthday, she was given numerous books, including a book of Tennyson; Mary Foote gave her daughter a book of Whittier's poems for her fourteenth birthday, the last she would have with her darling. Mary's brother Henry often gave books to his sister; the two were close, if not inseparable. Her mother frequently comments that they play chess together and that after Henry leaves home to attend Harvard College, he misses his sister a great deal. He wrote to his mother, "Give my love to Mary and tell her that I have repented ever since that I did not kiss her in the depot and that she must write to pay me for the disappointment" (September 2, 1855), and "I want to tell my darling Mary how much I shall value her letters" (November 11, 1856). Henry, who became a minister and subsequently a professor, died in 1889 at the age of fifty-one, well before his sister; his writing appears frequently in her devotionals.

A few years before Mary's fourteenth birthday, her mother wrote that Mary was "gentle, considerate & <u>bright</u> . . . only a comfort to me & help. I wish her steps might attend mine through life" (from the 1851 journal, Thursday, September 2). Here is another: "Mary grows more and more companionable every month—she reads to me—and talks with me—and I live over again my own 'little girl' life. . . . I am ever rejoicing that hers is so much more strictly sheltered than mine was— [I] without . . . a Mother's love and ever living sympathy and care" (November 5, 1854, to a Mrs. Tracy). Not only do we find a further comment about reading—literacy such a presence, such a way of life for Mary from her earliest years—but also a recurring theme, that Mary "can never have some of her mother's <u>chilly</u> experiences at that very tender age. God be thanked for this!" (August 20, 1851, journal). Recall that Mary Foote's mother died young, and Mary was raised by a stepmother, which resulted in her suffering "acutely from a want of perfect confidence in those with whom I was placed and my first effort as a Mother has been to break down every barrier between my child's heart & my own" (April 1, 1848). Her one concern was that her daughter not suffer the same sorrow, which appears to have contoured all her motherly anxieties and cares. How Mary responded to her mother's early death we do not know, though if her mother's evidence of their intimacy is to be believed, then we can only assume that it was as great a sorrow for her as her grandmother's death was for her mother—and thus may also have contributed to the shape Mary Wilder Tileston's lifework took, a desire to provide spiritual help through the valley of the shadow by daily readings from great, and occasionally not-so-great, literature.

Let me return to the letter about Mary's reading of *Undine* and cite what follows, for it demonstrates how intimate mother and daughter were, at least from her mother's perspective:

> She was diffident about expressing . . . [her views about *Undine*] to you. There is a natural reserve about her which for the present time prevents [?] her from opening herself <u>entirely</u> to any one but her mother. With me she is completely unreserved and I shall devote myself to the thought of making her always so. That is the only way in which I can hope to influence her. Henry finds it much more easy to communicate himself. And my knowledge of these two children <u>so different</u>, makes it very interesting to watch and speculate upon the developments of the little one who is as yet almost unknown [she had recently had another son]. . . . But enough of a Mother's talk.
>
> February 19, 1854

Mary's mother was, of course, too modest about "the only way" she could influence her daughter. However, she *was* anxious for her daughter, despite Mary's winning ways, comforts, and delights, as we know further from a letter to family friend Susan Higginson, written around this time (December 18, 1854):

> You always dwell upon the unknown anxieties of having boys to bring up and launch in this difficult world: but you don't know how much more I think about Mary than her elder brother in the way of anxiety. I find I am wishing too anxiously to help her over all the hard places— and that I long to have her future bright—& satisfying—and that I dwell upon all possible chances with a weakness which is quite inconsistent with my principles. . . . But the dear delights of a daughter cannot be exaggerated. Oh how I pity those who know nothing about it.

From the time Mary was four months short of being five years old, her mother claimed (April 1, 1848) that she could "see something of

[her] future character." It is frustrating, even irritating, that she spends the rest of the "memorandum" describing Henry, three months shy of ten, as if Henry were far more important, being a boy and the elder. And despite the deep joys Mary Foote expressed about her daughter, nevertheless her letters reveal a sense that the male heir stands in higher regard. Even in a journal entry written on Mary's birthday, Mary Foote devotes more space to discussing Henry's activities that day than Mary's.

However, despite the mild favoritism, common enough then (and now), from what we learn about Henry here and what we know of the siblings' close relationship, we can infer something of Mary's own character and upbringing. For instance, Mary Foote calls her son an "omnivorous reader," says when absorbed in a book he "never needs any other amusement," notes his "very marked intellectual traits"; now compare these statements with those about Mary quoted at the beginning of the chapter—"she enjoys studying . . . solitude, stories, history . . ." Of Henry's "marked intellectual traits" Mary Foote offers this evidence:

> When he was about 8 years old, his Father having reason to commu-
> nicate something to me that he did not choose to speak of, before the
> children, expressed himself in French. Henry's eye flashed with a look
> of complete understanding of the case as he said, "which is, (being
> interpreted), little pitchers have long ears."

Compare this comment with that about Mary's astute understanding of *Undine* or her request that she look up *de trop*. Clearly both children exhibited marked intellectual traits—and why not, living with parents who spoke French, were themselves omnivorous readers, not to mention omnivorous writers, and who gave and received books as naturally as they breathed.

And so, just as naturally, Mary Wilder Tileston early in her adult life began publishing compilations. Tileston saw herself and her books as contributing to her readers' education. For instance, in the preface to *The Children's Book of Ballads* (Little, Brown, 1883), Tileston wrote, "My object . . . has been to bring together from many sources the best and most stirring ballads of heroism and adventure. . . . Such poetry fills an important place in true education, by presenting a lofty ideal, and stimulating the heroic spirit." Or consider her preface to *The Blessed Life: Favorite Hymns* (Roberts Brothers, 1878):

My object in making this little collection has been to bring together in small compass a number of the best hymns, to which we are all attached, and such as are worth learning by heart. There are so many hours of sickness and sorrow, so many wakeful seasons in the night, when nothing soothes and calms the spirit so much as psalms and hymns, that it is well to store the mind with them, in readiness for the time of need. It is especially desirable to do this in childhood; for verses thoroughly learned then generally remain longest in memory.

Notice how easily she connects with her reader—citing hymns "to which we are all attached"—and the easy recommendation she makes to memorize the words, implicitly offering advice to parents that they and their children learn the hymns together. Would she and her parents not have done the same? Did she herself not know the benefit of reciting psalms and hymns?

A final example of Tileston's passion to teach, particularly to teach children, is from *The Children's Treasure Trove of Pearls* (published in 1908 by Little, Brown): "There have been many books dear to the hearts of children which have dropped out of existence, all the sooner if they were much loved, and therefore read to pieces. I have sought to rescue some of the stories in these books from oblivion, and to bring them together for a new generation to enjoy." Her words make me recall how she must have read *Undine* "to pieces." Her preface continues by noting worthy folktales from numerous cultures and she thanks the *American Folk-Lore Journal* for allowing her to use two of its stories. So in addition to reading Plato and Socrates and hymns and Julian of Norwich and a host of others, we can add an amateur's interest in folklore.

Tileston's Religious Views

Thus far I have explored the social and familial atmosphere that formed Mary Wilder Tileston, but I have said little about her religious upbringing, though for the Footes there was no separation between the social and familial and the religious, their religious values and practices ordering the other two. Nevertheless, there has been a reason for my silence: the difficulty in determining the family's specific theological views. Were they Unitarians, as several letters indicate ("the views of Unitarian Christianity are more sustaining & satisfying every year I live," wrote Mary Foote on October 8, 1852)? Or did they attend Unitarian churches but hold orthodox views, as other letters indicate?

Mary Foote's brother-in-law was a minister—a Unitarian?—who scheduled lectures by Ralph Waldo Emerson and Henry Ward Beecher, among others. The letters between Mary Foote and her sister Meggie deal almost exclusively with theology (contrast this with letters to her sister Eliza, which are filled with domestic details). The theological discussions are remarkable for a woman who claimed to be merely a mother; from the sisters' correspondence we can infer much, but much that is contradictory.

Mary Foote details the sermons she hears each week from a beloved minister; debates theological questions of the day (the letter of April 11, 1854, concerns her "impressions of Christ's supernatural existence"); and discusses the theological position of their new minister, whose views on the incarnation and the person of Christ she rejects: "You know I am old fashioned in my theology & of course must be aware that I could not assent to his views of Christ's nature—But I never heard the preacher who so aroused my whole spiritual being" (May 8, 1854).

In this regard, Mary Foote is more tolerant than many modern orthodox Christians who would find it hard to be spiritually "aroused" by a minister who rejected the fundamental tenet of the faith. Her sister defended such tolerance: "Miss Mary thinks . . . that I carry my toleration almost to the extent of a vice. But how much is gained if you can *love* & *trust* each other although poles apart in opinion and sentiment" (March 6, 1852); even so, the passion with which the sisters write about theology makes one think that when in conflict, each was trying to persuade the other to embrace, not simply to tolerate, the other's position. Not that the nature of Christ was unimportant to Mary Foote, for a few days later in another letter to her sister she refers to "Jesus Christ our Lord" (May 15, 1854); not that she disputed the evangelical conviction that one must choose or reject Christ; not that she failed to practice the disciplines of daily prayer and Bible reading; indeed, the evidence of her letters indicates how thoroughly she knew the Bible. Yet she was able to learn and grow spiritually from many, many sources, living and textual—to receive spiritual wisdom from them as from God. Mary Foote appeared truly to believe and *trust* that God can and does use all things and people for his children's edification, even using those who no longer believe.

Does she approve disbelief? On the contrary. "The one blessing I would ask for—our dear friend already has—a heart 'stayed upon God' and therefore in perfect peace. What is there in life to desire but this!" (August 5, 1856). However, I cannot stress enough how broadly and widely she looked for spiritual sustenance, not without questioning a person's theological position but without regarding "right" theology as the sine qua non, the litmus test, as if, ultimately, theology did not matter, despite how thoroughly theological questions obsessed her and how many hours she spent writing letters that are nothing less than deep and sophisticated theological disquisitions. Leave it to God, she implies, to separate the sheep from the goats.

Other Influences

I have been trying to trace the influences, underpinnings, and presuppositions that turned a bright and comforting five-year-old child into a woman who devoted her life to producing dozens of daily devotionals: to position Tileston's work within a tradition of devotional writing, to implicitly explain how that tradition helped shape Mrs. Cowman's *Streams in the Desert*, and not incidentally to give some insight into a woman about whom nothing has been written (at least that I have found). And nothing is more important than this tolerance of her mother, who could juxtapose Emerson and Elizabeth Barrett Browning, St. Paul and a Mrs. Huntington on the incarnation (wife of the minister William Reed Huntington?). But what are Mary Wilder Tileston's devotionals like? What, actually, do they *say?*

Before turning to these questions, however, let me first fill in the few details Tileston reveals about her adult life in writing the biography of her daughter, for they further demonstrate the breadth of Tileston's education and experience and show that just as her mother's family was interested in the politics of the Civil War, so was Tileston and her family interested and personally involved in the politics of the First World War. (The contrast to Charles and Lettie Cowman, who also lived through World War I and traveled to Europe, could not be sharper.)

Tileston and her husband lived first in Dorchester, Massachusetts. In 1874, two years after Amelia was born, the family moved to a 200-acre dairy farm in Concord, where they lived for eight years. It is hard to imagine the privileged daughter of a newspaper editor as a dairy farmer's wife; becoming a lawyer's wife might have been more predictable. I know something about what it takes to run a dairy farm. My grandparents owned a dairy farm, and my grandmother helped with the barn chores and in the field, cooked, canned, kept house, and raised only *two* children, not seven. No wonder that the Tilestons sold the farm after eight years, though Mary gives no reason and presents the setting, at least, positively: "It was a milk farm of two hundred acres, on the slope of Punkatesset Hill, running down to the Concord River, and it gave the children the freedom and varied interests of country life" (*Amelia Peabody Tileston*, 15). However, it must have been isolated, even lonely, as we can infer from this comment about life first in Salem and then in Brookline, "where [Amelia] enjoyed greatly the companionship of other children, which she had not had before." The family finally settled in Milton, but those early years and even the later years of Tileston's adult life have something of the nomad about them, as unlike her own settled childhood as possible. The numerous moves indicate restlessness, even rootlessness, not typical for that time or for those of her background. Yet they also reflect the turbulence of the times Tileston lived through. For her daughter, they set the stage for the greatest turbulence the world had yet seen and for her part in it.

Her daughter, like Tileston herself, attended private schools and finished at Miss Folsom's School in Boston.[2] Amelia made her first trip to Europe in 1895. After John Tileston died in 1898, Tileston took Amelia and three other daughters to Europe for a year, returning to Boston for eight years before moving back to Milton in 1907. Tileston's youngest daughter, Eleanor, died in 1912, followed a year later by another daughter Margaret. By 1915 Tileston had moved back to Brookline.

That is all she reveals—a series of deaths, a series of moves, all told in the plainest, most detached language, as if the events had happened to someone else: "After her father's death in 1898, she went abroad for a year with her mother and three of her sisters. On their return..." (19). Tileston expresses no emotion about the death of her husband or subsequently about the deaths of her daughters, even that of Amelia herself. She does not tell us where they went in Europe, though her comments about Italy in connection with her daughter's work there before going to Serbia make it clear that the family had spent some time there. Tileston says nothing about her own work or about how she lived after her husband died. Did she support herself by her publishing? Did her son, Henry Wilder Foote, himself a minister, support her? or her brother Arthur, who was an organist? What did she think of her daughter being given a military funeral with full honors or of the luminaries who attended it? How did an elderly woman cope with death after death after death? How many hymns and psalms did Tileston recite and how many wakeful nights did Tileston experience? There are no answers to these questions other than in the books Tileston produced, the ultimate themes of which are trust, fortitude, and joy—never despair. Never that. For in the very objectivity of the language Tileston chooses to describe her daughter's life and death, we hear echoed strength, pride, joy, and above all *stillness*, a central core of peace despite the chaos around her. These, no matter what else her devotionals say (as I discuss below), are the central message.

Tileston's Sources

Mary Wilder Tileston broke no new ground in producing devotionals, for women had been writing and compiling devotional books since the medieval period (I will have more to say about this in chapter 6). Copybooks like her mother's journals had an illustrious history during the Renaissance, and many educated people kept one (we might even say that it was the mark of an educated person); Shakespeare made Hamlet a dedicated copier, as we know from act one, scene five, when the Danish prince pulls out his daybook ("my tables") to record "that one may smile, and smile, and be a villain!" The copybook is also the source and heart of Montaigne's work and so the source and the heart of the essay. Copybooks were sometimes turned into daybooks, like Tileston's devotionals, and it was common for women to comment on the reading for the day—a movement from copying what one read, to assembling it in some order, to adding commentary about the quotations.

Although I have claimed that Tileston's foremost model was the work of her mother, nevertheless she could well have been inspired by St. Teresa of Avila or Julian of Norwich or St. Catherine of Siena— a few of the medieval women mystics she drew on—or later women of the seventeenth to the nineteenth centuries, like Madame Guyon, Mary Anne Schimmelpenninck, or Annie Keary, whose work may be little known or read today but which was well-known and read during their lives. Perhaps Tileston found inspiration in members of the pietist tradition, like Andrew Murray or John Keble. She may even have modeled her compilations on one of several textbooks she could have used in school, earlier examples of such books as *A Practical English Grammar*, by Albert N. Raub (1880) or *The Etymological Reader*, edited by Epes Sargent and Amasa May (1872), both of which taught language (personal pronouns, participles, suffixes, and prefixes) through excerpts from great writers: "Longfellow, Shakespeare, Milton, . . . Coleridge. . . . Addison, Cowper, Pope, Ossian, Scott, Ruskin, Thomson, Wordsworth, Trollope, Gray, Byron, Whittier, Lowell, Holmes, Moore, Collins, Hood, Goldsmith, Bryant, Dickens, Bacon, Franklin, Locke, the Bible."[3] Recall Tileston's object to educate and her advice about memorizing poetry.

Many of these same writers—Longfellow, Whittier, Ruskin, Wordsworth, Milton—appear in one or more of Tileston's books. History and the literary quality of her selections concerned Tileston, as we have noted and as she explained in her preface to *Great Souls at Prayer:* "This collection of prayers for daily use has been gathered from many sources, ancient and modern. It has historical interest, and the literary quality has been carefully considered, but the primary object is to nourish the spiritual life" (from the 1983 Keats edition).

Tileston is too modest. Anyone reading just this one book would receive a literary, historical, and theological education and, as Cynthia Ozick notes about Raub, an education in "language itself, language as texture, gesture, innateness . . . our common speech at its noblest."[4] "Elevated literature," Ozick continues, was the model for an educated tongue. Who could deny that most of Tileston's selections represent "elevated literature" in thought and in language?

Ozick asks:

> What did these demanding sentences do in and for society? First, they demanded to be studied. Second, they demanded sharpness and cadence in writing. They promoted, in short, literacy—and not merely literacy, but a vigorous and manifold recognition of literature as a *force*. They promoted an educated class. Not a hereditarily educated class, but one that had been introduced to the initiating and shaping texts early in life, almost like the hereditarily educated class itself.[5]

When I read Ozick, I recall Tileston's advice in *The Blessed Life:* Memorize early in life. Ozick, however, is bemoaning the loss of such literacy, such learning, such collections: "All that, we know, is gone."[6] But not entirely.

Ozick does not know about Mary Wilder Tileston or Lettie Cowman, whose books demand the kind of thoughtful reading Ozick values (though Ozick would reject their theological presuppositions), books that keep our gaze high or ask us to look long and deep. Who can read the following words lightly, swiftly, or casually?

> Grant me, O most loving Lord, to rest in Thee above all creatures, above all health and beauty, above all glory and honour, above all power and dignity, above all knowledge and subtlety, above all riches and art, above all fame and praise, above all sweetness and comfort, above all hope and promise, above all gifts and favours that Thou canst give and impart to us, above all jubilee that the mind of man can receive and feel; finally, above all angels and archangels, and above all things visible and invisible, and above all that Thou art not, O my God.
>
> Thomas Aquinas, quoted in *Great Souls at Prayer*, February 11, 42

The sweep of Thomas Aquinas's balanced and repeated prepositional phrases—"above all"—the whole moves, argumentatively, from the least to the greatest, and encompasses everything a human being might well rest in, then and today—even in those things God himself gives us and in which we might well rest (a profound, subtle theological insight). Aquinas could have stopped after the opening words, "Grant me, O most loving Lord, to rest in Thee," which is his petition. But would his prayer have the same power, the same passionate, imploring tone, without the list that follows? Would we know that resting in God is the utter sum of Aquinas's heart's desire, the utter sum and goal of his life? I doubt it.

Such language is not mean nor easy; it demands patience, care, deliberation. It demands, as Ozick rightly points out, to be studied; and it results in reflection, which is, fundamentally, the purpose of a daily devotional. No one who reads such prayers every day of the year will be the same person on December 31 as she was on January 1. I know. As I have read and studied these prayers—and entries from Tileston's other devotionals—my understanding of the nature of God has changed. So has my understanding of the *possibility* of faith, by which I mean the potential, what faith can encompass.

So not only do these daily devotionals fulfill Ozick's two claims about what Raub and Sargeant and May did to and for society, but the devotionals do something that Ozick's examples fail to do. Tileston's books preserve the writing of many, many women—well-known, little-known, unknown women—whose work deserves to be remembered; Ozick's two texts offer almost no examples from women writers. Yet it is rare *not* to find at least one woman excerpted in nearly every entry of Tileston's works. For instance, a prayer by Mary Carpenter follows that of Thomas Aquinas quoted above (even so, *Great Prayers* is the one exception to the ubiquity of women, for other than a prayer by Carpenter and one by Lady Jane Grey, the only other woman is Christina Rossetti—but Tileston uses more of her work than of any other writer).

The prayer of Carpenter, a nineteenth-century writer (Aquinas, thirteenth century), moves from verb to verb—calm, quiet, repress, correct, sanctify (another example of climax)—effectively uses parallelism, and also makes subtle distinctions: "So that we may *readily*, or even *joyfully*, give up whatever Thou dost ask for" (*Great Prayers*, February 12, 43, italics added). The nuances of meaning between the two adverbs remind me of Jesus' parable of the workers; God accepts even halfhearted sacrifice, but how much better *for us* to sacrifice joyfully?

The Compiler's Art

Obviously I cannot explicate every entry in every book by Tileston, but what I can do is explore particular, yet typical, entries, the part standing for the whole, as I have begun to do with these two prayers. First, I want to consider the entry in *Daily Strength* for December 8, not simply because it provides a good example of the far-reaching, educational (in Ozick's terms), and theologically diverse nature of the entries but also because it demonstrates in what ways it is legitimate to call Tileston an author, as *Publishers Weekly* does in its obituary, even though she (or her publisher) used the humbler, and deceptive, phrase, "selected by." To understand Tileston as an author—a composer—and not merely a selector or compiler is to understand what a devotional book is; or, to put it another way, a compiler or anthologizer is *also* an author.

Here is the entry, which I quote in full to make my discussion of it easier to follow and to (finally) display the devotional format for those who may be unfamiliar with it:

Blessed be the God and Father of our Lord Jesus Christ, who hath
blessed us with all spiritual blessing.

Eph. i.3

As sorrowful, yet alway rejoicing.
2 Cor. vi. 10

It is not happiness I seek,
Its name I hardly dare to speak;
It is not made for man or earth,
And Heaven alone can give it birth.

There is a something sweet and pure,
Through life, through death it may endure;
With steady foot I onward press,
And long to win that Blessedness.

Louisa J. Hall

The element of *happiness* in this present life no man can command,
even if he could command himself, for they depend on the action of
many wills, on the purity of many hearts, and by the highest law of God
the holiest must ever bear the sins and sorrows of the rest; but over
the *blessedness* of his own spirit circumstance need have no control;
God has therein given an unlimited power to the means of preserva-
tion, of grace and growth, at every man's command.

J. H. Thom

There is in man a higher than love of happiness: he can do without happiness, and instead thereof find blessedness!

T. Carlyle

As we see, Tileston begins December 8 with Ephesians 1:3, "Blessed
be the God and Father of our Lord Jesus Christ," then quotes 2 Corinthians 6:10 about sorrow and rejoicing—the two Bible verses establishing the theme for the entry on the nature of blessedness and the
possibility of happiness within the certainty of sorrow. Tileston picks
up the idea of happiness from the word *rejoicing* in Corinthians, for
happiness is not found in either verse. Two stanzas of verse about
happiness and blessedness by Louisa J. Hall follow. From the Reverend John Hamilton Thom, Tileston culls a brief commentary on happiness and blessedness to serve as a gloss on the poem and on the
Bible verses, the poem being the initial gloss on the biblical texts.

Finally, and surprisingly, comes Thomas Carlyle. Thus the entry begins with the verb "blessed" and ends with the noun "blessedness," demonstrating Tileston's careful crafting. However, not all entries have such an elliptical structure, though many do: December 7 begins "acquaint now thyself" and ends with "man's self"; October 11 "and when the people complained" ends "but complaint never."

Thematically, in the December 8 entry, Tileston begins with Paul blessing God for blessing *us* and ends with Thomas Carlyle, hardly a writer to put with Paul (theologically speaking), suggesting that we can find "blessedness" on our own—or at least that is one argument to be inferred. And indeed each of Tileston's entries *is* an argument, often more than one, for this entry contains at least another: that happiness and blessedness are distinct properties, that happiness is less important than blessedness, and that though happiness may not be in our control but in heaven's, at least according to the poem, blessedness nevertheless is. Or, as Thom puts it, our happiness depends on the actions of others—our "circumstances"—but circumstances cannot control ("need have no control over") our blessedness. God has given man "unlimited power" to command and thus insure our own blessedness.

Writers make arguments; that much is obvious, but less obvious is that compilers of devotional books also make arguments—365 small ones that add up to one or a few big ones, to which readers may assent without realizing the subtleties, incongruities, or fallacies of the arguments. Tileston, like any writer, wants her readers to think about the arguments, to consider the selections as a whole and not merely as a group of isolated sentences or paragraphs. Critics and scholars (or just educated readers) who have dismissed or ignored daily devotionals as being simplistic or simpleminded—and as I confessed I was one for a long time—simply don't understand the textual complexities that result when someone puts three or six or eight texts together on a page. (In talking with a contemporary anthologizer, I learned that what may appear to lack organization or purpose in a compilation is the result of much slow and careful thought.) For instance, what other printed page can and should be read from top to bottom and then again from bottom to top? Once we have read in the normal way of top to bottom, accruing texts like so much compounded interest, we then have to read backward, in the case of December 8, backward from Carlyle, who is the sum of Thom, Hall, and Paul; to Thom who multiples Hall who adds to Corinthians; and Corinthians to Ephesians, which started it all. In other words, we have something like exponential growth in Tileston's devotional entries: Carlyle increasing Thom, Hall, and Paul; Thom increasing Hall and Paul; Hall increasing Paul.

At the same time, we could say that Tileston has provided something for everyone, which accounts for her apparently universal appeal—from Episcopal Bishop William Lawrence to evangelicals Elisabeth Eliot and Ruth Bell Graham, who wrote in a preface that *Joy and Strength* "is a compilation of writings from God's choice servants down through the ages" (1986 edition). Charles Dodgson (Lewis Carroll), Ralph Waldo Emerson, Samuel Johnson, John Ruskin, Emanuel Swedenborg—"God's choice servants"? only if considered in Mary Wilder White Foote's and Mary Wilder Tileston's terms, but surely not in the terms of orthodox evangelicals.

Nevertheless, the juxtaposition of Swedenborg with Hannah Whitall Smith or Brother Lawrence characterizes Tileston's work as theologically eclectic or, more disparagingly, as theologically contorted or confused. We could, of course, count the number of entries each writer has, for instance, two for Swedenborg versus thirty-six for Edward Bouverie Pusey, who led the Oxford Movement after John Henry Newman converted to Catholicism. Would this quantitative evidence help us decide the theological leanings of Tileston? But then what do we make of the sixteen entries from Ralph Waldo Emerson or the nine entries from George Eliot in *Daily Strength*?

Let me consider Eliot more closely for a minute as an exemplary case. Although Eliot may have been raised in orthodoxy and even once professed orthodoxy, eventually she repudiated it. In fact she translated Strauss's *The Life of Jesus* and Feuerbach's *The Essence of Christianity*, the two most influential German texts of the late nineteenth century in higher criticism and the demythologizing of Christianity that, along with Darwin, caused deep and lasting disruptions in orthodoxy, so succinctly put by poet D. J. Enright: ". . . Once there were torrents to cross, / Forests to explore, and the nature of God" or "Job . . . Whose readiness to sing / Under the frequent scourge / Was a fine and sacred thing—/ But God was living then. . . ."[7] For the demythologizing of Christianity, we can in part thank Eliot, who said, "With the principles of Feuerbach I everywhere agree," as quoted by A. S. Byatt in her illuminating "George Eliot's Essays."[8] "The essential argument of *The Essence of Christianity* is that men invented religion—including the Persons of God, the sacraments and the Church—in order to be able to contemplate and worship their own nature."[9] Emerson might have agreed with Feuerbach, but would an orthodox Christian?

I am suggesting that for Tileston, as for her mother, such things did not matter. What counted was the aptness of a particular selection for a particular entry and for its bedfellows. All the entries, of course, are taken out of context, from the most to the least orthodox, which does not matter *because*, once put into another context, that of Tileston's own composition, the words change meaning, regardless of the original writer and her or his intentions and beliefs. I'm suggesting that the way Tileston and other compilers combine texts—the tense interplay of thought, contrary views, disjointed or disrupting juxtapositions—creates a tensile strength, surprisingly supple, lean, stretched, like thin-spun copper wire or membrane-thin gortex: textual skin. What they make as a whole, rather than what each is individually and was originally, tells.

Let us consider two more examples, this time from *Joy and Strength*.[10] The first of the two entries, June 16, includes the troublesome Swedenborg, along with the Psalms, Philippians, Lucy Larcom (more about her in chapter 5), and Thomas Erskine:

> Thy statutes have been my songs in the house of my pilgrimage.
> Psalms cxix. 54

> My God shall supply all your need according to His riches in glory by Christ Jesus.
> Philippians iv. 19

> How must the pilgrim's load be borne?
> With staggering limbs and look forlorn?
> His guide chose all that load within;
> There's need of everything but sin.
>
> So trusting Him whose love He knows,
> Singing along the road he goes;
> And nightly of his burden makes
> A pillow, till the morning breaks.
> Lucy Larcom

They live contented with what they have, whether it be little or much, because they know that they receive as much as is profitable for them; little, if little be profitable, and much, if much be profitable for them, but the Lord only can, who has an eternal end in view in all things which He provides.

Emmanuel Swedenborg

I hope you will learn, what I am always hoping to learn, to rejoice in God continually, knowing that He is really ordering all your circumstances to the one end of making you a partaker of His own goodness, and bringing you within His own sympathy.

Thomas Erskine

"Thy statutes have been my songs in the house of my pilgrimage" is juxtaposed to Paul's assurance that God supplies all our needs. At first, the connection seems tenuous, at best. The psalmist not only is writing metaphorically, as Paul is not, but also is addressing God to let him know that *he* knows the wonder of God's laws and at the same time reminding God that he, the psalmist, has been faithful—just in case God has overlooked this critical point.

Paul, on the other hand, is after a different kind of reminding because he has a different audience: members of the Philippian church who might be in the way of forgetting or maybe have not yet made the discovery that God will take care of them. And notice the play with pronouns: "*my* God" against "*your* need" and "*his* riches"; there is something deeply proprietorial about Paul's statement.

Two biblical passages, two writers, two immediate audiences here given to many, many other audiences. Then a third writer, Lucy Larcom, who not only glosses the two Bible verses but also brings them into harmony, just as did the third writer and text in the December 8 entry in *Daily Strength*. Larcom writes about "pilgrim" and "singing" and "road"—references to the psalmist—but also about "load," "Guide," "need," "trusting Him whose love He knows"—references to Paul. Thus we can interpret the two verses to mean that we can sing and travel our pilgrim road joyfully because no matter how many burdens we bear or needs we have, God will, in Christ, take care of them. Larcom's two pronouns, "Him" and "He," obviously refer to two different people—"Him" to God, "He" to Christ.

But Larcom's text adds to the biblical texts—or interprets them—by saying that the burden of the pilgrim contains nothing but what the

"Guide" chose for him and that the pilgrim needs every ounce of that burden, except, of course, "sin," which is the only part *not* provided by the Guide. Thus Larcom extends the Pauline passage: God will take care of a pilgrim's needs, translated as "load," which God himself brought into being in the first place. Without arguing this tetchy theological point, Tileston rushes us to her fourth text, Swedenborg.

What happens when Tileston adds Swedenborg? It seems as if the meaning of the devotional entry shifts again, for Swedenborg focuses on contentment. Then wouldn't Paul's famous passage on learning to be content regardless of circumstances have been more apt than that from Philippians? More predictable, certainly, which may be why Tileston did not choose it. But there are more problems with these two texts. Swedenborg is concerned solely with the material: "They live contented with what they have. . . ," whereas Paul seems concerned with the material *and* the spiritual. By juxtaposing these texts, Tileston has made an astounding move from God's statutes to mankind's need to burdens to contentment with one's material lot in life. With Swedenborg, we have Larcom's "burden" reduced to accepting one's social class or standing: If you've got a lot of stuff, then it's because it is "profitable," or good, for you to have it; if you don't have much, then it's because that is all you can reliably handle. But "profitable" also relates to investment, to earning ten dollars for every one dollar.

There seems to be some victimizing implied here, as well as some moral judgments: If someone is poor, he is so because this is what he deserves, because he has some moral deficiency; a rich and therefore morally superior person deserves his destiny too. Then that final, enigmatic line: "But the Lord only can, who has an eternal end in view in all things which He provides." The missing verb after "can" requires readers to fill it in—the Lord only can do what? *understand? justify? decide?* Or should we plug in Paul's verbs, "supply" and "provides"? But Paul does not hint of lordly class discrimination or imply that if a person is poor he only has himself to blame because he isn't good enough to be trusted with wealth.

Finally, we reach Erskine, which brings us nearly full circle, again, with the opening verses, but which also softens, to a degree, Swedenborg's harsh statement. "Rejoice" in God because his only goal is "making you a partaker of His own goodness." Rejoice means singing, as the psalmist urges, and the rest of Erskine is resonant with Paul's claim. Erskine also emphasizes the "living contented" of Swedenborg, not just because God has the long view but because in the end we'll be better off—all fairly straightforward orthodoxy. But Erskine is no less enigmatic than the other texts in this entry: "I hope you will learn, what I am always *hoping to learn*" (italics added). Erskine has not learned how to rejoice but is only *hoping* to, *always* hoping to. Is that enough, just hoping to learn? And why should his, or Tileston's, readers be able to go beyond him and actually succeed where he can only attempt? What's stopping him that should not stop the rest of us? Is this a case of the blind leading the blind or the parent who says do what I say, not what I do?

After all this, what are we left with? What theme do we have, what advice, what spiritual help? Maybe nothing more than "take the bitter with the better," which is far from the fervent cry of the psalmist: We've gone from "Ode to Joy" to a blues ballad, from a ringing assertion to a bloodless milksopian hope, a painful place to leave readers. Given the trials Tileston herself faced, I wonder that such an entry satisfied her. It certainly doesn't satisfy me; more than that, it disturbs me because I don't know how to read it. I would even suggest that it becomes unreadable as a result of the shifting meanings, like so many grains of sand slipping through my fingers. This is a troubling conclusion, given that the purpose of a devotional is to read and to reflect (however, might we not also say that the Bible itself often appears inscrutable?). Then I consider this entry from another perspective, the argument of the whole: We must learn to be content *despite* how little we understand; that if we make understanding a precondition to contentment, then surely we will never be content. And so, if Tileston wants us to learn this, if Tileston wants us to think about this as we go about our daily business, then I cannot imagine a better way for her to have accomplished her goal than by making the entry elusive; at least it has this effect on me. Its very lack of resolution brings me to the place where I am ready to learn, ready to turn the page.

It is not often in this or any devotional that one entry builds upon or directly connects to the previous one, but the entry for June 17 does just that:

None of them that trust in Him shall be desolate.
Psalm xxxiv. 22

That ye sorrow not, even as others who have no hope.
1 Thessalonians iv. 13

Are the consolations of God too small for thee?

Job xv. 11 (R.V.)

What shall make trouble? Not the holy thought
Of the departed; that will be a part
Of those undying things His peace hath wrought
Into a world of beauty in the heart.

Sarah J. Williams

She spoke of those who had walked with her long ago in her garden,
and for whose sake, now that they had all gone into the world of light,
every flower was doubly dear. Would it be a true proof of loyalty to
them if she lived gloomily or despondently because they were away?
She spoke of the duty of being ready to welcome happiness as well as
to endure pain, and of the strength that endurance wins by being grateful for small daily joys, like the evening light, and the smell of roses,
and the singing of birds. She spoke of the faith that rests on the Unseen
Wisdom and Love like a child on its mother's breast, and the melting
away of doubts in the warmth of an effort to do some good in the world.

Henry Van Dyke

The blues ballad of June 16 gives way immediately to the promise
that no one shall be desolate, that no one should sorrow as if he or
she has no hope, that no one should reject the consolations God offers
because they are always larger than we can imagine. Knowing the sorrow that Tileston faced in her own life, I find this entry particularly
poignant.

Recall how June 16 ended: Erskine's assurance that God arranges
all our circumstances, some of which, as Tileston points out in the
preface to *The Blessed Life*, include "wakeful seasons of the night."
But must we be stuck in sorrow, like a car, hubcap-deep in mud? No,
because God's goodness, in Erskine's words, is evidenced by God's
consolations. That is, God's goodness equals God's consolations during times of sorrow. And that is why, according to the logic of the June
17 entry, we cannot be desolate.

But not only do the three Bible passages, poem, and prose excerpts
answer Erskine but also the poem by Larcom. The burden of the pilgrim, which includes the deaths of loved ones referred to by Van Dyke,
is born lightly, with song. Again I recall Tileston's passion for hymns
and psalms and notice that both entries begin with verses from the
Psalms, the book she chooses most often to begin each entry (see,

for example, August 15, 16, and 29, or October 1, 4, 5; in fact it is hard to find an entry that does not include a verse from the Psalms).

As we have seen in the previous examples, each selection in this entry builds on and glosses the previous selection, in this case almost as if the selections become a conversation with the reader. I imagine Tileston selecting the first text and then the second and then thinking to herself, "but what about readers who will silently reject or question or argue with these verses? What of the reader who says, *I trust God, I have faith, so why do I feel so desolate, so hopeless? What's wrong with me?* Anticipating such a response, one she herself may well have had as she watched husband and children die, while she remained alive, she adds a line from Job—a question. The effect of that question is as if it leaped off the page and spoke itself directly to the reader because a question always implies a speaker and a listener. So not only does the question address the two previous verses, it addresses the skeptical, sorrowing reader. And more than that, for although "Are the consolations of God too small for you?" seems like a simple yes/no question, it is not. Answer no, and we must then ask, "Well, what are these consolations that are big enough?" Answer yes, and we still must ask, "What are these consolations that are too small?" Either way, the question from Job requires a question of our own— and a catalogue of consolations, which will be different for each reader. But just in case we can't think of any consolations, small or great, or have trouble recognizing consolations when they come, Tileston teaches us how by concluding with the selection from Van Dyke: "every flower was doubly dear," "the evening light, and the smell of roses, and the singing of birds. . . . the warmth of an effort to do some good in the world." As we end the reading, we can say, "So that's what she means" and list our own consolations—a hot shower, fresh coffee, blue sky, a dishwasher, turtleneck sweaters—my own eclectic, partial list of consolations in a world of sorrow. It is clear that Tileston intends us to participate actively in her devotionals, just as she urged readers to memorize hymns. We can't simply read and shut the book for another twenty-four hours. Her devotionals require something from us, just as faith itself does.

Am I giving Tileston far more compositional credit than she deserves? I don't think so. I don't picture her sitting in her house, thumbing aimlessly through books, magazines, Bible, to find a few selections per entry that sort of, more or less, might, loosely interpreted, go together. Rather, I imagine a conscious, thoughtful compiler, carefully choosing the selections for each entry and then considering how each entry reads, day by day, day after day. I hear her asking how June works, how all 365 entries add up—even the enigmatic entry for June 16 in *Joy and Strength.* I imagine her reliving her own experiences to test the usefulness of each entry and, as I indicated above, anticipating a reader's natural responses, skepticism and anger included. This, I argue, is the role of the devotional compiler.

As Bishop William Lawrence said, she understood the human condition. And that, perhaps, is the greatest asset any devotional writer can have.

From Mrs. Cowman's Library

TWO WOMEN IN BETWEEN

*B*ooks tell stories, sometimes more than the stories the authors have written. Sometimes a more important story comes in the notations a reader makes in a text. And so the books Mrs. Cowman read and studied not only help me understand her better but also help me better understand the genre of the daily devotional and the variety of devotionals available to women readers in the late nineteenth century.

The books she owned help me trace the reading habits of women then and continue my investigation of what makes a devotional succeed. Mrs. Cowman's books reinforce what an odd book a devotional is, how unexpected the contents, how democratic its impulses. Anyone can compile a devotional book, and anything can be included. Time, geography, political persuasion or theological disposition, class, gender, even race (though this latter is the most problematic) do not seem to matter. A devotional book, I begin to realize, is a container or a mystery box like those one finds at estate sales: Buy the box for a dollar and discover what treasures lie therein—or what white elephants. The two devotionals I consider here fit this description to a T.

Ellen M. Dyer

> The sincere and earnest worker will take every statement of truth and build it into his body and into his life, through right thinking, right speaking, right acting. He will be as accurate in applying his knowledge of

truth as in following any rule in algebra or music, thus mastering every detail of the laws of life.

These words preface Ellen M. Dyer's *Daily Suggestions for Workers: Many Thoughts Borrowed from Many Minds,* published in 1898 by Harper. Several things are worth noting about this exhortation, which is the only word to describe it. First, it is not particularly religious. It could be the motto of any progressive organization with a goal of helping people improve their lives. Or it could be introducing any one of a number of contemporary pop-psychology or self-help books. Second, it implies that there are systematic rules for improvement through application of the truth and that success depends on accuracy, doing one's sums correctly, solving a double equation, or practicing the C-minor scale. Building a better life, a successful life, this implies, is straightforward, accessible to all, even easy. Third, these words come from a teacher and though we have no source given, must surely be those of Ellen M. Dyer herself.

The flyleaf opposite the title page of the copy of *Daily Suggestions for Workers* that I am reading is stamped "Chas. E. Cowman, 156 So. Hobart Blvd., Los Angeles, Calif. January 18, 1923." The words "Mamma Anna" have been written in pencil but in a different hand than the margin notes in the text itself. But does this book belong to Charles Cowman, who is only a year and a half away from death? Or does it really belong to his wife? It is her handwriting that I find throughout the book.

Does Mrs. Cowman receive this book from one of her many well-wishers, as her diary records that so many devotional books came into her possession? Hundreds of people send her tracts, poems, hymns, and letters, hoping to lighten her burden or share their own. Is this a book she carries in her purse or keeps in the pocket of a bed jacket? It is certainly small enough, only 104 pages, with dimensions smaller than those of a mass-market paperback. Although the book has readings for each day of the year, most are no more than two or three lines. Some have quotation marks around them; others do not. Because no author is identified, does Mrs. Cowman assume that Ellen M. Dyer wrote some of the entries herself, those without quotations, as I assume that Dyer wrote the opening words? I wonder whether Mrs. Cowman uses Dyer's approach as her own model, providing sources for some but not all entries and thus obscuring her own contributions.

Mrs. Cowman could have found Dyer's book in a used bookstore or at a church rummage sale; but she could not have purchased it new. Not only do the penciled words "Mamma Anna" indicate a previous owner but by 1923 the book would have been out of print—1923, a pivotal year. Charlie is dying; Mrs. Cowman's diary shows their desperate longing for supernatural healing; Mrs. Cowman publishes *Streams.* Recall the advertisement:

Just the Very Book You Will Want for Christmas

Mrs. Chas. E. Cowman has compiled one of the choicest books of Daily Readings that is on the market (365 pages). They comprise gatherings of years, special things that will help one in their perplexities and trials. It is a book full of heart-throbs and victories. Be sure to send in your order early. Price $1.50 post paid.[1]

"A book full of heart-throbs and victories," a book for help in "perplexities and trials." And in 1923 Mrs. Cowman was reading Dyer's book, among other things, or so I assume, given the stamped date and the marginalia. Some of Dyer worked its way into Cowman's own devotional, in spirit and theme if not in actual words cited.

I imagine Lettie next to Charlie's bed, book in hand, late into the night, reading the short entries aloud—entries that would provide nourishment without overtaxing a sick man's ability to concentrate, the way poached eggs or milk toast coddle a sensitive digestion. She holds a pen; she marks passages; she may even copy them elsewhere, as had been her habit since girlhood. She and Charlie talk about the entries, using them as springboards for prayer, particularly those that concern sickness, like that of March 25th: "In any moment of trouble and sickness, when we need help it is better to open out like the flower, . . ." next to which is the word "good" and a line drawn down the left side of the text. Or an earlier entry for February 25th, next to which Mrs. Cowman writes "Healing," puts a right-hand bracket around the whole, and underlines the three central lines: "Making yourself free and relaxed, porous, as it were, that God's love may freely penetrate. Be still, listen, and you will hear. . . . give voice to that message and healing follows."

These words, noted by Mrs. Cowman, provide another commentary on *Streams in the Desert,* another reason why Mrs. Cowman publishes the book. If, as I said earlier, a devotional writer or compiler first addresses herself—the initial audience—then these words must have struck Mrs. Cowman like the swift incision of a surgeon: Give voice . . . healing follows. And nothing so occupies Mrs. Cowman in 1923 than the healing of her husband. Could her words in *Streams*—her voice—lead to Charlie's healing? Given her diaries, she may well have believed Dyer. Thus she publishes *Streams* so that Charlie will be healed.

Yet *Daily Suggestions for Workers* is a strange little book, indeed, for a devotional. No passages from the Bible are included, no poetry, no multiple comments per day. When I found it in the Zondervan-owned Cowman library in Grand Rapids, Michigan (I found nothing like it in the Cowman library housed at OMS headquarters), I wondered what in the book attracted Mrs. Cowman. The title alone seems so pedantic if not narrow, even classist, so un-Victorian, off-putting for someone like Mrs. Cowman, who never thought of herself as a "worker"; even in 1898 the word had blue-collar connotations (actually, even earlier than that, if one thinks of Lucy Larcom and the magazines the female mill workers wrote and published in the mid- to late-1800s, as I discuss in chapter 5). Had the title ended with the words "in God's Vineyard," then I would understand its attraction. But attract her it did, for the book has been well read, at least until October 29, as evidenced by how many entries have been underlined in black ink; how many have a word or two of response recorded in the margins; perhaps the brevity of the entries commended it to her. The comments provide a record of Mrs. Cowman's thinking, correlate with her diaries, show how and what she was reading while Charlie lay dying, so for these reasons alone the book and its author are worth a pause.

The title page of this little book provides the following facts about publication: Philadelphia, Press of Harper & Brothers, 200 S. Tenth Street, 1898; there was also an 1894 edition. And there is this tantalizing detail: Ellen M. Dyer, 1516 Locust Street—another Philadelphia address, listed on local maps of the time and in the city directory next to the author's name as a school, though the directory indicates her as a resident only for 1897 and 1898; she does not appear in the 1900 census for Pennsylvania.

What school did she run? No information exists. Dyer's school, which apparently was also her home, was about eight blocks from the Harper offices. I imagine the author walking to Harper with her small manuscript and high hopes that an editor would find it meritorious, which someone apparently did, given its publication and subsequent printings. The world was on the verge of a new millennium; the Cowmans of leaving for Japan Mrs. Cowman getting her feet wet as a public speaker; England of a new monarch; the country in financial panic, workers restless. Perhaps Harper saw an opportunity or a market or a social role to play by publishing Ellen M. Dyer's schoolmarmish book.

More about this author I cannot write for, as I said, she appears in the Philadelphia city directory for two years and then disappears. Does her school, most likely of the primary grades (as were most such small, private schools of the time), fail to attract enough students? Does she move? die? marry? I assume that Ellen M. Dyer was unmarried when she ran her school because a married woman would probably not have been so occupied.

Could she have been distantly related to Mary Ellen Dyer, who was hanged in Boston early in our history for her Quaker beliefs?[2] Mary Ellen and Ellen M. are so similar that I find myself consistently interchanging the one name for the other. The surname Dyer, I learn, is a well-known Quaker name, as sure a mark (and all related) as the Anabaptist, Amish, and Mennonite names so ubiquitous in Pennsylvania and Indiana. But neither the city archives nor the archives at Quaker headquarters in Philadelphia list an Ellen M. Dyer. The librarian of the latter tells me that nevertheless Ellen must have been a Quaker, her school run on Quaker principles. Perhaps that is the source of her failure, if indeed it was: a school for poor or working-class children, or for the children of former slaves or recent immigrants. If Ellen M. Dyer was raised as a Quaker and still practiced her faith, it would explain the numerous references to rest, to silence, to quietude, to God within all human beings. I am drawn to such references because Mrs. Cowman herself was drawn to them, marking them in some way.

Perhaps at another time in her life Mrs. Cowman would not have been so drawn to such texts, but at this time the need for rest, for peace, for patience overshadows everything else, including the insistence on "right doctrine." And Cowman's own book is evidence of this, as well, just as it sounds on nearly every page the themes and concerns that Cowman notes in Dyer's book.

For instance, she writes "praise God," next to August 6, part of which reads "a new outpouring of the Spirit follows each Gethsemane hour." We have already seen how the image and metaphor of Gethsemane permeates her biography of Charles, her diaries, and her devotional. Or, next to July 23, she responds "Amen": "Grow as the lilies of the field, nothing doubting. . . ." Mrs. Cowman writes and underlines "fine" next to an entry about the majesty of God within us all, calls "lovely" a passage about murmuring brooks and rustling corn, declares "<u>Amen!</u>" to advice on prayer and "Wonderful!" this entry: "The creation of a thousand forests is in one acorn, so the future of many lives may be folded in the victory gained to-day" (June 30); she also dog-ears the page. As she underlines it, I imagine her thinking that Charlie's future lay folded in the victory she gains over doubt and fear and pain. Throughout her diary, she gives evidence that she links Charlie's healing to *her* faith: Victory of and in the spirit would lead to victory of and in the body.

Perhaps because Dyer's audience are workers, the aphorisms so frequently focus on the body and the intimate connection of body and spirit: What happens to the one happens to or affects the other. How thoroughly Mrs. Cowman believed this and suffered from it. Such a concern for the physical, however, not only goes against what we might think is the common grain of devotional literature but also is quintessentially medieval, as we shall see in chapter 6. The medieval women who wrote devotionals sometimes suffered incapacitating physical diseases; the demands of the body were consistently uppermost in their minds, and so they persistently draw our attention to our physical being.

Mrs. Cowman could not escape thinking about the body. In some ways, it was all she did think of in the early 1920s, for she was a prisoner of Charlie's body, though she would not have used the word *prisoner*. Nevertheless, she undoubtedly craved any advice or thoughts about the body, whether they diminished the significance of the body or heightened its significance by making its well-being the prerequisite of a healthy soul. And in Dyer, Cowman would have found both views expressed—from the underlined August 12 entry that declares "the human body is but a mask that conceals or reveals the reality of our spirit" to those about the body being an artist's canvas or learning "to embody" sublime ideas (January 28). Could the former mean that an unhealthy body reveals an unhealthy spirit? There are passages in Dyer that lean in that direction, and these would have pained and depressed Mrs. Cowman without the counterargument that resting and relaxing the body provides ease for the spirit. It is not insignificant that she is drawn to a physical image as the controlling theme for her own work—a thirsting, dying man finding water in the desert, not a mirage but reality. An oasis.

An oasis is always the same, yet never the same, because each visitor brings her own pains and illnesses and reasons for thirst to be quenched. What crosses all experience is the joy in finding water where none would be expected. In so many ways a devotional (re)produces this experience, and Dyer's is no exception. If anything, it is more like a sudden stream than any of the other devotionals, simply because it and Dyer herself are so unprepossessing. It was Cowman's good grace to find it, her good sense to read it, her good instinct to use it.

Mrs. C. S. DeRose

Dyer's book leads me to look for other devotionals that Mrs. Cowman might have read and imitated because to understand the devotional means discovering how writers and compilers come by their ideas; reading is so crucial to the genre. With Mrs. Cowman, almost her only escape from suffering is through books. However, other than Tileston's *Daily Strength*, in the Cowman library at Zondervan, I find only one other devotional book by a woman.[3]

The devotional I find is Victorian in outlook, source material, and style, which the publisher has dressed appropriately in purple cloth with silver embossing for the title, *A Daily Staff for Life's Pathway*. If I know little about Ellen Dyer, I know even less about Mrs. C. S. DeRose, designated on the title page as selector and arranger—not even her first name given. That she was married is obvious, but I imagine her a widow, given the choices for her devotional, given the dedication of her book: "To the Memory of My Mother."

I see Mrs. DeRose at her mother's bedside with a book in her hand, perhaps a book of Shelley's verse or Tennyson's. Or could that be "The Stones of Venice" by John Ruskin she holds? The room is dim, the draperies blood velvet, the furniture ornately carved mahogany. The tops of the dresser and nightstand are marble, the handles cut glass. Next to the bed is a bellpull within reach, so that her mother can call for the servant girl or for her daughter at need. Like most sick, elderly people, she can be querulous, but Mrs. DeRose knows what to do. Every afternoon, every evening before her mother falls asleep, Mrs. DeRose reads to her. The rich cadences of Carlyle or the mesmerizing rhythms of Robert Browning's "Fra Lippo Lippi" soothe her mother, help her forget her pain. They share a cup of tea, they share thoughts, they share a love of reading. Then her mother dies. Having cared for her mother so many years, having had her daily routines and rhythms determined by her mother's needs, Mrs. DeRose would have felt the loss more acutely than most of us would today, we who seldom watch a parent die. How could she profitably fill the hours once filled caring for her mother? What, she wonders, would best memorialize the life of her mother? What would have pleased her mother most had she still been alive?

A book dedicated to her.

A book that includes some of the writers and passages that her mother loved best.

A Daily Staff for Life's Pathways is born.

With this perhaps too sentimental picture before me of the imposing Mrs. DeRose—now dressed in black satin with a gold and onyx brooch at the collar—and her circumstances, I want to know the real story. I also want to admire this book as I've come to admire the others.

When I began this study, I had assumed that no life that had a public aspect could be lost, yet with Mrs. DeRose this has happened. Although she publishes a book in 1895, there are no records of her, nothing in the old lists of books published in the 1800s, not even the title of her devotional. And who publishes it? A vanity press? No, indeed, but a well-known, well-respected, and highly successful old house, Frederick A. Stokes, with offices in New York and London. And it was illustrated by Izora C. Chandler in a nostalgic pen and ink style, display type and design equally nostalgic. As I said, the book is high Victorian—one of those ubiquitous and lucrative devotionals published during the mid- to late-1800s.[4]

It would have competed with Tileston's own books, and perhaps that is why it died while *Daily Strength* lives on. Or perhaps Mrs. DeRose, whose reading taste runs predominantly to such writers as Kingsley, Shelley, Tennyson, Carlyle, Ruskin, and George Eliot was out of step with the audience. On the other hand, Tileston too uses most of these writers, Shelley being the exception. So it could not be the Victorians who put readers off. Perhaps the writers whom no other devotionalists include were the culprits: Ovid, for instance, Alexander Pope, John Locke, Pythagoras, Seneca, even George Bernard Shaw, the latter hardly a friend to Christianity. Or maybe there were simply too many devotionals by the time DeRose compiled her own. Although breadth is a characteristic of all daily devotionals, too much breadth results in a lack of focus or purpose. Unlike Tileston and Cowman, who sound the consistent themes of suffering, perseverance, and hope, such consistency is lacking in DeRose. Nevertheless, the wide-ranging entries evidence a breadth of reading or a sharp memory of the school primers she would have read as a girl. DeRose's emphasis on reading is evident from the start. On the title page we find the following quote from Samuel Smiles: "Sometimes a book containing a noble exemplar of life, taken up at random, merely with the object of reading it as a pastime, has been known to call forth energies whose existence had not before been suspected."

But what kind of reading is DeRose thereby recommending? or assuming? Is it an approach to reading that is actually antithetical to the book that she has produced? As I pointed out in the two previous chapters, Cowman and Tileston assume their audience will read daily and systematically, using the devotionals for study and reflection. In this sense, the devotionals are textbooks, not books for casual entertainment. In fact nowhere do we find the slightest hint that reading is a "random" activity, a mere "pastime." Reading for Cowman and Tileston is always purposeful; they tell their readers, in effect, to read as they read. DeRose, on the other hand, appears to read by happenstance; and if her book affects readers, it will be almost accidental. She assumes her readers will open her book at random, occasionally, to pass the time. Asking less of her readers, does she receive less? It is almost as if she belittles or undercuts her very own work. Or it might be that as a gift book, which the binding, design, and illustrations all indicate, she could have no other aspirations for it.

It is difficult to draw conclusions about DeRose's religious perspectives, even more difficult than for Tileston, had we only her book as evidence of her life, or for Mrs. Cowman, who despite some anomalous entries nevertheless definitely leans toward Low Church Protestantism. In fact given the numerous nonreligious entries in

DeRose, we might conclude that she merely reflects that strong-minded, flinty morality of the mid-Victorians, or the late Greeks. Yet DeRose uses numerous Catholic writers, but then so does Tileston. Is Thomas Aquinas more or less "Catholic" than Catherine Adorna? Although DeRose may have known about medieval women mystics, she nevertheless found Margaret Fuller and Madame de Staël more to her liking. If there is more of Anna Shipton than in Tileston or Cowman, there is less of Elizabeth Barrett Browning, Christina Rossetti, or some popular nineteenth-century women authors like Lydia Maria Child; yet Adelaide Procter appears prominently (see chapters 4 and 5 for a discussion of some of these women and a more thorough comparison of the devotionals). It is also noteworthy that Harriet Beecher Stowe, the single most popular midcentury author, appears only once.

But what did Mrs. Cowman make of DeRose's book? She didn't pick up a fondness for Shakespeare or Goethe or Matthew Arnold or the *Wisdom of the Brahmins*. She didn't write in the margins, as she did in Dyer's book, except for marking a couple of entries with an x. But she did leave us evidence of what she found significant, for she had two ways of marking books: She wrote in them, or she turned down a corner, top or bottom. There are numerous dog-eared pages in DeRose's book: January 16 and 17, February 10, May 17, August 2. The top part of the entry for February 21 has been cut out; perhaps Mrs. Cowman wanted to use it in a speech or as one of her own entries. From the numerous fragments she stuck in books, I know that she often cut out sections from magazines, though cutting something from a book is unusual. These marked passages have a common theme: understanding, accepting, and trusting God's will, the same theme that permeates Mrs. Cowman's diaries during the early 1920s and one of the themes in *Streams in the Desert*.

One of the checked passages is even more significant. Mrs. Cowman marks a passage from Stopford Brooke that closes the reading for February 26:

> A sorrow comes upon you. . . . Meet the dreadful hour with prayer, cast your care on God, claim him as your Father,—and the degrading, paralyzing, embittering effects of pain and sorrow pass away, a stream of sanctifying and softening thought pours into the soul, and that which might have wrought your fall but works in you the peaceful fruits of righteousness.

That such a passage moved Mrs. Cowman we should well expect. And how similar this is to so much of her diary, in which night after night she records how paralyzed and degraded and near embitterment she and Charlie are, but through prayer the brittle is made pliant again.

What of the rest of this entry? DeRose did not exaggerate when she assumed that her audience would read randomly, for there is no other way to read, despite the dates. Not even hermeneutical sleight of hand could infer a connection among Psalm 32:22 on joy, three lines from Sir Walter Scott on the difference between waking and dreaming, or the words of John Henry Newman on watching for the second coming of Christ. Unlike the entries in Cowman and Tileston, DeRose's selections show no pattern, no sense of one selection building or commenting on the previous selection. Occasionally two selections may connect, but the others do not. Because the entries give the sense of reading a series of non sequiturs, DeRose's devotional lacks a sense of purpose. But I keep searching.

In my search, I turn to one of the entries, May 17, marked by Mrs. Cowman in three ways: the upper left-hand corner is turned over, the last selection for the day is checked, and there is an unusual bookmark at the page. Although I understand why Mrs. Cowman would note the Bible passage, I cannot find a connection from Matthew 11:30, "For my yoke is easy, and my burden is light," to "Convey thy love to thy friend as an arrow to the mark." Yet each of the four selections taken alone would have had great resonance for Mrs. Cowman, regardless of how disjointedly they fit together. The selection from Matthew is obvious, as is another from Samuel Smiles on the difference between genius and character, a distinction that Mrs. Cowman carefully developed in the biography of her husband. And finally F. W. Faber's comments on deeds as thoughts that influence so many people we do not know sound very like Mrs. Cowman's view of her own devotional.

Mrs. Cowman's bookmark, however, is more interesting than her notation on friendship because it is the only evidence of domesticity among her papers. Did Mrs. Cowman clean? do laundry? cook? Was she ever occupied or preoccupied by the concerns of most women? It does not appear so. Raised with servants (or day help for her mother), she continued to have servants in one guise or another; during Charlie's illness the servant would have been the nurse. Thus it is quite a surprise to find "A Meatless Menu" serving as a bookmark. Women don't save menus or recipes unless they want to try them, even if they never do. And what a menu it is, a company, not an everyday meal: cream of corn soup, bran biscuit, baked potatoes, mashed hubbard squash, mock veal loaf with white sauce, fruit salad, mayonnaise dressing, pineapple tapioca pudding, bran bread, zwieback, minute brew, and cream. Just typing it makes me full. It also makes me realize how white American diets used to be; even the fruit salad is whitened with mayonnaise. (Many of the ingredients are white: milk and cream feature prominently.) Three recipes then follow, for the mock veal loaf and two alternatives, Rice à la Carolina and Protose Cutlets. Protose is the main ingredient of each recipe, which makes me think that this menu, rather than coming from a women's magazine, was included with the protose or was in a magazine for Seventh-Day Adventists. But what is it? And what is cero-vita, another ingredient? They sound like the health food forerunners of tofu or a wartime exigency, though the numbers 5-15-20 at the bottom could well be the date the menu was published.

But why mention this other than for its insight into earlier eating habits or Mrs. Cowman's one dash of domesticity? The menu serves as an apt metaphor for, commentary on, even evaluation of DeRose's devotional, whether or not Mrs. Cowman had such in mind when she stuck it in the book. The menu reminds me of Paul's words about milk and pablum and being too young for meat, and so many of DeRose's entries too have that effect. The menu also sounds a false and incoherent note, with imitation veal or other meat substitutes, all no doubt cheaper than the real thing, but hardly as satisfying. There is a sense of the false and incoherent about DeRose's devotional also: a lack of purpose or harmony, as I said, despite an occasional, emerging theme. Cowman's meatless menu also lacks harmony, unless we think that beginning with cream of corn soup and ending with cream is harmonious (monotonous, yes, exciting, no). The menu, too, is high on starch and filler, again a characteristic of DeRose's devotional; another word might be sentimental or nostalgic. And despite the occasional hardedged insight, it is no more sinewy than the soft, squishy combination of foods on the menu. DeRose and this menu have no texture and give us nothing much to chew on.

A Daily Staff for Life's Pathway lacks the robustness of Tileston and Cowman because, finally, it lacks the themes of suffering and triumph that imbue the other two devotionals (themes that their fore-runners of the medieval era had, as I discuss in chapter 6). An occasional entry may hit these themes, but we do not find them in entry after entry after entry. Even Dyer's, as brief as it is, emphasizes how to overcome life's nagging, if not dramatic, trials.

My puzzlement over and speculation about Mrs. DeRose and her devotional end when I study "A Meatless Menu." There is a reason why the combination of such food is no longer found on most American tables, and it is the same reason why no bookstore can stock *A Daily Staff* when Cowman and Tileston remain staples on devotional shelves.

four

The Company of British Women

Christina Rossetti
Adelaide Procter
Anna Shipton
Dinah Muloch Craik
Mary Ann Schimmelpennick

I knock at the stone's front door.
"It's only me, let me come in. I want to enter your insides,
have a look round,
breathe my fill of you."
Wislawa Szymborska, "Conversation with a Stone"

When I first read this poem, I thought immediately of Lettie Cowman, Mary Tileston, Ellen Dyer, Mrs. DeRose. I thought immediately of the women they knew and read and anthologized, the reason for this and the subsequent chapters. Szymborska's stone becomes a metaphor for the women I am studying. I say to them, "Let me in, have a look round, breathe my fill of you." Most of the time they say to me what the stone replies, "'Go away,' . . . / 'I'm shut tight. / Even if you break me to pieces, we'll all still be closed.'" But like the speaker in the poem, I keep knocking, asking the women to let me in. I want to know the women who appear in Cowman and Tileston.

It would be misleading, though, for me to imply that my devotionalists draw exclusively from women because they don't. In their work as much as in their culture, we find fewer women than men. The odd thing is that I easily recognize most of them, from men like Emerson and Carlyle to theologians and preachers, just as most readers would. On the other hand, most of us won't and don't recognize the majority of the women included. Even so, it is noteworthy to find so many women cited, so many now obscure women, who originally showed up in large and small magazines or, occasionally, in books—sentimental novels, religious novels, collections of poetry, hymns, short stories, all now long out of print, out of sight, out of mind. We come across a name in Tileston or Cowman or DeRose and wonder, *Who was she? Where did she come from? What did she write? Where did she publish?* It is noteworthy too that along with women from the eighteenth and nineteenth centuries, we find so many women from the medieval era: Julian of Norwich or Catherine of Siena, who were hardly household names, at least among Protestants. How accessible were the works of these women in the mid- to late-1800s?

Some women, like Adelaide Procter, Anna Shipton, or Christina Rossetti, show up in Tileston, DeRose, and Cowman (since Dyer provides no authors I do not know whom she anthologizes, and given that the citations are not well known a book of quotations is no help); others, like Lucy Larcom or Madame Guyon, occur in Tileston and Cowman, or Dinah Maria Craik only in DeRose and Tileston; still others are unique to the individual volumes, like Juliana Horatia Ewing or Lydia Maria Child in DeRose, Mary Anne Schimmelpenninck in Tileston, Margaret Bottome in Cowman. (I am only referring here to Tileston's *Daily Strength;* if I include her other anthologies, or even just *Joy and Strength*, then the overlap becomes more complicated; for instance, Tileston also uses Juliana Ewing and both Tileston and DeRose anthologize Madame Swetchine.)

It would also be misleading to imply that only now-invisible women caper and dart in these devotionals, for we find Frances Ridley Havergal, Harriet Beecher Stowe, Elizabeth Barrett Browning, Charlotte and Emily Brontë, George Eliot, Hannah Whitall Smith, and Hannah More, who need no introduction other than to note that they have found their way into the devotional milieu. Although well known, I include Rossetti on the basis of her own little-known devotional—an unknown within the known.

I imagine these women as a great company, all assembled in a ballroom, and I want to know them, talk with them, watch them dance and listen to them recite or tell their stories. I want to see them on stage, performing as they once performed, see them take their bows and curtain calls, so that I can applaud their work. And I want readers to know at least a little about them, so they too can applaud. Unfortunately, for some of these women no more *can* be known. I knock, but when I open the door and enter so many of them have their backs to me. How often have I read the words "Not much is known about the life of...." They published; they perished. I have, therefore, been unable to trace every woman mentioned in these devotionals; nor would it be possible to tell the stories of every woman even had I been able to find references to them. It would not even be possible to list all the women anthologized in Tileston alone, for this would then become a different book.

However, it is possible to provide commentary on a representative sample of women, starting with the women found in DeRose, Tileston, and Cowman, to indicate the scope and breadth of their reading habits, to explore the women who inspired them, to establish the women other women were reading in late-nineteenth and early-twentieth-century America—and this I have done. As I read the magazines they would have read and consider the praise heaped on the writers they anthologized, I learn what values for women predominated. In other words, the review articles in particular demonstrated on what grounds women's writing was valued and by extension on what grounds women's lives were valued and valuable. Although I don't compare the reviews given to women and to men to detail how different the judgments were, let me say that they *are* different, women in general praised for the usefulness, goodness, or high moral tone of their work and not necessarily for their plotting, their character development, their use of language.

Obscurity is a strange and shape-shifting characteristic of the women the devotional compilers anthologized. When I chose the women I discuss below, I did not know this about obscurity; I did not know that women like Lucy Larcom or Lydia Maria Child had been undergoing a shape-shift, even though I knew that scholars in women's studies were heading back to the nineteenth century on a search and rescue mission. I chose my examples *solely* on the basis of how important they seemed to me as I read DeRose, Tileston, and Cowman— which is to say how important they seemed to them. Yet some of the women I chose for textual reasons have indeed been resuscitated—

or at least rescue attempts have been made in the past ten years or so.[1] If I don't review contemporary scholarship about these women, as is standard academic practice (though I do refer below to some of these texts), it is because I am pursuing the religious links of women writers to DeRose, Tileston, and Cowman and what the women's nineteenth-century contemporaries thought of them.

In addition, in this chapter where I talk about British writers and in the next chapter where I move to three American and one European, I offer an anthology of women without making overt links among them, which would have proved artificial or manufactured, for their commonality lies in their appearance in the devotionals already discussed and not in their lives, their interests, their themes and concerns as writers—or so it appears at first. Although any reader could, with some searching, find out about Lucy Larcom or Adeline Whitney or Lydia Child, no book that I know attempts to sample as many women writers as I do here. Only such an anthology can provide us with an understanding of how saturated the nineteenth century was with women writers and of how well thought of they were. Including these women in two chapters, therefore, makes a great impact and will lead readers to find out more about the women who interest them the most.[2]

Because so many women appear in two or more devotionals, we might expect to find overlapping citations. For instance, I had assumed that Mrs. Cowman, being the most recent compiler and a magnet around texts, would simply have duplicated citations from Tileston and DeRose. If Tileston cites verses from Lucy Larcom or from Madame Guyon, then I expected to find the same verses in Cowman. Not so. Where Tileston chose verse, in the case of Madame Guyon, for instance, Cowman chose prose. With only one exception, when Tileston, DeRose, and Cowman have anthologized the same writer, each chose a different passage if using the same genre, or, as I just noted, a different genre entirely; the genres could be poetry, hymns, rhymed children's verse, letters, diaries, devotional or theological commentary, novels. The exception is a verse from Mary Frances Butts, born in 1836 according to Tileston, which both she and Cowman use, Tileston for February 27, Cowman November 12.

What does their choosing different passages from the same writers mean? It means that, contrary to my stereotypes and limited expectations of these compilers, they didn't simply consult a bedside book of quotations for an appropriate uplifting thought on sorrow or temptation or work or joy. No. It means that they read the texts they cite—probably in their entirety.[3]

Unfortunately we can no longer read many of the women our main subjects anthologized. As much as I would like to, I cannot duplicate Tileston's or DeRose's reading, even on a small scale—not even by checking *Poole's Index*, which goes back to the early 1800s. In the case of the better-known, less obscure women, I find references to poetry or reviews of their work but often no copies of the magazines, for instance little-known religious periodicals. Or I find no references to particular women and so can only speculate where Tileston or Cowman may have found them (some of them, I know, wrote hymns and thus would not be found in the pages of *Poole's*). On the other hand, I locate several women, whom Cowman anthologized, in *Poole's* and the other indexes.

Such a search is anthropological as much as historical. What magazines must Tileston or DeRose or Cowman have read? Only religious magazines? only religious magazines of a particular theological stripe? women's magazines popular at the time, like *Godey's*? Or did they read middlebrow literary magazines? What cultural light does that shed on the place women occupied in the publishing of the time? Patterns emerge: Unitarian and Methodist and Catholic magazines like *Unitarian Review, Christian Examiner, Christian Remembrancer, Christian Observer, Catholic World*. Some periodicals were anthologizers themselves like *Littell's Living Age* or some periodicals from the United Kingdom. *North American Review*, that "august literary periodical," to use John Tebbell's words, shows up frequently.[4] Then come magazines still published today: *Atlantic Monthly, Harper's, Ladies Home Journal, St. Nicholas*. Many women, poets especially, published in all categories, from religious magazines (of all theological hues) to children's magazines, and were regularly anthologized in *Littell's*. Many of the women, like Dinah Maria Craik or Mary Anne Schimmelpenninck, received high accolades from (mostly) male reviewers, almost always with the prediction that the writer would still be read in a hundred years—which shows why reviewers shouldn't speculate about future reading tastes. When was the last time you curled up with a novel by Annie Keary, Elizabeth Sewell, or Adeline Whitney? Of Whitney's novel *The Gayworthys*, a reviewer wrote, "One who can write thus is far higher than a mere author or artist . . . we only close with the hope that a writer so gifted will not peril her . . . excellence by becoming a mere servant of the booksellers, and writing too much."[5] When have you run across the work of Larcom, Craik, and Child, despite the attempts that have been made to bring some of their work back into print? Even when their work has been reprinted, it has been largely for an academic audience—certainly not for readers of devotionals—and local bookstores don't usually stock texts published by university presses. The writers of these new biographies or the editors of new editions are not interested in that genre.

It is too easy—has been too easy—to dismiss these women as not worth knowing because, in a tautological argument, if they had been worth knowing we would know them, so the question would never arise—only those worth knowing *are* known.[6]

Christina Rossetti

O Lord, who art our Guide even unto death, grant us, I pray Thee, grace to follow Thee whithersoever Thou goest. . . .

In Tileston, January 23

> In the bleak midwinter,
> Frosty wind made moan,
> Earth stood hard as iron,
> Water like a stone;
> Snow had fallen, snow on snow,
> Snow on snow,
> In the bleak midwinter long ago.

As I type Rossetti's words, it is two weeks before Christmas, and I am thinking about playing some of my favorite carols; "In the Bleak Midwinter" stands at the head of a very long list. I have sung it at carol services on Christmas Eve; I have sung it as a choral arrangement with me as mezzo soloist. I sing it in my head as I reread the words. But not until I began reading Tileston and Cowman did I realize that the mid-nineteenth-century poet whom I had studied when an undergraduate English major—studied and disliked—wrote the words to the carol I love so much.

Rossetti was a prolific writer, and not just of poetry but also of prayers and children's verse, though today she is best known, in addition to being the sister of poet-painter Dante Gabriel Rossetti, a founder of the Pre-Raphaelite movement, as one of the finest religious poets of the nineteenth century. Nevertheless, it is hard for me to think of mid–nineteenth-century England as the place or the era of Rossetti or religious poetry or daily devotionals because Charles Dickens, who so detested the Pre-Raphaelites, dominates those decades. (I will return to Dickens later.)

However, knowing Rossetti as a poet and hymn writer, I find it odd that Tileston in *Daily Strength for Daily Needs* selects three of Rossetti's prayers and Mrs. Cowman in *Streams in the Desert* a single prose line. Why odd? Because of Tileston's passion for hymns (she uses so many verses of hymns, particularly by Anna Waring and Anna Warner) and Cowman's passionate nature, which would have resonated more with Rossetti than with the stodgy though redoubtable Baptist preacher F. B. Meyer, whom she cites frequently. And surely it is her love of the dramatic that inclines her to Canadian poet Annie Johnson Flint, the darling of late nineteenth- and early twentieth-century magazine editors. Yet when I read Rossetti's poem for January 19 from her devotional, *Time Flies*, I cannot help thinking of Mrs. Cowman:

> Joy is but sorrow,
> While we know
> It ends to-morrow:—
> Even so!
> Joy with lifted veil
> Shows a face as pale . . .
> Page 16

"Lifted veil" and its opposite, "drawing the veil," were two of Cowman's favorite phrases.

From Tileston, Cowman knew at least three of Rossetti's prayers, might even have read Rossetti's own "reading diary," the poet's name for her daily devotional, published as *Time Flies* in 1902 after her death in 1894 by the Society for Promoting Christian Knowledge; but whether Rossetti composed it herself or an editor compiled it after her death is unclear from the title page. Certainly no editor is listed.

Time Flies includes Rossetti's meditations, poetry, prayers, and Bible passages for every day of the year, though it does not follow the format of the traditional devotionals of Tileston and Cowman. Also,

111

unlike their work, Rossetti notes Catholic feasts and other holy days, like the well-known Epiphany (January 6) or the little-known (at least to Protestants) Feast of St. Prisca, Virgin Martyr (January 18).

With Rossetti we have what most people would call a *real* author, not to mention one of the best known today of the company of women in which we find ourselves when we read Tileston and Cowman and DeRose. Rossetti has had the greatest fame and the widest circulation, and has been the subject of the largest critical scrutiny; she is even undergoing something of a renaissance right now—all reasons to begin meeting our company with her. For me, though, the carol is reason enough.

I wonder how long before an editor rediscovers *Time Flies* and produces a new, even a scholarly, edition.

Adelaide Procter

> It isn't the thing you do, dear,
>   It's the thing you leave undone,
> That gives you the bitter heartache
>   At the setting of the sun;
> The tender word unspoken,
>   The letter you did not write,
> The flower you might have sent, dear,
>   Are your haunting ghosts at night.
>   In Cowman,
>   *Streams in the Desert*, July 30

When I began my search for obscure women, I started with those shared by Cowman and Tileston. At the top of my list is Adelaide Procter.[7]

Cowman chooses two of Procter's complete poems for separate entries; Tileston, three verses from different poems for three entries. The pedestrian rhythms and obvious rhymes of the Cowman selection above might bother a reader of contemporary poetry by Nobel Laureates Seamus Heany or Wislawa Szymborska—two poets who also treat religious themes—nor is it necessarily the best example of Procter's work. The selection for January 26 in Tileston is somewhat more complex, with its play on the conditionals for its theme: "No star is ever lost we once have seen, / We always may be what we might have been. . . ." But recall Mrs. Cowman's promise in her little ad:

"help" for "perplexities and trials," "a book full of heart-throbs and victories." Procter's poetry helps fulfill her claim. If nothing else, her selection from Procter captures a common human failing and echoes St. Paul's own complaint (not to mention my own) about leaving things undone.

But who was Adelaide Procter? Fortunately Tileston in her index provides Procter's dates, 1825–1864, thus making my search in *Poole's* easier: starting with obituaries or retrospectives. When the name Charles Dickens shows up in connection with Procter, I am startled and turn to Peter Ackroyd's monumentally definitive biography *Dickens*. If she isn't in Ackroyd, then she really can't have been that important, no matter that commentators at the time called her Dickens's protegée. Unfortunately Ackroyd has a lone reference to Adelaide Anne Procter, quoting the following from Dickens's introduction to her collection, *Legends and Lyrics:*

> To have saved her life, then, by taking action on the warning that shone in her eyes and sounded in her voice, would have been impossible, without changing her nature. As long as the power of moving about in the old way was left to her, she must exercise it, or be killed by the restraint.[8]

Ackroyd is "quot[ing] back" at Dickens his own words. So much for Adelaide Procter.[9]

Although Ackroyd provides little information about Procter, he is exhaustive about the publication in which she published most of her poetry.[10]Always in need of ready cash, Dickens turned to journalism to supplement what he earned on his novels and edited—or "conducted," as he called it—a variety of magazines throughout his life. In 1849, disappointed with the sales of *Dombey and Son*, he began to think of a new journalistic venture, even as he was working on *David Copperfield*. That venture, which he announced in December 1849 as a "WEEKLY MISCELLANY OF General Literature"[11] became *Household Words*, the name lifted from a line in Shakespeare's *Henry V*, the first issue appearing March 30, 1850. During its lifetime, Dickens published Wilkie Collins, serialized Mrs. Gaskill's novel *North and South*, and serialized his own novel *Hard Times*. He wanted, so he claimed in the first issue, "to illuminate the Fancy and demonstrate that 'in all familiar things, even in those which are repellent on the surface, there is Romance enough, if we will find it out. . . .'"[12]Had the magazine been available to Mrs. Cowman, she would have been a receptive reader, Dickens's goals and tastes and hers so much in concert, particularly in poetry. Both of them understood what appealed to their readers; or, as Ackroyd more pointedly if not pejoratively puts it, "As for poetry, Dickens seems to have possessed ordinary middle-class taste *in excelsis*. . . ."[13] So is that why Adelaide Procter finds her work accepted by Dickens and published in *Household Words*? Is it her mediocrity or accessibility (often another word for mediocrity or middle class) that recommends her? Was it simply *easy* to get published there?

The year before Procter first appears, in 1852, Dickens estimated that "he read nine hundred manuscripts of which only eleven were suitable for publication, and that after substantial rewriting by himself."[14] And yet "in the spring of the year 1853," writes Dickens in his introduction to Procter's *Legends and Lyrics* and published in the December 1865 edition of *Atlantic Monthly*, "I observed . . . a short poem among the proffered contributions, very different, as I thought, from the shoal of verses perpetually setting through the office of such a periodical, and possessing much more merit."[15] Apparently there were as many unsolicited poems as prose pieces.

Dickens did not know the poet, one Mary Berwick, who gave her address as a circulating library in the west of London. Dickens duly wrote her there, accepted her poem, and requested more submissions. And Mary Berwick duly sent more. Dickens, ever the novelist, could not help creating a character out of her name and her poems. He decided "that she was a governess in a family; that she went to Italy in that capacity, and returned; and that she had long been in the same family,"[16] when all he knew was her "businesslike, punctual, self-reliant, and reliable" characteristics (how we all stereotype), despite which, he adds, Mary Berwick was no less real to him than his own mother. Something of the same process occurred with me as I read and studied Mary Ellen Dyer and Mrs. C. S. DeRose. As soon as I learned that "1815 Locust Street," Dyer's address, was listed as a school, I created a "businesslike, punctual, self-reliant, reliable" schoolmarm, who, given her name, was also a Quaker. And I could be just as wrong as was Dickens.

Through an accident involving the galley proofs of the December 1854 issue, Dickens discovered that Mary Berwick was really the eldest daughter of an intimate of Dickens, a literary figure known to the reading public as "Barry Cornwall." Dickens had taken the proofs to dinner at the Cornwall house and in typical Dickensian fashion began to read aloud some of the issue, including a Christmas poem of Mary Berwick. And there sat the author and her mother, who knew the secret, which Dickens learned the next day. He had known Mary from a child and she, apparently not wanting publication on such grounds, had used a pseudonym. Dickens, then, is much more forthcoming than is Ackroyd about Procter's identity. (And obviously *Atlantic Monthly* thought well enough of her to reprint Dickens's personality sketch.)

Procter was born in Bedford Square, London, on October 30, 1825. She loved poetry from an early age and carried a copybook of favorite passages with her much as "another little girl might have carried a doll." Dickens, Thackery, and Tennyson, among other Victorian notables, were regular household visitors. Never married, she learned to speak French, German, and Italian, including the Piedmontese dialect. When she was twenty-six, she converted to Catholicism, and, though she wrote many more poems than just religious verse, she became best known for *A Chaplet of Verses*, published in 1862—two years before her death of consumption—to benefit a night refuge for homeless women and children in London, a charity she supported. Clearly both Mrs. Cowman and Mary Wilder Tileston knew the book, Tileston anthologizing the first four lines of the closing stanza of "Per Pacem ad Lucem," the whole of which reads:

> I do not ask my cross to understand,
> My way to see;
> Better in darkness just to feel Thy hand,
> And follow Thee.
> Joy is like restless day; but peace divine
> Like quiet night;
> Lead me, O Lord, till perfect Day shall shine
> Through Peace to Light.[17]

Dickens, hardly an orthodox Christian as Ackroyd and other biographers point out, nevertheless praises her for the "deep sense of her Christian duty to her neighbor" and her devotion to "a variety of benevolent objects":

Now it was the visitation of the sick that had possession of her; now it was the sheltering of the houseless; now it was the elementary teach-

115

ing of the densely ignorant; now it was the raising up of those who had wandered and got trodden under foot; now it was the wider employment of her own sex in the general business of life; now it was all these things at once.[18]

Not only does she sound thoroughly modern in her concerns, but she reminds me of Mrs. Cowman's claims for herself and her husband, in that, hints Dickens, her "incessant occupation," killed her. She was only thirty-nine when she died, February 2, 1864.

Anna Shipton

> Sow ye beside all waters,
>   Where the dew of heaven may fall;
> Ye shall reap, if ye be not weary;
>   For the spirit breathes o'er all.
>   In DeRose,
>   *A Daily Staff for Life's Pathway*,
>   September 3

> Sow, though the thorns may wound thee;
>   One wore the thorns for thee;
> And, though the cold world scorn thee,
>   Patient and helpful be.
>   In DeRose, September 4

> Sow ye beside all waters,
>   With a blessing and a prayer;
> Name Him whose hand upholds thee,
>   And sow thou every where.
>   In DeRose, October 27

Anna Shipton earns six curtain calls on Mrs. DeRose's devotional stage, the three cited above, obviously three stanzas from the same poem, an economical, efficient way to compile a devotional, but whether these are in the order of the original I have no way of knowing, other than to judge by the logic of the text and the dates DeRose uses them.

Anna Shipton earns two curtain calls in Mary Wilder Tileston, also verse, and in Mrs. Cowman, Anna Shipton takes one long, prose bow on March 19 where the subject is waiting on God during suffering, a subject close to Mrs. Cowman's heart.

Having said this, however, there is not much more I can say, for who Anna Shipton was, where she published, when she published, and what she published, I do not know. She is not listed in *Poole's* or in early volumes of *The Reader's Guide*. She is not listed in most of the standard indexes for American letters (major or minor) or the bibliographical and biographical references devoted to obscure women writers, which leaves me with nine references—six verses, one piece of prose—in three devotional books out of which to construct an Anna Shipton.

That Tileston uses her three times and DeRose six times tells me that Shipton was well known in the 1880s and 1890s; recall that the initial copyright for Tileston's *Daily Strength* is 1884, and on Cowman's copy of DeRose's book the copyright date is 1895. Clearly they were reading Shipton, and if they were, then so were others. Did Shipton's popularity grow in the ten years between the first publication of *Daily Strength* and that of *A Daily Staff for Life's Pathway*? Did her publishing output also grow?

Although it may seem obvious that she published poetry, I am not sure, for the verses found in DeRose and Tileston could just as well be hymns, particularly the three stanzas quoted above. I can hear them being sung. If so, it would explain why Shipton is not to be found in the standard indexes of periodical literature. (The other reason could be that she published in such small religious magazines that *Poole's* didn't bother to index her works. Or no one bothered to review her books.) However, checking various sources on hymn writers is no more successful than checking *Poole's*.

So why write about such an obscure woman?

This book is about failure and obscurity as much as it is about bringing the obscure to light. An implicit or underlying theme is the way that once well-known women writers—well known enough for three different compilers in three successive generations to anthologize her—have simply disappeared with only the eeriest textual traces remaining. As I look for historical evidence of Anna Shipton's life and enlist the help of editors and reference librarians, I keep wondering how such a thing could happen or whether a published writer today could pretty much disappear from the records. Somehow I doubt it, for we are a record-hungry people, chewing data and spitting it onto hard drives and floppies and CD-roms and even card catalogues like so many famished and desperate beavers attacking pristine forest.

The Victorians, apparently, were not nearly so starved for or dedicated to facts as we are.

So I risk the possibility that someone out there knows Anna Shipton, cherishes one of her early books, roomed with her great-great granddaughter at Wellesley, Smith, Bowdoin. Maybe someone will cry, "Anna Shipton! She wrote my favorite novel when I was growing up," and then rummage through the attic and find a copy. Of course none of this may happen, but if it does so much the better; introduce me to Anna Shipton, for I do want to get to know her.

Until someone does, though, I am left to imitate Charles Dickens once more and invent a character based on the gossamer facts I do have. This is risky, I know. As David Quammen says about scientists, they "are chary of guesswork. They do it, but they do it in private. Guesswork in public makes them look intellectually whimsical whereas a scientist . . . needs to be taken seriously by her professional peers."[19] Scholars of all stripes are chary of looking intellectually whimsical. On the other hand, I could take heart from Szymborska's stone, which says "You shall not enter, you have only . . . its seed, imagination."[20] Imagine the following:

> Anna Shipton lived in New England, her name common there.
>
> Anna Shipton knew her Bible. Her verses include numerous biblical allusions, like "love thrown upon the waters comes again" (Tileston, June 4), "the Lord of the harvest" (DeRose, October 1), "beside the waters still" and "the living waters flow" (DeRose, September 22). Shipton also quotes Philippians and Romans in the excerpt found in Cowman.
>
> Anna Shipton was theologically conservative. Had she grown up in the early twentieth century, we would call her a fundamentalist. Fundamentalists were (are) fond of quoting St. Paul, particularly such passages as that in Romans advising us to be conformed to the image of God and explaining what that means—suffering as Christ suffered. Pushing my inference a step farther, I decide that . . .
>
> Anna Shipton was a revivalist. She urges us to sow and reap and not be weary. She believed in the resurrection—"the seed burst from its tomb" (DeRose, October 1).
>
> Anna Shipton never married (there go those great grandchildren I imagined a few minutes ago). The convention at the time was

to refer to married women by Mrs. and their married name. Witness the only name we have of DeRose (Mrs. C. S.) and Cowman (Mrs. Charles E.). None of our three writers refer to Anna Shipton as Mrs. Shipton.

Anna Shipton did write hymns, I've decided, after rereading the six stanzas of anthologized verse. The use of well-loved biblical language and themes is too similar to other nineteenth-century hymns to discount this possibility. I imagine her whipping them out in time for the evening revival service; she preaches and plays the piano. I may try humming some common hymn tunes to find a fit.

Such speculation, however, is dissatisfying, for I want to know the facts. Dissatisfaction leads to desperation, and I call a reference librarian. Perhaps he can succeed where I have failed, being more adept at computer searches than I. I tell him I'm not expecting much, which is about what he finds, though I do learn that Shipton is mentioned briefly in *Childhood in Poetry*, an annotated bibliography of the Shaw Childhood in Poetry Collection found at Florida State University. I also learn that one S. Austin Allibone in his *Critical Dictionary of English Literature: British and American Authors Living and Deceased from the Earliest Accounts to the Latter Half of the Nineteenth Century* and its supplement, published by Lippincott in 1871 and 1891, mentions her. In the Hobart and William Smith Colleges library, I stop to look at the Shaw on my way to Allibone, I grab the author volume, I hover over the *S*s, but the computer is wrong. No Shiptons of any kind. Disappointed, I walk to the third floor, north, head down the Z aisle, and look for 2010.A431.

To my surprise when I pull *S* off the lower shelf and open to the appropriate page, there she is, Shipton, Anna. S. Austin Allibone comes through. Sort of.

Allibone kindly lists several of her London publications, like *Footsteps of the Flock* (1870) or *The Lord Was There: Incidents from My Journal*, an intriguing title. But where are the biographical bits he provides for his other authors? If only Anna were Helen, who follows her, I would know her father's name, his occupation (minister), her place and date of birth, something to help me create a persona. Could they be sisters? Allibone keeps his mouth shut.

I check a second volume. More references to her publications, including—I was right—collections of hymns: *Whispers in the Psalms: Hymns and Meditations* (the third edition by 1855) and *Brook in the Way: Original Hymns and Poems* (1864), all first published in Great Britain. But still no biographical information. I decide to request some of her books through interlibrary loan. *Poems*, published by Thomas Crowell (no publication date), arrives from the library of the University of North Carolina. *Waiting Hours*, published by Henry Holt (no publication date), comes from Roberts Wesleyan College. A final volume, *Tell Jesus: Recollections of Emily Gosse*, published by Mrs. Jane Hamilton who in 1868 lived at 1344 Chestnut Street in Philadelphia, is sent from Gordon-Conwell Theological Seminary—the libraries that own at least one of Shipton's books as odd a collection as her own work.

Poems is a beautiful book, cloth-bound with gold etching on the cover, the name "Anna Shipton" the only words on it. The pages have gilt edges and borders with red lines. At the back of the book, Crowell prints a one-page advertisement for its "Red Line Poets" series, of which this volume of Shipton is a part. Crowell claims it is "the only complete line of poets published in this country": "the New Designs for the covers are especially attractive and in keeping with the *superior quality of paper, presswork and binding*, which combine to make this series so justly popular with the trade and the general public, whose demands during the past year have severely taxed our ability to supply promptly." Then comes the list of the poets, and there is Shipton (Anna), right after Shakespeare and Shelley, and right before Spenser. Some poets like Shakespeare and Shelley can also be purchased in an alligator leather binding, including, I am startled to find, "Procter." Is this Adelaide or her father, Barry Cornwall? (I also note that Crowell in its red line series included Cook, Eliza, a DeRose favorite.)

So what does Anna Shipton say for herself about her collection of poems? She says that she wrote them "to cheer and soothe my own heart," that she had long wanted to see her poems in "large type, that I may administer to the old, and sick, and feeble." She also says that "this edition, prepared for America, and chartered with many a prayer, I commit to *Him* who gave me songs in the night, and taught me to sing them." And she asks people "on the other side of the Atlantic" to bless the book. So obviously I am wrong about her nationality—not a hard-nosed Yankee New Englander but a proper Victorian English-woman. She ends her brief preface with an enigmatic statement about being a "now silent singer." Was Anna Shipton handicapped? I wonder. Had she been a professional singer as well as poet?

Hoping for more biographical information, I turn to *Waiting Hours*, a devotional book, not a daily or anthologized book but one of Shipton's own composition, which includes several of her poems. What I learn makes me want more, for it hints and whispers at an unusual life more than it elucidates. Here is what I discover.

She has seen Mount Etna.

She had been "disabled by an accident" (17) and become lame on a trip from the German baths to visit a dying friend.

She visited Switzerland and the Alps.

She spoke French, Italian, and English, but not German.

She spent some considerable time in Italy and carried an Italian New Testament and read Italian well.

She didn't like the heat of southern Italy.

She had enough money in England to employ a "laundress."

She laid "no claim to rhetoric" (217), but knew how to write a compelling narrative (*Waiting Hours* is largely about her European travels).

When I turn to the third volume, *Tell Jesus*, I am mystified by the title page. "New Edition, Enlarged," it says, and then the publisher's information, the Jane Hamilton mentioned above. Apparently Mrs. Hamilton paid to have the book printed and distributed in this country (appropriately she used Caxton Press of Sherman & Co., Philadelphia). This particular copy was given to Sophia M. Lawson with the inscription "Happy New Year, M.B.S., 1871," so it obviously stayed in print for several years.

Just as *Waiting Hours* is about Shipton's European travels, so *Tell Jesus* fits the same category of memoir, only this time about a close friend who has recently died, Emily Gosse. Could this be the dying friend whom Shipton visits in Italy? Perhaps not, though it is hard to tell, for Shipton gives almost no factual information, other than the place and date of her friend's burial, Agney Park Cemetery, Friday, the 13th of February, 1857. That Mrs. Gosse was ill for some time is clear, that she was fervent and pious obvious. But the purpose of this book, like Shipton's others, is not to give biographical or factual information but to give spiritual guidance to readers who are suffering from grief or guilt. She, like Mrs. Cowman and Mary Wilder Tileston, wants to offer consolation and an escape from despair.

But what narrative can I make of these mere whispers—a word she loved.

I start to hum "Whispering hope, Oh how welcome thy vo-oice . . . making my sorrow rejoice."

"Do you know it? 'Whispering Hope'?" I ask my husband after the tune has been haunting me for hours.

"Fanny Crosby," he responds immediately. "I think Fanny Crosby wrote it."

Fanny Crosby, another favorite of my devotional compilers. How many hymns will I hum before I'm done?

Dinah Muloch Craik

> I sometimes feel the thread of life is slender,
> And soon with me the labor will be wrought;
> Then grows my heart to other hearts more tender.
> The time is short.
>> In Tileston, *Daily Strength for Daily Needs*,
>> July 29

> Why do we heap huge mounds of years
> Before us and behind,
> And scorn the little days that pass
> Like angels on the wind?
>> In DeRose,
>> *A Daily Staff for Life's Pathway*,
>> August 2

Even if I hadn't already been curious about Dinah Maria Muloch Craik, to give her wonder-full name, the August 2 entry in DeRose would have called my attention to her. As I said in chapter 3, Mrs. Cowman had an odd habit of dog-earing bottom as well as top corners of the pages of her books. She turned back the bottom right-hand corner of the August 2 entry, and so I need to pay attention to the entry that prompted such a response. In addition to Craik, the page includes a verse from Proverbs about humility, a prose passage from one Annie H. Ryder, and an aphorism from "Trapp." I know that any one of these selections could be the one that attracted Mrs. Cowman, but I reject Ryder and Trapp because of their topics (working toward perfection); I know she wasn't much interested in Proverbs, since she used only six verses from it. That leaves me with Craik, whose subject is one Mrs. Cowman frequently addresses and whose genre— poetry—was Mrs. Cowman's favorite. Add to this that Tileston also quotes Craik, and there is reason enough to argue her importance.

Dinah Craik lived to be sixty-one (1826–1887; she died of a heart attack); she published numerous novels and had great influence and popularity among Victorians. A partial computer printout runs to seven pages for her novels, children's books, and poetry in England and in the United States. Even so, much of her devotional work hints at bitterness or dissatisfaction with life. Given her sales record, she should have thought that life was more like a rope than a slender thread, to return to the quote at the beginning of this section. Yet it is true that she never received much critical acclaim, then or now. Maybe she wanted praise from Dickens and failed to get it, or he turned down the poetry and fiction she submitted to one of his magazines. Maybe he wrote bad reviews of her novels. Ackroyd certainly never mentions Craik. Today her work is not widely available, even her well-known children's book, *The Little Lame Prince*—a favorite of Christina Rossetti.

Recently, feminist scholar Elaine Showalter has edited *Maude / On Sisterhoods and a Woman's Thoughts about Women*, the latter two by Craik (the former by Christina Rossetti), for New York University's women's classics series. The volume was originally published in London by William Pickering (Pickering and Ingalls was until a few years ago a large religious publishing house), which is the edition I received from Ohio State University. Showalter says that Christina Rossetti and Dinah Craik lived near each other in London and belonged to the same literary generation. But there the similarities end. Rossetti was a cosseted and highly praised poet, as well as a recluse.[21] Craik, on the other hand, was hardly cosseted or reclusive. She began writing for a living at the age of nineteen, providing food, clothing, and shelter for herself and two younger brothers. Her nonconformist preacher father had deserted his children after his wife died and Craik was not yet twenty. She wrote the same kinds of things Charles Dickens wrote—novels, stories, essays, magazine pieces—and for the same reason: money. According to Showalter, Craik was dismissed by some of the best writers of the day, like George Eliot who declared Craik "a writer who is read only by novel readers, pure and simple, never by people of high culture (in a letter to_____)."[22] And yet Craik herself corresponded with Oscar Wilde to defend her views on women and knew well the mid–nineteenth-century literary scene of London.

Some writers and compilers have themes that occupy them, that crop up no matter what they are writing or during what part of their life they are writing. Cowman, among her many concerns, always returned to the theme of refreshment in a bitter land and to the practice of active waiting; Tileston emphasized praise and worship as a way to strengthen spiritual muscle; Larcom, whom I discuss in the next chapter, wrote about work over and over (one book is called *An Idyl of Work*). Dinah Maria Muloch Craik, at least in the two excerpts that interested DeRose and Tileston, felt the passing of time, oppressively so. She plays with spatial quantities for time— "slender" and "mounds of years," the latter such a provocative image, as if time is so much bread dough we heap onto the counters of our lives.

The anthologizers of a contemporary devotional *Companions for the Soul*[23] include "Psalm for New Year's Eve," a poem Craik wrote in 1855, which confirms that she was, indeed, concerned about how quickly time passes and how much a person ought to accomplish before heading "tombward," as she put it. Of course, this theme preoccupied the Victorians, and Dickens is the master of its exploration.

Was the theme of time her most pervasive? Given her need to earn a living, given her concern with time passing her by, it would appear so. In the quotes above, she urges time to slow down, just as she urges her female readers to pay attention to "the little days" and not focus solely on the big events. In *A Woman's Thoughts* Craik says that the "whole energies" of women

> are devoted to the massacre of old Time. They prick him to death with crochet and embroidery needles; strum him deaf with piano and harp playing . . . and they will never recognize his murder till, on the confines of this world, or from the unknown shores of the next, the question meets them: "What have you done with Time?"—Time, the only mortal gift bestowed equally on every living soul.
>
> Page 67

Craik doesn't blame women for killing time; rather she blames women's parents, the educational system, and the current values of her culture in denying women what God so clearly ordered at humanity's expulsion from the Garden.

What was their godly role? marriage? children? Perhaps, but more significantly, Craik believes that women have a right and a godly necessity for meaningful work just as men do, which can offer consolation and solace for life's disappointments. She *fights* for a woman's right to work at a time when such a fight was frowned on. Duty is not a dirty word in her vocabulary, any more than for Cowman or Tileston. As I read *A Woman's Thoughts*, I am startled by the consistently similar themes to Tileston and even Cowman, who did not cite her. As I argue that Cowman wants her readers to know active waiting and contentment, so Craik argues for her generation:

> A principle agent in this [middle age for women] is a blessing which rarely comes till then—contentment: not mere resignation, a passive acquiescence in what cannot be removed, but active contentment; bought, and cheaply, too, by a personal share in that daily account of joy and pain, which the longer one lives the more one sees is pretty equally balanced in all lives. . . . Alas! It is the slowest and most painful lesson that Faith has to learn—Faith, not Indifference—to do steadfastly and patiently all that lies to her hand; and there leave it, believe that the Almighty is able to govern His own world.
>
> Pages 210–11

Underlying these seemingly positive sentiments, however, it is possible to sense a woman who has suffered and struggled and worked to learn the lesson she so eloquently explains here. Showalter hears the same anxiety and claims that "her advice rests on an ideal of Christian resignation, often grim in its denial of the importance of happiness and personal fulfillment."[24] Because of this and Craik's heavy-handed dismissal of the women's movement, "American feminists . . . classed [Craik] with the prosings of such writers as Sarah Ellis on the duties of women in all the roles and obligations of their lives."[25] Again we have the scholarly prejudice against women of faith, of orthodoxy.

To find out more about Craik from the perspective of her contemporaries, consider that marvelous anthologizer *Littell's Living Age*, which in its May 12, 1877, issue published an article on "Miss Muloch" from *The Victorian Magazine*. It seems indeed that the reading public couldn't get enough of Craik's fiction. "This lady's works," writes "Ella" in *Victorian Magazine*, "are much read, which fact is corroborated by the testimony of certain articles in the shape of well-worn, well-soiled library volumes."[26] This must have been a favorite way of proving popularity during the Victorian era, for a reviewer of Larcom says much the same thing about her books. And Tileston, recall, uses that same refrain about books children read. If nothing else tells us that we are indeed in a different era, a comparison of the look of library books then and now would do so.

So who was reading these books into such a state? We immediately think of women when we think of lending libraries, the Victorian era, and women novelists of Victorian sentimentality—women readers on both sides of the Atlantic. Certainly, if we listen to George Eliot's dismissive comment, only people who read "novels," and not "high culture," read Craik. Children may have been reading Craik's collection of fairy tales (she too an anthologizer). Although Ella doesn't deny that Craik appealed to women, she makes it clear that Craik was not simply a woman's writer but reached a wide audience, from young people to old men, who, she claims, have been known to cry over Craik's best-known and best-selling sentimental novel, *John Halifax, Gentleman*, which was published in 1857; Ella calls it "a landmark in the literary life of its author."[27]

According to Ella, Craik's first novel, *The Ogilvies*, appeared when Craik was only twenty-three (1849) and others quickly followed: *Olive* (1850), *The Head of the Family* (1852), *Agatha's Husband* (1853), *A Life for a Life* (1859). In 1864 she received a Civil List Pension of sixty pounds a year, and with that financial security, in 1865 she married. In 1875 *The Little Lame Prince* was issued. Her early publisher was the distinguished Chapman and Hall, then Hurst and Blackett, and finally Macmillan.

Did early success spoil her? *Olive: And, the Half-Caste* was equally successful (now available through Oxford's Popular Fiction series). After *John Halifax* and her marriage, she kept writing and also kept her full name, a forward-looking gesture. The year 1865 was noteworthy for more than just her marriage, for she published several books, including *Christian's Mistakes*, which Ella likes better than some of the others, though she reserves her highest praise for the story, "My Mother and I," and says that Craik wrote most of it where she had set the story, a small village near Bath. The village claimed the best butter, the best eggs, the best violets, the best primroses, and, by extension, the best writers. The best in sentiment, in moral uplift, in a close rendering of the human heart, characteristics also evident in Craik's poetry: "A large-hearted charity and a sublime philosophy are to be found in her books, and are always guided by a calm, clear-sighted judgment."[28] In short, she "understands the human heart."

Craik herself might say that if true, it is true because of her Christian beliefs. She knew her Bible well, for instance, citing Isaiah in her New Year's poem, which she calls a psalm. Craik may have even wondered, as I do, why Ella ignores Craik's religious beliefs. Clearly they were the most important aspect of her life, the central, controlling perspective revealed in her fiction and in her writing about women. Her religious views mattered to DeRose and Tileston; despite Craik's reputation as a novelist they chose Craik's poetry, where Craik's religious views are presented much more compactly, which makes them more excerptable than the prose. Did Victorian reviewers expect everyone to be at least nominal Christians and so found a writer's religious beliefs unremarkable? If so, that would explain why Ella mentions Craik's bad grammar but passes over her Christian beliefs. Victorians did not expect the former but took good grammar for granted; whereas we cannot take either for granted. Living in an age of disbelief, I think the mention of a writer's religious views essential. Who, for instance, could rightly review a novel of Madeleine L'Engle without mentioning her Christianity? or the stories of Isaac Bashevis Singer without mentioning his Judaism?

So what else does Ella reveal about Dinah? She doesn't mention her sales figures or the names of her publisher or the titles of all her books or the order in which they were published and subsequently reprinted in the States by Harper and by Ticknor and Fields; for that information I needed to consult other sources. The Ticknor and Fields volume *Poems*[29] is surely the one Tileston and DeRose read. Nevertheless, Ella, speaking for other Victorian readers, tells me that despite Craik's flaws she admires Craik's intellect, her understanding of the human heart (read human nature), and her ability to delight readers as she instructs them because for Ella and other Victorians the purpose of a novelist was to do good.

But when it comes to praising a Victorian novelist, the touchstone always was Dickens; and Ella, knowing this, says that Craik may well share a eulogy given to Dickens: He had never written anything a child could not read. I can imagine Tileston reading *Littell's* and nodding her head and marking the passage for future use. Although we may not judge writers today by their suitability for children, for a compiler like Tileston, however, who published so much for children, this would have been high praise indeed.

Mary Anne Schimmelpenninck

I believe that no Divine truth can truly dwell in any heart, without an external testimony in manner, bearing, and appearance. . . .
    In Tileston, *Daily Strength for Daily Needs*, March 13

Nothing at Dudson was esteemed too little to be cared for, and nothing too great to be undertaken at the command of God; and for this they daily exercised their mental and bodily powers. . . .
    In Tileston, *Daily Strength for Daily Needs*, October 9

No one could be farther removed in the circumstances of their lives and in their theological persuasions than Anna Shipton, for example, and Mary Anne Schimmelpenninck; including them both here demonstrates the cultural and religious turmoil of the mid–nineteenth century as it further reinforces my view of the breadth of reading represented in and by the daily devotional. Mary Wilder Tileston, nearly thirty years away from publishing *Daily Strength for Daily Needs*, found—somehow, somewhere—the remarkable Mary Anne Schimmelpenninck's spiritual writings.

When the *Life of Mary Anne Schimmelpenninck* was published by Longmans in 1858 (she was born in 1778 and died in 1856), numerous periodicals published reviews. *Littell's Living Age* reprinted one review of the *Life* from the *Examiner* in September 1858 and another in the spring of 1859 from the *Christian Remembrancer*, which included extensive excerpts, unlike our reviews today. But surely Tileston would have been too young—fifteen or sixteen—to have read the reviews, even though *Littell's* was a likely staple in the Tileston household, as in most mid–nineteenth-century middle-class American homes. The fact that *Littell's* reprinted so close together two reviews of the same book demonstrates how important that journal's editors thought Mrs. Schimmelpenninck and her religious memoirs were. Had Tileston read the reviews, would this fact have prompted her to ask for a copy? Schimmelpenninck in her will had asked that all her writings be issued in a uniform edition. Along with the autobiography, a new edition of her memoirs of Port Royal was to be published in two volumes, and one volume each of her essays, *Principles of Beauty* and *Essays on the Temperaments, on Gothic and Grecian Architecture, and Other Subjects*—wide-ranging interests indeed (how interesting it would be for students to read her essays about architecture alongside Ruskin's). It was the first two volumes of these writings that Longman published in 1858; volume one is the autobiography she dictated to her relative, Christiana C. Hankin, between 1854 and 1856; volume two contains Hankin's reminiscences (she calls it a memoir) as well as selections from Schimmelpenninck's correspondence and diaries.

Perhaps Schimmelpenninck's importance comes not so much directly from her as from those she knew and the events she witnessed. She grew up in a wealthy Quaker home in Birmingham. Her father, Samuel Galton, was a member of the Royal Society and one of the first members of the Linnean Society. He knew the leading men of science—Priestly, Watt, Erasmus, Darwin—and introduced his daughter to them early, to science and scientific inquiry, to scientific skepticism. She was not given fairy tales, just facts. Her mother writing to her around 1798 said, "Talk about matters of fact."[30] Her father could not have been pleased when Mary Anne chose a religious life over that of scientific skepticism. Initially drawn to the Moravian church but disturbed by the church policy to draw lots in admitting members, Mary Anne was baptized a Methodist and joined a Wesleyan congregation, where she worshiped for ten years; eventually, however, she did become a Moravian, writing *Memoirs of Port Royal*, her appreciative look at the piety of the movement, and living in one of their communities after her husband died. The reviewer in the *Remembrancer* spoke of the memoir's publication "some thirty years earlier . . ." as exciting "considerable attention" and said that readers "have probably been attracted recently by her very inharmonious and unpronounceable name in the lists of new books, and already are aware of her connection, by birth and education, with the leading Quaker families."[31] I too am drawn to her because of her name, which is not German but Dutch, her husband's family that of Count Schimmelpenninck, a stadtholder of Holland.

Although Schimmelpenninck may not have shared Lydia Child's religious beliefs (see next chapter), they did share a wide-ranging intellect and breadth of learning along with the domestic necessity of making a living to support a husband. When the Schimmelpennincks suffered a drastic reversal of fortune, Mary Anne chose the same livelihood as Child—writing. When so many women writers today find it difficult to live on what they earn as writers, it is astonishing how many women in the 1800s on both sides of the Atlantic were able to support themselves through print. And this fact makes it even more unfortunate that today we know so little about women who were household names back then.

Schimmelpenninck's sales were not hurt by her having so many amusing anecdotes to tell about Darwin and other well-known scientists. Her portraits of Darwin show her not at all intimidated by his reputation; indeed, without expressly criticizing him but simply in telling stories about him, she conveys a self-centered, self-indulgent character: "His figure was vast . . . his head was almost buried on his shoulders, and he wore a scratch wig, as it was then called, tied up in a little bob-tail. . . . A habit of stammering made it" hard to understand him.[32] He ate prodigious quantities of food, particularly sweets, such as (for luncheon) hothouse fruits, West Country sweetmeats, clotted cream, and Stilton cheese, but would not touch fermented liquors. It dismayed him to watch the dishes around him being emptied. "But what was my amusement," she writes, "when at the end of the three hours during which the [luncheon] had lasted, he expressed his joy at hearing the dressing bell, and that dinner would soon be announced." Schimmelpenninck also describes his "sagacious" eye and his keen observation.[33]

Obviously, she herself was no mean observer and had a gift for description. No doubt Schimmelpenninck could thank both her parents, who may not have allowed her to read fairy tales but encouraged her to read almost everything else. Excelling in languages, she read Latin well enough for Virgil, could make her way around an Anglo-Saxon text, understood German, spoke French with her family (so similar to Tileston), learned Hebrew as an adult. "Her mother," writes the reviewer in *Remembrancer,* "made a great point of style, read our best authors with her, taught her to throw all her heart into Pope's Homer . . . [and] particularly impressed on her the beauty of our translation of the Bible, of which she seems to have been a most careful student."[34] Not only did the young Mary Anne read widely, but she memorized much of what she read, reminiscent of Mary Wilder

Tileston's practice. The conversations that she heard growing up—about science, about the French Revolution, about the rights of man—influenced her adult beliefs and led her to be concerned about slavery, another similarity she shares with Child and Tileston, and to oppose war and capital punishment.

But Schimmelpenninck's work is religious—her memoirs, her essays, her autobiography. Darwin, the French Revolution, Priestley: They are all significant to and for her as they helped shape the adult convert she became. The French Revolution and Priestly, for instance, plunged her into a period of unbelief from which she emerged several years later, thanks in part to meeting some Moravians, to claim with Paul that "Christ is all in all." From that point on, she sought, as one of the excerpts in Tileston declares, to take "out of the hand of our Lord every little blessing and brightness on our path" (*Daily Strength for Daily Needs*, May 1).

When she talks of every little blessing, we are hearing the words of someone who suffered a great deal, whose health, ever precarious, failed her completely in the last twenty years of her life after a paralytic seizure left her bedridden but not bitter. Writing to a friend, she exclaims:

> Has not our Lord led us through all the steps of our pilgrimage, even now, until its close? We began in doubt, we end in certainty; we began by opinion, we end by experience; we began in conflict, we end in peace. Oh! shall we not end in joyful thanksgiving: and, when we compare the past with the present, feel that his gracious love and unmerited mercy have indeed encompassed us with songs of deliverance.... I am yet daily learning more of, and how great an unpaid debt of grateful love we owe to all our friends; yea, and to all our enemies too; for we owe most to those who have most often been the means of sending us to our Lord....
>
> *Memoirs of Port Royal*, 171

This beautifully written letter with its balanced cadences so reminiscent of the prayer Tileston uses from Thomas Aquinas in *Great Souls at Prayer* could well have inspired Tileston, who also was "daily learning" about the love that provides strength for all one's needs, who encouraged the spiritual discipline of daily contemplation, and who wanted readers to discover the riches of the daybook as an anchor in the midst of conflict.

Although Schimmelpenninck did not herself compose or compile a daybook, she nevertheless focused on the day-to-day, without, however, neglecting the political events of her day; but the daily comes first. Could this ubiquitous concern for daily experience be peculiar to women writers? She wrote:

> I have long thought that the experiences of daily life, and the ample and vivid page of history, form, as it were, a lock and key to those who take the trouble to apply them. How small an incident in our own private life may throw light on volumes of cruelty. . . . that the horrors which were raging around me in the period of the French Revolution, and the political state of things with us, taught me a deep and ineffable lesson, of how evil is man, and how great and glorious is God.
>
> Pages 311–12, volume 1

Political and private concerns led her to disregard her duty, almost the greatest sin any of these women could confess to, and "disputatious against . . . authority," as she puts it (312, volume 1).

As with women like Procter and Craik, Schimmelpenninck's life and work crosses the life and work of so many of the great men of the mid-Victorian era; yet when the stories of Dickens or Darwin are told, no one consults the women who knew them for the insights they might or could provide. Because of Schimmelpenninck, however, I now have a different perspective on Darwin. And because of Tileston, I now know Schimmelpenninck.

five

In American and French Company

Lucy Larcom
Lydia Maria Child
Margaret Bottome
Madame Guyon

*T*he previous chapter considered some of the British women writers preserved by Tileston, Cowman, and DeRose. Here we look at four more women, three Americans and a Frenchwoman, whom they anthologized and who are closest in spirit and in time to women writers of the medieval period, the subject of chapter 6.

Lucy Larcom

> Thy universe, O God, is home,
> In height or depth, to me . . .
> Content am I to be. . . .
> From "A Strip of Blue"[1]

> Yet the world is Thy field, Thy garden;
> On earth art Thou still at home.
> In Tileston,
> *Daily Strength for Daily Needs,*
> October 1

> Is it raining, little flower? . . .
> In sorrow, sweetest virtues grow,
> As flowers in rain.
>
> In Cowman,
> *Streams in the Desert,*
> June 12

> Success in writing may mean many different things. I do not know that
> I have ever reached it, except in the sense of liking better and better
> to write, and of finding expression easier.
>
> *A New England Girlhood,* 272

Lucy Larcom is just the kind of writer I might have read growing up. But I did not know Lucy Larcom. I have only recently learned of her through Tileston and Cowman, who sent me to libraries, indexes, and those aging female actors, the wrinkled and disdained card catalogues. I discovered that Larcom published a lot of poetry, and at first it appears that poetry is all she published. We can see from the excerpts above that she tended toward garden verse and garden metaphors, in keeping with Northeastern transcendentalism. I learn that much of her poetry appeared in *Atlantic Monthly;* then I stumble on the magazine's review of her best-known book, *A New England Girlhood, Outlined from Memory,* published in 1889 by the venerable Boston house Houghton Mifflin; reading it now I know how much I would have loved it as a child. Not only did Houghton Mifflin reprint it several times and issue a new edition in 1924, but Northeastern University Press reprinted it in 1986 with a foreword by Nancy Cott. How appropriate, given our current obsession with memoir; Larcom would be right at home in the publishing world today. The biography *Life, Letters, and Diary* (in some sense a sequel to *A New England Girlhood*) was written by the Reverend Daniel Dulany Addison, rector of St. Peter's Episcopal Church in Beverly, Massachusetts, and published shortly after her death by Houghton Mifflin in 1895 (a recent edition published in 1994 is once more out of print).

For a few years after she died, magazines continued to publish her poetry; in a local library I find a copy of the 1889 edition of *New England Girlhood* and an 1884 edition of *The Poetical Works: Household Edition.* (According to Houghton Mifflin printing records, 9,000 copies of that book were issued, 8,000 of *New England Girlhood,* 6,980 of *As*

It Is in Heaven, to sample some of Larcom's printing history.) I love the subtitle of *The Poetical Works,* so domestic, so practical, so useful. When I read it, I imagine the book propped up in the kitchen, open, being read while someone stirs a long-simmering sauce. I think of it shoved next to the pots and pans or a copy of Mrs. D. A. Lincoln's *Boston Cook Book: What to Do and What Not to Do in Cooking.* "Household edition" indicates that Larcom wanted the book to be a tool, just like other household items—a ladle, a feather duster, a cookbook. She included nearly three hundred poems, from her earlier poems and "Childhood Songs" to her later poems, but not the poem Mrs. Cowman anthologized. She and Tileston would have had their pick of religious poems, for so many of them retell such Bible stories as Jacob and the ladder or commemorate Christmas and Easter. "Daily Bread" would have stirred Tileston and Cowman, and how Mrs. Cowman would have welcomed two early sonnets, "Drought" and "Springs in the Desert," so close to the title of her own book (Mrs. Cowman called a subsequent devotional *Springs in the Valley*).

So if Anna Shipton is a missing needle in an imaginary haystack, Lucy Larcom is a bushelful of needles. Between 1890 and the end of the decade, *Poole's* can't get enough of Larcom. Here's an eclectic sample of her publishers: *Atlantic Monthly, Book News, Critic, Dial, Outlook, Journal of Education, Kindergarten Primary Monthly, Ladies Home Journal.* Just this list of periodicals indicates what a broad audience Larcom reached and makes me wonder where Tileston and Cowman read her. Was it in *Outlook,* subtitled *A Family Paper,* a new series of the *Christian Union,* the publisher of which was the well-known minister Lyman Abbott (a favorite of DeRose)? Or did they read her in *Ladies Home Journal* or the *Atlantic Monthly*? Although they may have read Larcom's memoirs, they nevertheless chose her poetry, not her prose, to anthologize.[2]

A New England Girlhood tells the story of Larcom's early years, first in Exeter and then in Lowell, Massachusetts, after her father died, which left her mother with eight children to support, though the oldest three (in their teens) soon found work. Because her mother was so downcast, Larcom took it on herself to console her mother subtly and indirectly by singing such hymns as "Come, Ye Disconsolate" or "How Firm a Foundation," emphasizing the most pertinent words so that her mother wouldn't miss the point. Soon her mother decided to open a boardinghouse in Lowell for mill girls: "Some of the family objected," she writes, "for the Old World traditions about factory life were anything but attractive" (*A New England Girlhood*, 146). She does not tell us what the family thought when she herself became a mill girl at the age of eleven.

From 5 A.M. until 7 P.M. she worked, changing bobbins, for which she earned two dollars a week plus board. At night she studied and wrote poetry, also contributing to the fortnightly magazines published by her mother's boarders—the mill-girl magazines, an unusual accomplishment then or now. When Charles Dickens on his first American tour visited her mill, she missed meeting him but later received a sketch done by a friend who became known as "Boz." On the walls of the factory, she pasted newspaper clippings of her favorite poems. Because her job required her attention only once every forty-five minutes, she was able to read and talk to the other girls and think. The mill owners even encouraged the girls to bring books and to read while at work. And what did she read besides the newspapers?

According to the reviewer in the *Outlook*, Larcom read what she called "the genuine thing": *Pilgrim's Progress, Gulliver's Travels*, the novels of Sir Walter Scott, and the poetry of Spenser, Southey, Wordsworth, and Coleridge.[3] In her memoir she also lists Shakespeare, Milton, Tennyson, and Carlyle; she copied "passages from Jeremy Taylor and the old theologians into my note-books and have found them useful even recently, in preparing compilations"—yet another woman who kept a commonplace book (238). She also memorized much of what she read, poetry especially. Later in life, Larcom dismissed the notion that children in the early 1800s had nothing to read and called herself as witness. She credits books as her "earliest educators"; at the same time, she dismisses the fluff that by the 1880s and '90s was passing for children's literature. I imagine her in the classroom where she spent twenty years, urging her students to read and imitate what they read. *Life, Letters, and Diary* even offers advice about learning to write: "Interest yourself in something, and just say your simple say about it."[4]

Larcom is yet another example of a little-known woman writer who defies our expectations and stereotypes. Who would suspect the poor, working-class background of the woman who wrote the poems Cowman and Tileston anthologized? Or, knowing Larcom's background *only*, who would predict such literary breadth? In this respect, Larcom and Cowman are similar. What readers coming cold to *Streams in the Desert* would suspect that Mrs. Cowman had studied opera or read Tennyson and Browning? These women were readers, and everywhere I turn this fact confronts me.

The *Atlantic Monthly* review of *A New England Girlhood* gives the book high praise and not solely because of its writing. Rather, writes the reviewer, "we have been so impressed by the value of this book as a contribution to sociology": the sociology of Essex and Lowell and Lawrence and Wellesley during the shift from agriculture to manufacturing of that region and the "brave Puritanism" of the communities.[5] His evaluation has been echoed by recent scholars after reading the memoir. What puzzles me about the reviews, however, is their silence about Lucy Larcom's religious views and her religious poetry. In her memoir Larcom devotes considerable space to religion. She calls her church, the First Congregational of Lowell (she wrote a history of its first fifty years in 1876), her "home-centre" (209): "Work, study, and worship were interblended in our life." She explains what sustained her as a child and as an adult:

> To draw near to the One All-Beautiful Being, Christ, to know Him as our spirits may know The Spirit, to receive the breath of His infinitely loving Life into mine, that I might breathe out that fragrance again into the lives of those around me,—this was the longing wish that, half hidden from myself, lay deep beneath all other desires of my soul. This was what religion grew to mean to me, what it is still growing to mean, more simply and more clearly as the years go on.
>
> *A New England Girlhood*, 208

Tileston's and Cowman's selections are witness to Larcom's religious poetry; so much of her writing was religious; and yet the reviewers say nothing, a peculiar silence, unless I am to interpret the following as an implicit reference to her religious beliefs: "Every girl should read this life . . . of a strong, sweet womanly woman, who lived each day at a time; who accepted disagreeable employment in such a spirit that those about her never knew it was disagreeable, doing her duty so faithfully that she was credited with an enthusiasm for her profession."[6] This could well reflect Paul's advice to be content in all circumstances or Jesus' words not to worry about tomorrow; or it could be the late-Victorian Pollyanna perspective of what a woman should be. Shirley Marchalonis, who has written a biography of Larcom, claims that Larcom along with her contemporaries was "preoccupied with spiritual matters";[7] if so, then the reviewers are an exception.

But whatever is the truth about Larcom's preoccupation, the silence about religion reminds me again how uncomfortable critics are today in dealing with religion. For Tileston and Cowman, on the other hand, Larcom's theological musings, in prose and poetry, provide the reason to value Larcom, as the theme(s) of their devotionals demonstrate. In fact the opening entry of Cowman's devotional sounds so much like the conclusion of Larcom's chapter "Reading and Studying" in *A New England Girlhood:* "I had early been saved from a great mistake; for it is the greatest of mistakes to begin life with the expectation that it is going to be easy. . . . What a world it would be, if there were no hills to climb! . . . I knew that there was no joy like the joy of pressing forward" (246).

Larcom was not only a memoirist of note and a poet and a writer of fiction and a historian and a teacher (she attended Wheaton Seminary, which became Wheaton College, and wrote commemorative exercises, addresses, and poetry for its fiftieth anniversary). She too compiled devotional or daybooks. Recall what she said about copying Taylor and the old theologians into her notebooks and how useful they became when she started compiling her own daybooks for publication (unlike Tileston or Cowman, Larcom admits that once her health failed and she could no longer teach she had to earn a living as a writer). Her compilations include *Beckonings for Every Day: A Calendar of Thought, Breathings of the Better Life*, which went through at least six editions, and *The Cross and the Grail*, with selections from Shakespeare, Longfellow, Whittier, and Phoebe and Alice Cary. The first two works Houghton Mifflin published; the last was published by the Women's Temperance Publishing Association.

Then and now daily books of devotional and inspirational words not only were lucrative—why else would the premier publishers of the day issue so many devotionals?—but also were a way to educate and encourage women to read and think and aspire to noble actions. Witness what Larcom says in the preface to *Breathings of the Better Life* (Ticknor and Fields, 1867): "As a volume of extracts it may win a welcome from those who cannot own many books, for bringing them into acquaintance with authors who, in ages and regions widely separated, have spoken clearly of the unselfish life which Jesus came to teach and to inspire" (iii).

Further, Larcom wants "to inspire the traveller struggling upward to a better life" (iii). Unlike Tileston and Cowman, for instance, Larcom states up front that she has no theological axe to grind, paying "no regard . . . to peculiarities of name or sect in making quotations. Whatever thought has seemed spiritually deepest, or of strongest practical force, has been written down as a sure word of prophecy from heart to heart" (iv). Yet like Tileston and Cowman, Larcom wanted "to shape an every-day manual, answering to a general need; one of those small books, filled with great thoughts, which are a real help to men and women, and which may accompany them to the workshop, the camp, or the sick-room, unobtrusive and restful as the presence of a friend" (iv).

Breathings, however, is not arranged as a daily devotional but arranged by such themes as "Life Eternal" and "Bearing the Cross," central spiritual themes for Larcom that proved central for her readers, for the book went through several editions (though she earned no money from it) and Larcom received numerous letters from grateful readers. According to Marchalonis, Larcom considered this devotional her most important book and most lasting contribution to American letters. In fact she cared about every aspect of its publication, writing to Houghton Mifflin about binding and color: "I think that at least my little books, *Breathings Beckonings*, &c, should be obtainable in the same style. People *want* a handsomely bound book for a holiday-gift, and my friends have always said they wished mine were to be had in nicer binding. If it is too late to put them upon the market now, might there not be some ready for Easter and another Christmas?"[8]

Although *Breathings* is not a daily devotional, Larcom did not neglect that form of the genre. *Beckonings for Every Day*, which she mentions above, was a daily devotional, suggested to her by her publisher on the sales strength of the former collection. She conceived of the book not just in terms of the thoughts collected but also in terms of its appearance. She fought her editors for her vision of page layout and design, dividing the months with blank pages, the title, and the color of the binding. It was important to the reading experience, she believed, that quotations not be carried to a new page and that when possible each page should begin with a new paragraph.[9] She may have won at the time, but the edition I hold has none of the features she thought so essential to a daily devotional.

Because Larcom knew the fierce competition her book faced, in the introduction she tries to distinguish it from others: "It has features sufficiently distinctive to give it a reason for being" (1). Could she have had layout and design in mind? Whether that be the case, she recommends her devotional because of the process she used in putting it together, and in so doing offers readers a way of reading hers or any devotional book. "Such a book," she writes, "to be really valuable, must be a growth, and scarcely a rapid one" (1). Implicit here is a definition of the spiritual life itself and of how reading and studying devotional literature ought to proceed: slowly and steadily.

What else distinguishes her devotional from others? Each month has a theme that focuses the selections ("something of coherence would make the book more useful to the reader" [3]), and, claims Larcom, she has chosen more widely than other devotionals on the market (but hardly more widely than her heirs). She makes a final claim that she hasn't just chosen texts of consolation but of challenge, and I hear echoes of Cowman in Larcom's words: "It is not good for us to breathe always the soft atmosphere of the valley, however soothing it may be: the bracing air of spiritual heights strengthen the soul to ascend toward the grandeur of its immortal destiny" (2).

I have no physical evidence that Tileston and Cowman knew Larcom's devotional books, but even if they did not know them how appropriate it is that they anthologized the poetry of a fellow compiler. The rich possibilities of this genre, as I have explained in previous chapters, appealed and continues to appeal to women readers, those readers who Larcom explicitly says are her audience, those readers who are implicitly part of the Tileston and Cowman texts. The numerous editions of Larcom's own devotionals and the letters from her readers offer further evidence of the significance this genre has had for American readers for more than a hundred years.

Lydia Maria Child

Over the river and through the woods, to grandmother's house we go. . . .

Lydia Maria Child

Active participation in the duties of *this* world seems to be the surest safe the health of body and mind.

In DeRose, *A Daily Staff for Life's Pathway*, December 18

Mrs. DeRose includes Child in her December 18 entry, but what does Romans 8:14, "For as many as are led by the Spirit of God, they are the sons of God," have to do with Lydia Child's solidly middle-class, respectable advice about fulfilling one's duty? What does it have to do with Acts 17:28, "For in him we live, and move, and have our being"? The connection between Child and John Henry Newman is clear, for they speak the same language—"Prune thou thy words, thy thoughts control..."—or N. L. Frothingham "Every day is a life, fresh with reinstated power, setting out on its allotted labor and limited path ... the sun rises, and lights up the world to do his part in it." Now we're down to duty and how to have a healthy body and mind—the marrow of the nineteenth century.

Because the connections escape me, I jot down Child's name on a handy scrap of paper, planning to look for her in Tileston and in Cowman; even though I don't find her, I decide that Child is worth investigating. After a few days' search, I conclude that Tileston missed an opportunity (and she didn't miss many); temperamentally, if not theologically, she and Child have so much in common. But there is another reason for surprise—the connection between Tileston's family and Child through Child's best friend, the more conservative Lucy Osgood, twelve years her senior; their friendship lasted sixty years and involved lengthy correspondence about theology, among other subjects. During the 1840s and 1850s Tileston's mother too corresponded frequently with Lucy Osgood and occasionally with her sister, Mary. It would have been odd indeed for Lucy not to have written about her close friend Lydia, whose growing literary reputation as a writer for children and adults would have made her noteworthy, particularly given the Footes' love of literature. Add to that Child's work for the abolitionist cause, as we have seen a cause that also concerned the Foote family, and we can surmise that the Footes knew (of) and read Lydia Maria Child.

Lydia Child's interests were as broad as Tileston's. Child wrote not only novels but also essays, as well as biographies of some well-known women like Madame de Staël and Madame Guyon, whom Tileston read and anthologized. Child published the widely read and highly successful magazine *Juvenile Miscellany;* editing and writing most of its stories. A reviewer in *North American Review*, writing in July 1833, said that "the power alone of producing such a series of instructive stories ... so well calculated to captivate the youthful attention, and to fix youthful sympathy, argue a remarkable power of invention. In fact, it is one of the best proofs of the author's capacity for higher things."[10] Wouldn't Tileston have agreed?

Tileston and her family may well have read Harriet Jacobs's *Incidents in the Life of a Slave Girl*, edited by Child, or Child's *An Appeal in Favor of That Class of Americans Called Africans*, which Carolyn L. Karcher has edited for the University of Massachusetts Press (1996). Karcher has also written an 804-page study, *The First Woman in the Republic: A Cultural Biography of Lydia Maria Child*, published in 1994 by Duke University Press.[11] In 1997 Duke published *A Lydia Maria Child Reader*, as part of its "New Americanists" series and again edited by Karcher, some small evidence of the renewed interest among scholars, at least, in Child.[12] Nevertheless, for those who want to know more about Child than her Thanksgiving song cited above, the *Reader* is a good introductory collection, including samples of her Indian stories, children's books, and journalism, among other categories.

Child was born in 1802 and died in 1880, living almost exclusively in New England, as did Tileston, and influenced by Unitarianism, as were Tileston and Larcom. Also like Tileston and Larcom, Child appears to have been a one-woman publishing show, and she needed to be, for her husband ran up debts faster than a gambling addict at a Las Vegas casino. For instance, the year the two were married, 1828, Child owed $15,000 for his newspaper, the *Massachusetts Journal*. According to a review of *Letters of Lydia Maria Child* in the *Atlantic Monthly:*

> Mr. Child was a visionary, who always saw before him a pot of gold at the foot of the rainbow. Now it was one thing and now another, and while there was perfect accord between the husband and wife, Mrs. Child's native good sense and sound judgment were sometimes sorely tried by the vagaries which her husband followed.[13]

(In the same issue and immediately preceding the review, there is a story by Nathaniel Hawthorne, putting Child in good company, indeed.)

Compare David Child's publishing venture with her own publication for children, which quickly earned her enough to make her self-sufficient, and, indeed, to marry, despite the warnings about her future husband's profligacy. The *Juvenile Miscellany* began in September 1826, and in five months the bimonthly had 850 subscribers (within a year it had earned three hundred dollars in profits); Lydia Child published the magazine for eight years. Caroline Healy Dall described the eagerness with which children waited for each edition:

> The children sat on the stone steps of their house doors . . . all the way up and down Chestnut Street in Boston, waiting for the carrier (it always came on Saturday). He used to cross the street, going from door to door in zig zag fashion; and the fortunate possessor of the first copy found a crowd of little ones hanging over her shoulder from the steps above. . . . How forlorn we were if the carrier was late![14]

Although eight years may strike us as a short life for a magazine, its influence continued throughout the nineteenth century in the work of Louisa May Alcott and in the children's magazine *Our Young Folks*, which James T. Fields of Ticknor and Fields published. Lucy Larcom was at first one of three editors, she in charge of the puzzle pages; eventually she became editor-in-chief. Highly successful from the start, during its first year the magazine printed essays or stories by Lydia Maria Child as well as Louisa May Alcott and Harriet Beecher Stowe. Larcom herself published four poems in the magazine, and Longfellow's "Christmas Bells" appeared. Child's children's magazine also influenced Larcom's mill-girl magazine, the *Lowell Offering*.

The assertion by the *North American Review* that Child and her husband were in "perfect accord" may strike modern readers as more wishful thinking than fact; eventually she admitted that her marriage had failed and the two of them went their separate ways.[15] Yet however much David Child's extravagances and debts may have burdened her life, in at least one instance they proved beneficial; his "vagaries" in 1842 led to Child's becoming editor of a new antislavery publication, the *Standard*, because her husband, who had been offered the job, wouldn't leave his sugar-beet experiment in Northampton. Child accepted the job and moved alone to New York City; she needed the money if not the time away from her husband. But if at first money more than the cause of abolition motivated her, that soon reversed, so much so that the reviewer of *Letters of Lydia Maria Child* claims that it "has genuine value as a transcript in glowing language of a period of our national life when a woman's sympathy was a powerful lever in the great upheaval which followed."[16]

The publication of Child's letters indicates the esteem in which she was held at the time; John Greenleaf Whittier wrote the biographical introduction and another noted abolitionist, Wendell Phillips, prepared the appendix; Houghton Mifflin published it (as they did Larcom). Whatever we may think of Whittier today, at the time he was a celebrity, an author courted by Henry O. Houghton (the firm owned *Atlantic Monthly* and subsequently bought Mifflin and Garrison to become Houghton Mifflin). It was no mean thing to have Whittier introduce a collection of letters by a woman writer, no mean thing to have the collection—and everything else one wrote—published by Houghton Mifflin, whose Riverside imprint was a mark of excellence, according to John Tebbell.[17] Tebbell lists as evidence for his claim Longfellow, Whittier, Emerson, Holmes, Lowell, Thoreau, Hawthorne, Tennyson, Browning, Dickens, and many other well-known writers—all on Houghton's list, but Tebbell does not, unfortunately, include Lydia Maria Child, despite her obvious success, significance, influence. Although Tebbell couldn't include everyone, nevertheless, considering that he emphasizes the Civil War era and that Child is considered one of the foremost female abolitionists, she surely merited a mention.

In the long term, her work for the abolitionist cause might be her most significant legacy,[18] but in the short term one of her most significant and certainly most lucrative ventures came with what we now call advice or self-help books. Her first was *The Frugal Housewife* (1829), which, according to *North American Review*, had gone through ten editions: "It was to be found making its way into the boudoir of the fashionable, as well as into the farmhouse"[19] (imagine a comparably august literary journal today reviewing such a book). In its first year *The Frugal Housewife* sold six thousand copies and eventually had thirty-three editions in the United States and twelve in England and Scotland. It was translated into French and sold in Paris bookshops. Every woman, so claims the review, knew the book and every daughter received it before setting up a household. If anyone knew the necessity of frugality, it was Child, thanks to her husband. A sequel called *The Family Nurse* followed.[20] Child wrote advice books for women at every stage of life, from childhood through marriage, for instance *The Girl's Book* and *The Mother's Book*. Lydia Child must have been the Martha Stewart of her day.

I am beginning to understand the citation DeRose uses because Child's life centered on doing her duty, and her publishing focused on giving other women advice on how to do theirs. Given her husband, she must have struggled to maintain her mental, if not also her physical, health. However, I am still puzzled by the connections DeRose makes to Paul; perhaps DeRose knows something I have yet to learn and reviewers' comments about Child's high moral tone are beginning to sound a little shopworn, since I've read the same thing about every woman included here. Was Child more concerned with duty and morality than with Christianity? Would she have been comfortable with Paul as a textual companion? Like so many of her contemporaries, she fled from Calvinism, tippled Unitarian transcendentalism, soon dallied with Swedenborgianism, but because none satisfied her she spent her life searching for some religious faith, investigating in addition both Catholicism and Judaism.

So, although Lydia Maria Child never published devotional literature, nevertheless she was as preoccupied with religion as her contemporaries. Her restless spiritual quest led to a three-volume study of the major religions, *The Progress of Religious Ideas, Through Successive Ages* (1855), an essay for *Atlantic Monthly* called "An Intermingling of Religions" (1871), and two years before her death an "Eclectic Bible," called *Aspirations of the World: A Chain of Opals*. Earlier in her career, about the same time as she was writing advice books for women, she published a biography of the French convert and devotional writer Madame Guyon.[21] The reviewer for *Atlantic Monthly* described Child's religion this way: "[It] may be summed up in the words that she bore other people's burdens. She had a warm religious nature, but it was untrained and disposed to run off into eccentricities,"[22] but not disposed to run off to a "historic church."

The irony here is that the reviewer alludes to Paul (bearing one another's burdens), yet Paul's proclamation of the death and resurrection of Jesus Christ as the sole means of salvation was far, far from Child's own beliefs. For the man who proclaimed the shame of the cross, Lydia Maria Child makes a very strange devotional companion indeed.

Margaret Bottome

There are seasons when to be *still* demands immeasureably higher strength than to act. Composure is often the highest result of power.
In Cowman, *Streams in the Desert*, February 10

Christ's triumph was *in* his humiliation. Possibly our triumph, also, is to be made manifest in what seems to others humiliation.
In Cowman, *Streams in the Desert*, April 3

Mrs. Cowman and Margaret Bottome are soul mates and kindred spirits. Each of the five unusually long excerpts from Margaret Bottome in Cowman's devotional concerns the stoical bearing of one's burdens—the harsh realities of life and the satisfaction one receives from meeting harshness head on, looking it in the eye, squaring one's shoulders, and shouting, "You won't defeat me, try as you might." Picture Mrs. Cowman after a particularly difficult night with her husband, coming across the passage she chose for February 10 and writing "exactly" or "excellent" in the margins or simply underlining it in the blue ink she favored. Picture her taking stock of the situation—she is powerless in the face of her husband's illness, nothing she can do— and then she repeats aloud to herself those words: "seasons . . . to be *still* . . . composure . . . power" and determining yet again that she will learn the lesson God is trying to teach her through her husband's unfair illness. (Why us, Lord? Weren't we your obedient servants?)

But who was Margaret Bottome? Given the excerpts in Cowman, I expect to find a "traditional" woman with traditional values—wife, mother, quoter of 2 Timothy or Genesis 2: perhaps a minister's wife, or a missionary's, like Mrs. Cowman herself. The facts surprise me.

Opening the first page of the January 1907 edition of *New England Magazine*, I find myself face-to-face with "the late Margaret Bottome." Studying the photograph, I find a person of strong presence: broad features, piercing, dark eyes, large hands, erect carriage. She reminds me of an imposing, early twentieth-century opera singer. She wears a dark suit, white blouse; a large flower is pinned to one of the lapels and from the stem hangs a small purse with a gold chain and a filigree clasp. Above the flower on the satin lapel is a pin, which appears to be an insignia pin (something like a Phi Beta Kappa key, for instance): a circle with a cross hanging from it. Although Margaret Bottome is facing the camera, it is as if she has been caught in the act of reading, for to her left is a desk, with an open book on which her hand rests; her other hand holds the folds of her skirt. Perhaps the open book is only a prop or perhaps it is an emblem of her life, as it could be an emblem of the lives of every woman in this marvelous company.

The caption beneath the photo identifies her as (when alive) the president of the International Order of King's Daughters and Sons, an organization I have never heard of, though it is refreshing to see daughters come first. The editors of the magazine direct me to the story by

H. O. McCrillis, which is not about Margaret Bottome per se, I discover, but about the organization she founded on January 13, 1886, in her home in New York City. Nine other women were present at that meeting.[23] The group elected Mrs. Bottome president and Mrs. Dickinson secretary. McCrillis says that "by the recent death of Mrs. Bottome the order has lost one of its ablest and most useful members."[24] The women adopted a constitution to develop "spiritual life and [stimulate] Christian activities" and a badge—the silver Maltese cross with the letters I. H. N. (In His Name) engraved on it, the insignia I noted on Mrs. Bottome's lapel.

At first, the group limited its membership to women, but in 1887 it changed the rules to admit men and boys, though McCrillis notes they are few in number. Also at first the membership of each circle, as the local chapters were called, was limited to ten; by McCrillis's writing, the twenty-first anniversary, the size limit had been dispensed with and membership in the organization itself had grown to the hundreds of thousands (one estimate is five hundred thousand). In 1891 the word *international* was added to the name, reflecting the worldwide work of the group. Each of five Canadian provinces (and twenty-six U.S. states) held its own annual or biennial convention. The original ten women believed that there were "multitudes of women eager and desirous of making their lives of value to themselves and of use to the world, and that what they needed was not stimulation to make them willing to work, but education in the world's needs, and instruction as to the best methods of battling with its misery and sin."[25]

So much constitutes sin and misery; they saw it everywhere. Although at first a woman-to-woman ministry (one gathered ten and then each of those gathered ten more and so on), as their numbers grew, so did the work they took on: "Work for the aged; work among seamen . . . the establishment of libraries and a home study system; work in home and foreign missions; providing outings and vacations for worthy women and children. . . ."[26] McCrillis also provides examples of what we would now call relief work: the India famine, Armenia, the flood in Galveston, the San Francisco earthquake, Cuban relief—"misery and sin." McCrillis also lists such institutions as nurseries (we would call them day-care centers) that the King's Daughters and Sons helped found, including the "Frank Bottome Memorial Settlement," obviously named for Mrs. Bottome's husband. All of this activity reminds me of Adelaide Procter's work with homeless women and children in London, or Lydia Child's work as an abolitionist. What of Mrs. Cowman's own work?

Mrs. Cowman may not have agreed entirely with the broad definition of misery and sin with which the group operated, but she certainly would have agreed that women want to find their lives "of value and of use." Wasn't that the driving impulse behind her devotional— to demonstrate to women that their lives do have meaning no matter how dreadful their circumstances? And though Mrs. Cowman and her husband did not found the Oriental Missionary Society to relieve suffering from natural disasters, or to give women primarily a philanthropic outlet, nevertheless the similarity between Mrs. Bottome and Mrs. Cowman is notable. But would she have cheered Mrs. Bottome's goal "to make somebody better, happier, healthier, and more able to meet life's problems," in the words of McCrillis?[27] Certainly the latter, or if not "more able," then at least to accept life's trials, even enthusiastically, as Mrs. Bottome herself recommended. But I doubt that Mrs. Cowman cared about making someone "better," as McCrillis means that expression (the first page of the article espouses the philosophy that every day in every way we are getting better and better, so ironic considering the horrors of this century and his standing unknowingly on the precipice of World War I). Mrs. Cowman knows firsthand that "better, happier, healthier" are deceptions, impossibilities. But from first to last McCrillis is determined to stay cheery, so unlike Mrs. Bottome herself, who recognizes the inescapability of suffering. He declares that "It ought to make every one feel safer to know about this work. The forces of evil do not have it all their own way."[28]

I do not know where Mrs. Cowman read Mrs. Bottome perhaps in *The Silver Cross*, the organization's monthly magazine. Perhaps Mrs. Cowman encountered Margaret Bottome on the latter's trip to Asia. Did she know anything of Mrs. Bottome's work, and if she did, how did she reconcile the belief in suffering in silence and stillness with the do-good action plans of the International Order of King's Daughters and Sons? How would she have responded to Mrs. Bottome's activities in the area that I least expected to find her involved in—the rights of women.

The *North American Review* published a highly censorious essay, "Petticoat Government," by a Max O'Rell, who begins, "I loathe the domination of woman,"[29] and continues, "the new woman," that creature he so detests, is simply another word for "ugly women, old maids, and disappointed wives."[30] "She wants to be a man and to remain a woman. She will fail to become a man, but she may succeed in ceasing to be a woman." It is to be expected that O'Rell thinks women have only one purpose in life, "to be a mother,"[31] which of course means first becoming a wife. Pity Mrs. Cowman, who never had children; or Adelaide Procter or Lucy Larcom, who never married; or the women who joined Margaret Bottome's organization. Were they all "thin"? Did they all have "sallow complexion[s], eyes without lustre, wrinkled, mouth sulky, haughty, the disgust of life written on every feature"?[32] That is hardly a description of Mrs. Bottome or of any of the nine original members of her group. It is hardly a description of Mrs. Cowman either.

The editors of the *North American Review* asked H. P. Spofford, presumably a man, and Margaret Bottome to respond. And respond she does. We need more new women, she cries; we need more new men. We need women who "want to help right the wrongs," to help "in the interest of good government."[33] How contemporary this sounds; latter-day feminists have made the same appeals, but how comfortable would they make Mrs. Cowman? Bottome concludes by quoting Lucy Stone that "what a woman can do well, she has a right to do"— and she has a right to find out what it is that she can do well. I doubt that Mrs. Cowman would have quarreled with this, given her own leadership after her husband's death.

Madame Guyon

> Possess yourself as much as you possibly can in peace; not by any effort, but by letting all things fall to the ground which trouble or excite you. This is no work, but is, as it were, a setting down a fluid to settle that has become turbid through agitation.
>
> In Tileston, May 20

> I have learnt to love the darkness of sorrow; there you see the brightness of His face.
>
> In Cowman, *Streams in the Desert*, October 12

The mystic Madame Guyon serves as a land bridge between the continents of the Middle Ages and the "modern" nineteenth century where we have found ourselves so far. What intrigues me is how a French Catholic mystic found her way into two Protestant and decidedly unmystical devotionals.[34] Tileston chose six passages from Madame Guyon and Cowman four; and one of the best ways to distinguish between the devotionals of Mary Wilder Tileston and Mrs.

Cowman is to study the themes in the writers they both excerpt. The Tileston passages deal with peace and spiritual nourishment, the Cowman passages with joy in the face of pain or degradation. Given the circumstances of the composition of *Streams*, I understand why Mrs. Cowman was drawn to passages about darkness, pain, anguish, despair. Given the upbringing Mary Tileston received, I understand her attraction to passages about silence, contemplation, meditation.

Madame Guyon lived in the late seventeenth and early eighteenth centuries (1648–1717), a devout Roman Catholic and aristocrat, author of the spiritual *Autobiography of Madame Guyon*. Today she is undergoing something of a revival, her work having been discovered by Protestant fundamentalists and evangelicals.[35] Of Madame Guyon's autobiography, Ruth Bell Graham writes, "This is a strange autobiography, deeply inspiring, at times disturbing, always intensely personal."[36] She wonders how any Christian living during the time of the decadent Louis XIV at Versailles could have remained unsullied; yet Madame Guyon did, no doubt, thanks in part to her exceptional spiritual director. Today women of means have personal trainers; in seventeenth-century France aristocratic women had spiritual directors to whom they took their cares and concerns and questions.

Madame Guyon lived an unremarkable life until age twenty-eight. By unremarkable I mean typical, traditional, uneventful. Married at sixteen without her consent to a wealthy aristocrat eighteen years older than she, Guyon suffered under the autocratic rule of her mother-in-law until her husband died twelve years after they married. Then not only did she and her mother-in-law reconcile, but her mother-in-law became devoted to her. A cynic might credit Madame Guyon's annual income of seventy thousand livres as the impetus for the elder's change of heart. Madame Guyon could have remarried, moved to Paris, founded a convent, or led a religious order, any of which would have been seen as normal. She chose none of those paths, however, and because she did not, her life became the remarkable one we know.

Five years after her husband's death, Madame Guyon left her home and spent the next five years—1681–1686—looking for the mission she was convinced God had called her to fulfill. Or to put it more precisely, she knew that God had a mission for her, though she did not in 1681 yet know what that mission was to be. While she was searching, she moved from Paris to Thonon to Turin to Grenoble, haunted and hassled by enemies and rumors of witchcraft and other theological heresies, none of which was true. Also during this time, Guyon managed to begin her career as an inspirational and theological writer; her books were those that inspired and galvanized women devotional compilers of the nineteenth and early twentieth centuries. First came *Les Torrents spirituels*, then *Explication et réflexions sur la Bible. Moyen Court* followed and then *Examen de l'Ecriture Sainte*, "a meditative interpretation of the Bible," as scholar Marie-Florine Bruneau puts it.[37]

Given the era and the daring of a woman writing theological explication of Scripture, it is no wonder that clerics like Bishop d'Arenthon d'Alex of Geneva and others sought to discredit her and worse; in late 1687 the bishop issued a pastoral letter condemning *Moyen Court*. The archbishop of Paris, François Harlay de Champvallon, added his voice, accusing her of heretical teachings about prayer. Knowing this background, we easily understand why Guyon wrote in *Experience God through Prayer*, "I do not criticize the divine leadings of others. It is my purpose through the writing of this book to influence the world to love God and to serve Him successfully" (Whitaker House edition, 1984, page 7).

Guyon claims to write for the unlearned, the ordinary person "to dispel any myths and discuss the advantages of prayer" (8): "Dear reader, study this book with a sincere spirit and a humble mind. If you read to criticize, you will fail to profit from it" (9). What follows is a remarkable series of short essays on how to pray, her first essay explaining the process: meditating on less than half a page of Scripture at a time or perhaps merely a verse or two, think about it, connect it to other passages, memorize it, study it, consider commentary, and then, as she puts it, "pray the Word" (17). In the next essay, "Beginning the Journey," she takes readers step-by-step through the process, using the Lord's Prayer as the model text.

Madame Guyon is describing the purpose and process for which nineteenth- and twentieth-century devotionals were designed and published. She is, in effect, *establishing* the genre, building on the work of medieval women mystics and anticipating the devotional compilations of subsequent generations of religious women. Madame Guyon recommends solitude, silence, surrender. She writes of the themes of consolation, suffering, patience, active waiting; she emphasizes grace and the work of God, not the work of human beings. These are the familiar themes of Mary Wilder Tileston and Mrs. Cowman. No wonder Protestants have found Madame Guyon so close to their own concerns; no wonder she has been described as a female Martin Luther.

Accused of promoting such doctrinal errors as convincing members of various religious orders to follow their own spiritual insights rather than the rules of the order (which does, indeed, sound much like Martin Luther), her writing was condemned as heretical, and she was arrested and eventually imprisoned in the infamous Bastille from June 4, 1698, to March 24, 1703; because of her, one of her servants also served twelve years there. As Bruneau says, Guyon's enemies used "slander, forgery of documents, insinuations, lies, subterfuge, imprisonment, psychological brutalization"[38] to destroy her; during her imprisonment she was interrogated eighty times for eight to ten hours an interrogation. Unfortunately for her, her life became the nexus of political and familial as well as religious intrigue, partly the result of her wealth, partly the result of her connections, partly the result of her refusal to give people what they wanted. She had to be removed, and her religious work and writing provided church and state the perfect reason to do so. Thrust into the center of the maelstrom was Guyon's friend François Fénelon, who, while defending his own theological position to his enemy Bishop Jacques Bénigne of Meaux, refused to condemn Guyon's.

Of what was she really charged? She was accused of being part of the quietist movement, or, in short, of being a mystic, of promoting meditation, of "quieting reason and of discursive thought . . . to reach new insights. For mystics of this school, the uses of discourses, thoughts, or operations of the mind adhered to by other forms of meditation, prevents the operation of the divine."[39] The antimystics in the Catholic Church, who eventually defeated the mystics, were convinced that such mysticism was a slippery slope leading to a rejection of church hierarchy, authority, dogma. (And they may well have been right in their fears.) When the church repudiated mysticism, it also repudiated its own history and some of its most profound and influential adherents, such as Teresa of Avila, whom I discuss in the next chapter. Yet Guyon hardly rejects the use of discourse, thought, or the mind; rather she recommends the opposite: reading and memorizing Scripture, reading other religious writers—she quoted frequently from Augustine, among others. And, of course, she recommends that her readers *study* her own books.

Guyon fought for the spiritual rights of average people. She preached throughout her travels; she urged that at least the Gospels and prayers be available in the vernacular and not solely in Latin. She objected to the power dimensions of church hierarchy, which failed to serve the spiritual needs of parishioners, her sole concern. So not only was Guyon criticizing the system the church had established but she was a woman doing so. The combination proved too great for church leaders to ignore. Perhaps part of her success with average Catholics resulted from her persecution. When she wrote or talked about suffering or temptation to despair, they knew and we know that her advice had been hard-won. Eventually she found followers not only in France but in Scotland, Holland, and Germany, and not only among Catholics; even during her lifetime she influenced Protestants of numerous theological persuasions. In the scope of her vision and in her commitment to individual spirituality and personal accountability to God, she did indeed anticipate the devotional work of Tileston and Cowman.

All along I expected to encounter women who quietly and retiringly published sweet poems or saccharine prose that advocated, among other things, a traditional role for women. Most explicit in Margaret Bottome, but implicit in the lives of the others, the opposite message comes through. We find women discovering what they do well, what gifts God has given them, what messages they want to give to other women. And these messages influenced generations of women, even if most of their work is no longer in print, or if in print not readily accessible.

Throughout these chapters I have tried to put these women together into a cultural context and to emphasize their similarities while recognizing each woman's distinctive contributions. None fits the standard mold or matches the stereotypes of women in the nineteenth century. As I reviewed each life again after completing this anthology, another fact became obvious. None except Madame Guyon and Mary Wilder Tileston had children, and several never married. I cannot give a reason why these women "failed" to fulfill the fundamental role assigned to women (then and now), but it is as if their readers were their children. In this and in so many other ways, the women whom Mrs. DeRose, Mary Wilder Tileston, and Mrs. Cowman culled for their devotionals are fitting progenitors of women like Kathleen Norris and fitting heirs of the medieval devotional tradition among women.

A Venerable Devotional Tradition

Teresa of Avila (1515–1582)
Catherine of Genoa (also called Adorna, 1447–1510)
Margery Kempe (ca. 1373–ca. 1440)
Catherine of Siena (1347–1380)
Julian of Norwich (ca. 1342–ca. 1413)

everal years ago, driven by a reference to Catherine Adorna in Tileston's *Daily Strength*, a reference to Catherine of Siena and to Teresa of Avila in Tileston's *Joy and Strength*, and a reference to "Mother Julian" in *Daily Strength* and Cowman's *Handfuls of Purpose*, I began to read these women mystical writers as well as books about them. Most contemporary scholarship, I discovered, focused not on their spirituality but rather on the physical results of that spirituality: in short, the starvation some of these women underwent. Feminist scholars argued among themselves as to whether the Catherines, for instance, suffered from anorexia nervosa or other eating disorders. They read women (and men) mystics to define the medieval view of "the body," not to define the mystics' understanding of spirituality—of the incarnation, of salvation and the atonement, of grace, of sin and repentance, and the second birth. The scholars were not looking for help in practicing the Christian faith or in understanding what daily spiritual discipline means to women with children to raise,

155

husbands to feed, ends to meet. Not that the *lives* of women mystics necessarily focused on domesticity, though some of their lives did, but that their theological understanding of "lived religion" through daily devotional practice was embedded in domesticity and so provided help for women who did have domestic lives to lead.

Although the work of feminist scholars was interesting, certainly, it seemed to me ultimately beside the point, for I had before me just a few tantalizing references to women mystical writers and wanted to know how the nineteenth-century genre of daily devotionals connected to the devotional mysticism of the medieval period. I found it intriguing and significant that the earliest work by women writers focused on the daily practice of spiritual discipline, whether that work came in the form of letters, diaries, prayers, extended metaphors, or brief meditations meant to be read slowly and pondered deeply: *lectio divina*, the Catholic version of intense meditative reading. I connected their work with the numerous women writers of devotional literature in the nineteenth and twentieth centuries, the subject and form apparently acceptable for women to publish (except for Madame Guyon, of course). Indeed, at least in the case of Teresa of Avila, she was *ordered* to write and publish.

I was also curious about where Mary Wilder Tileston discovered Catherine Adorna or Catherine of Siena, for I had assumed that their work would not have been widely accessible in the late nineteenth century. A computer search on the publishing history of several of the women revealed that not until the *late* nineteenth century were editions of the work of these women available. I wondered where Mrs. Cowman discovered Julian of Norwich, for Mrs. Cowman's Holiness tradition is far, far removed from Catholic mysticism (not to mention the abhorrence with which fundamentalists in the early and well into the mid-twentieth century held Roman Catholicism). Nevertheless, Mrs. Cowman uses a sentence from Julian to define the purpose of *Handfuls of Purpose:* "In the year 1373 Julian of Norwich wrote: 'He said not thou shalt not be tempted; thou shalt not be afflicted, but He did say, thou shalt not be overcome.' We are to rise unvanquished after every blow—we are to laugh the laugh of faith, not fear" (v). It is interesting that Cowman here near the end of her life writes about the laughter of faith, using Julian as her touchstone (and a passage not used by Tileston, who in *Joy and Strength* cites her six times and once in *Daily Strength*), when so much of her previous work focuses on the tears of faith.

Other than that one reference to Julian, Mrs. Cowman does not cite the women mystics, but she does include Madame Guyon, François Fénelon, and Francis de Sales, all of whom wrote in the tradition of the medieval mystics of the church and knew them well. And as we saw in the previous chapter, Madame Guyon and François Fénelon suffered for this. Ultimately the church rejected its mystical tradition—or should I say that the mystical tradition, which had once been mainstream, became a tributary only. Nevertheless, the early mystics influenced Madame Guyon, who in turn influenced Tileston and Cowman and their numerous readers.

So far from being dead or absent in the nineteenth century, somehow the women mystics found their way into the daily devotionals so popular then. Although today we might assume that Julian of Norwich had the greatest influence, it was Catherine Adorna with whom the nineteenth century was fascinated (but how did they learn of her?). We might think of her as the fulcrum for the women listed at the beginning of this chapter. In so many ways, the women mystics who lived before Adorna lead to her, and she in turn leads to the daily devotional as it came to be written by Mrs. DeRose or Lucy Larcom. Yet Teresa of Avila too found some small favor with the Victorians, according to the lively new biography by Cathleen Medwick, who notes that George Eliot "made Teresa the genius loci of her novel *Middlemarch.*"[1]

Today the popularity of the medieval women mystics demonstrates the renewed interest in spirituality among general readers, if not among scholars, and accounts in part for the continued success of the Cowman and Tileston daily devotionals, for contemporary spiritual writers like Kathleen Norris, for the appropriation or adoption of the genre for nonreligious purposes. The daily devotional as a form is so far from disappearing that editors are creating books of "daily readings" for the current most popular medieval mystic, Julian of Norwich.

But how can one account for the popularity of a genre or a writer? Although it is possible to suggest reasons, in the final analysis no one can really say why. When I asked minister Jim Kerr, he said, "In the circles I have been running in of late (spiritual formation . . .), Julian of Norwich, Catherine of Siena, et cetera, are all the rage. I think this is so, not only because they are women . . . but because (especially with Julian) they are great theologians." If they are great theologians, it is a theology of a different stripe—not systematic theology, certainly, because the women were not interested in developing a *sys-*

tem to understand God. Rather, they wrote out of an existential need to understand the deepest, most personal, most immediate concerns of their life, which they believed others would share. They wrote of practice and practicality, and they wrote with and through domestic images and metaphors. They could not be farther removed from systematic theologians and could not be closer to the homely stories of Jesus. The only writer who comes close to writing systematically is also the most recent in time, Teresa of Avila, whose work on the pilgrimage of the soul, *Interior Castle*, uses a consistent metaphor to explain the religious life. And, as I said, she wrote under orders.

I would like to look briefly at the work of each woman and how that work intersects with that of the others and with the compilers of daily devotionals. Rather than working chronologically, however, as I list the women at the beginning of the chapter, I start in the middle, with Margery Kempe, followed by the two women whose life spans overlap with hers, for these three women alone demonstrate the breadth and scope of devotional writing and writers in terms of theme, style, theological perspective, socioeconomic class, education, and devotional response.

Three Mystics of the Middle Ages

Margery Kempe, Julian of Norwich, and Catherine of Siena were contemporaries (Kempe was seven when Catherine died). Margery Kempe and Catherine shared a similar background; Margery's father was a cloth merchant, Catherine's a cloth-dyer, though Margery's father was wealthy—a burgess and a five-time mayor of their town of Lynn in England; he also served as a member of parliament six times. But of Julian we know nothing, not even her real name, for she refused to reveal any personal details apart from her life as an anchorite in Norwich, a town close to Lynn. As do Mrs. DeRose and Ellen M. Dyer, Julian lives only in her work, from which we deduce her concerns and personality (if personality in part is the result of what a person thinks about each day). However, we do have Kempe's account of her visit to Julian to add to the anchorite's own work concerning the revelation she received from God in 1373.

All three women lived during the political, social, and theological tumult of the late fourteenth century—the end of the Middle Ages, the beginning of the Renaissance. For example, the seeds that eventually led to the Reformation had already been sown. In England John Wycliffe had died in 1384, and his English translation of the Bible was secretly being used by the Lollards; Norwich was a particular stronghold for them. Near the end of her life, Kempe (like Madame Guyon) was charged with heresy through an accidental connection with a leading Lollard. Henry V had defeated the French at Agincourt, and to protest the heavy taxes that Henry had imposed to finance his war, the peasants revolted. But of these events Kempe, like Mrs. Cowman who seemed to ignore the current events of her day, remained silent, as did Julian. What mattered were the personal, spiritual issues facing Kempe; what mattered to Julian were her revelations. Temporal affairs were irrelevant.

Catherine also lived through numerous wars, the spread of the black plague (it began sweeping Europe a year after her birth), and the increasing corruption of the church and its clergy. But unlike the other two, Catherine did concern herself with theological current events at least. In her *Dialogue* she describes in detail the church corruption of her day; before she died, the church had split in two. She also composed several prayers for the purification and renewal of the church, one of which she read in Rome soon after the schism began.

Although Margery Kempe could not read or write, she was nevertheless an astute and successful businesswoman, who for a time ran the largest brewery in Lynn, East Anglia; perhaps she inherited her father's business acumen. Unlike Catherine and Julian, she was married and mother of fourteen, both of which facts eventually mortified her, given the equation of virginity and spirituality. After becoming a Christian, or as she says, a bride of Christ, she became obsessed with the idea of wearing only white as a sign of her spiritual marriage, but her worldly marriage seemed to stand in the way of her desire, making her fear that she was unworthy to wear the sign of virginity. Eventually, however, she became convinced that it was indeed God's direction and so for the rest of her life she dressed only in white. She also became convinced that she was called to go on a pilgrimage, like the folk in Chaucer's *Canterbury Tales*. What a spectacle she must have been, tramping through all kinds of mud and dirt and stormy weather in her white clothes! But she went much farther than holy Canterbury, traveling to the Holy Land, to Rome, and to Santiago di Compostela in Spain, one of the most famous of all sites for pilgrimage in the Middle Ages; even today thousands of pilgrims a year go there. Kempe also visited Julian in her cell at Norwich.

Julian, some thirty years Kempe's senior, composed *Revelation of Love* (in some translations called *The Revelation of Divine Love*), the first known book to be written by a woman in English, after she received her spiritual insight in 1373, the year of Kempe's birth. At the time, like Kempe and Catherine, she was "unlettered," to use her word, though somehow she learned to read and write, spending the next twenty years writing her book. Kempe and Catherine, on the other hand, dictated their works, Kempe using two different scribes, Catherine using those of her followers who were literate.

Margery Kempe

John Skinner, who has recently translated Margery Kempe's rough Middle English into modern idiom, describes Kempe's book as a "diary of the soul," lacking the sophistication or polish of Catherine's writing on prayer, for instance. Skinner calls Kempe's vocabulary "impoverished."[2] The second of Kempe's scribes was better educated than the first, and he, according to Skinner, "virtually rewrote the book aided by Margery's memory and fresh dictation" (4). As often happens in rewriting, the book grew—by ten chapters, necessitating a book two. At the end of book one, Kempe (or the second scribe) says:

> This book ends here, for God took to his mercy the man who wrote the original draft of what has been copied out again here. He did not write at all clearly nor was he accurate in recording, in any kind of exact detail, what had been told to him; moreover, his handwriting and his spelling made very little sense. So now here at last, with God's help and the efforts of she who felt and experienced all these happenings, is a faithful account all contained and set down in this little book.
>
> Page 298

One has the impression that either Kempe or her new scribe or both were quite pleased with God's mercy in taking the first scribe out of this world, so bad was his handwriting and spelling, a strange criticism considering that spelling would not be standardized for some time.

As this and other examples show, the book lacks the theological force of Julian's work, which in tone and style is much closer to Catherine's *Dialogue* and to the daily devotionals of the nineteenth century, though Kempe, like Catherine, recorded the dialogues she had with God: what he tells her, what she tells him—a devotional, medieval twist on "he said, she said". But Kempe has what the other two lack—a narrative power and authorial presence, a freshness and immediacy that appeal to early twenty-first-century readers, who have made the memoir a best-selling genre; not even in Catherine's letters do we have anything approximating the lively discourse of Kempe.

Although it would probably be anachronistic to call Kempe's book a memoir or an autobiography, nevertheless (and despite Skinner's disclaimer), it fits that category best. Not only does Skinner criticize her vocabulary, but he deplores "the repetitive echoes of common talk, as if we were merely listening to any chance conversation in the streets of fifteenth-century Lynn" (4), which makes Kempe sound like a querulous old gossip and strikes me as a disapproval of the domestic. And what if his estimation is correct? Is it not marvelous to imagine chance conversations about the work of God in the world? The very ordinariness of her comments, which Skinner disparages, I find most appealing and suspect that other early twenty-first-century women readers will as well. For instance: "I went back to visit her regularly, praying with her and offering her what comfort I might, asking God to fortify her against the enemy. And I have every reason to suppose that he did so, blessed may he be" (248). The last sentence in particular may not have elevated, theological language, to be sure, but what better expression of faith could Kempe have made?

Kempe lets us eavesdrop on her conversations with God—her running dialogue with him throughout the book—and with herself. She makes us want to know what adventures she will have next or how she will fare on her latest pilgrimage, say to the Holy Land, or during her latest illness. We shiver when she talks about the cold winter, about her poverty and debts (154). We hear echoes of the Book of Job in the taunts of her friends, "Why ever did you give all your money away?" they ask, when she talks about raising money for a pilgrimage to Santiago. Her anecdotes, such as the following, make for lively reading:

One time a silly man, who was quite indifferent to his reputation, purposefully poured a bowl of slops down upon my head as I was walking along the street below him. I was not upset in the least but said to him, "God make you a good and holy man." And I went on my way, thanking God for the accident; such was my way of accepting many similar things that happened to me all the time.

Pages 196–97

161

Kempe's experience smacks of slapstick because none of us has had (or ever will have) such an experience. But then I think of all the times I have been splashed by a truck or car, and who hasn't had this happen, either deliberately or accidentally, and I doubt that our reaction has been one of gratitude to God and a prayer for the perpetrator. Kempe's reaction reflects themes found in Tileston and Cowman: No matter what the circumstances, profound or trivial, thank God for them. As the title of Tileston's devotional makes clear, we need strength for daily, ordinary, domestic needs, and we need access to this strength in ordinary, plain language.

And Margery Kempe is a plainspoken, no-nonsense kind of woman. Who could fail to be charmed by the following homely analogy? "Daughter," God says to her, "you obey my will and cling fast to me like the skin of a stockfish sticks to your hand when you have boiled it tender" (134). Now, some readers may not understand this image, but anyone who has ever tried to remove the sticky skin of a fish from her hands will recognize the power of Kempe's words. Illiterate she may have been, but hardly unimaginative or unskillful. Or consider her description of the Holy Spirit as "the kind of noise a pair of bellows make. . . . And then our Lord changed this sound into the cooing of a dove; and later he turned it into the song of a robin redbreast, who would often sing very merrily in my right ear" (134). Kempe has an unerring sense of how to explain abstract ideas in concrete, domestic terms, a gift all the more striking when we consider that she is dictating, not composing. (Skinner's translation no doubt deserves some of the credit.)

Readers familiar with Chaucer would be tempted to call Kempe a mystical Wife of Bath based on the conversation she has with God about the relative merits of virginity and wifehood. God has just announced that she will have another child, and she responds, "I still make love to my husband and that upsets me greatly and makes me feel guilty" (66). God assures Kempe of two things: that he loves wives as much as he does any virgin and that loving her husband "brings you reward and fresh merit." Given the times and the teachings of the church, Kempe's perspective is extraordinary.

Because of her tone, her style, and her concerns, Kempe is a fitting forerunner of Tileston and Cowman, for she is an ordinary wife and mother trying to understand and accept the big and small frustrations of life; and she concerns herself with the domestic affairs of those she meets, for instance a man she encounters one day in Saint Margaret's Church, whose "wife had just had a baby and gone out of her mind" (248). If Kempe knew anything, it was childbirth, and she immediately goes with the man to his home.

Of course, some of her frustrations, she admits, were of her own making. Her honesty and lack of self-pity are as refreshing as her conversational style; even her ubiquitous pious language (as in the full text of the above example) doesn't sound overwrought or romantic or strained, the way Lucy Larcom's or Anna Shipton's sometimes does. At the same time, Kempe's stories about Rome remind us of those Anna Shipton tells about her own far more comfortable Italian travel. Both women tell of providential encounters with local residents and of humorous, if awkward, language barriers. Kempe traveled close to Catherine's home, but if she knew of Catherine or visited Siena as a holy site, she does not mention it (the possibility intrigues me). Kempe anticipates not only the spiritual memoir of, say, Kathleen Norris but also the genre of travel writing.

Of course, *we* can read Margery Kempe, but Mrs. Cowman, Mary Wilder Tileston, or Anna Shipton could not. On December 27, 1934, medievalist Hope Emily Allen announced in a letter to the *Times* of London the discovery of a four-hundred-year-old manuscript that had been languishing in an old Catholic library. Allen subsequently collaborated with another medieval scholar to produce *The Book of Margery Kempe*, published by the Early English Text Society. Based on textual evidence, they decided that the recently discovered manuscript had been copied shortly after Kempe's death.

If no one before the twentieth century would have been able to read Kempe's book, then why include her? I do not claim that Kempe influenced anyone under consideration here, but I am trying to show that there are persistent and consistent themes shared by all women who wrote (and write) of the spiritual life and to introduce readers to wonderful women writers of the past. Kempe argues with God and suffers acute worries about her spiritual inferiority; she seems to rush from one holy man to another, including the holy woman Dame Julian (who took a man's name, after all). Kempe was seeking reassurance, and her need for such reassurance reminds me of Mrs. Cowman's own need, which lies just beneath the surface of *Streams in the Desert*. But beyond this, if only because of her connection to Julian, Kempe should not be left out of a chapter exploring the roots and connections between the Middle Ages and the late nineteenth- and early twentieth-century fascination with devotional discourse.

So what does Kempe tell us about Julian of Norwich? At the very least we learn that she was well-known as a mystic and spiritual leader. Kempe in chapter 18 of her book recounts what she told Julian about her devotions, her meditations, her understanding of grace, her conversations with God: "I also told her in detail of the numerous and wonderful revelations; for what I wanted to learn from this anchoress was whether I had been deceived by them. For I knew she was an expert in this very field so I knew she would offer me very good advice" (74). As Kempe recalls, Julian said:

> The Holy Spirit can never urge us to do anything against charity; for if he did so, he would be acting against his own self for he is the sum of all charity. And so it is that he leads a soul to chastity, for those who live chaste lives are named as temples of the Holy Spirit; and the Holy Spirit grounds the soul, making it steadfast in true faith and right belief.
>
> Page 74

Kempe's quotations of Julian continue for several more paragraphs, notable for Julian's frequent citations from the Bible, demonstrating her knowledge of and grounding in Scripture. Kempe concludes by saying, "The anchoress and I had a great deal to say to each other about all these sacred and holy matters. Dwelling on the love of our Lord Jesus kept us absorbed for the many days we spent together" (75). These two make a strange and marvelous pair, the garrulous woman and the recluse.

Julian of Norwich

In the centuries following Kempe's visit to Julian, Julian's reputation waned, and her book, *Revelation of Love*, was little known, making Tileston's frequent citations—in an early modern translation (using thee, thy, -eth, like the King James Bible)—all the more remarkable. We might forget these facts, given how her reputation soared in the last half of the twentieth century. Thomas Merton called her the greatest of the English mystics, and C. S. Lewis said that Julian's book was "dangerous," meaning potent, demanding. Today the Church of St. Julian in Norwich is visited by scores of pilgrims each year. Among the recent editions of her work are Sheila Upjohn's *All Shall Be Well:*

Daily Readings from Julian of Norwich,[3] two small volumes of daily readings (published by the Julian Shrine in 1980), and a new translation of her work by John Skinner.[4] Many people now recognize her analogy of creation to "something small, about the size of a hazelnut" (9). Unfortunately that's all many people know about Julian's magisterial, masterly work—and there is much more to know.

Skinner provides a brief introduction to the life of an anchorite, and the medieval *Ancrene Riwle* gives a primary account of the requirements. All who sought their bishop to become an anchorite had to demonstrate a true calling and the financial wherewithal to support themselves. Most applicants dedicated themselves to lives as hermits, though some worked in the community for charitable reasons. All anchorites were single and committed to celibacy and chastity; they all had two servants to care for their needs—more, says Skinner, to protect them from intruders, such as Margery Kempe, than as a luxury. Julian's own cell consisted of two rooms connected to the St. Julian Church, at the time one of the humblest churches in a very rich town.

On May 8, 1347, Julian received what she called "showings," sixteen of them, each of which dealt with a particular theme or theological issue: the Trinity, the incarnation, the death and resurrection of Jesus, worship, prayer; she lists them in her first chapter. The rest of the book explains each of the showings in turn. The first fifteen occurred in one day, beginning at 4 A.M. and ending at 3 P.M., while she was awake. The final showing "was in conclusion and a confirmation of all fifteen" (147) and took place the following night while she slept. She was "thirty and a half years old" (5) and had been so ill for three days and nights that on the fourth, believing she would die, she asked for the last rites. Three days later her visions began.

Regardless of the showing, whether of Christ's death or of her grateful response, a spirit of intense joy hovers over the pages. For instance, in chapter 14, the sixth showing, she writes, "I saw him rule royally there, filling it full of joy and mirth. He himself presided by endlessly gladdening and entertaining his very close friends with every warmth and courtesy . . ." (32). There is so much domestic significance in this scene and so much elegant metaphor. Julian sees Christ as the consummate host, in charge of his home, yes, whose only purpose in gathering his friends together is to entertain them, to show them rich hospitality, to make sure they are treated to the very best with the greatest sincerity and care. This picture of heaven echoes the parables Jesus told of the great feasts and banquets he intends to serve us. It also reflects Jesus' model of being the first servant among many servants. What better illustration of Jesus' ruling and serving simultaneously than Julian's vision—her very practical, even ordinary, view of heavenly bliss: God having a good time, making sure everyone else is having a good time. It also reinforces the passage cited by Cowman, making me wonder whether she had read the entire book rather than just a passage or two anthologized or quoted in a sermon she had heard or read. Her interpretation—"We are to laugh the laugh of faith, not fear"—is so in keeping with Julian's book, but without the context of the whole book the interpretation seems a stretch, given what Cowman cites. Yet she got it just right. Repeatedly Julian talks about joy, bliss, merriment, and if she herself doesn't use the words *laugh* or *laughter*, nevertheless, that is the force of her theological perspective.

Julian, in the explanation of the first showing, establishes the central theological truths learned from God's revelation to her, and it establishes her rhetorical style. The Lord is "so homely with a sinful creature" and offers "courteous love." That is, as in the passage cited above, the Lord behaves with familiarity and with civility toward humankind—homely, of the home, the hearth. Julian's theology, therefore, is grounded in domesticity, and this distinguishes her work and the other women mystics from male mystical writers, just as it is a distinguishing characteristic of nineteenth-century daily devotionals.

Julian warns us, however, that familiarity is no excuse for discourtesy, as it is so often in families. "But we must take care not to be so familiar that we neglect courtesy. For our Lord himself is sovereign homeliness; yet as homely as he is, so is he courteous, and he is utterly courteous" (169)—and utterly to be our example. "Sovereign homeliness" has the effect of an oxymoron or at the least a paradox, the adjective usually connected to the state (and so public), the noun with the hearth (and so private).

How familiar, though, does Julian think God is with his creatures? The answer comes through metaphor, one of the significant rhetorical characteristics of her prose: "He is the ground of all that is good and supporting for us. He is our clothing that lovingly wraps and folds us about; it embraces us and closes us all around as it hangs upon us with such tender love" (9; this passage immediately precedes the hazelnut analogy). Julian uses two fundamental metaphors, ground (or earth) and clothes, which even the poorest can understand. A few pages later she uses the clothing metaphor in a slightly different way to explain how God clothes us in his goodness: "For just as the body is clad in clothes, and the flesh in skin and the bones in flesh with the heart in the breast, so are we, soul and body, clothed and wrapped around in the goodness of God" (13). Julian wants us to know that we can experience nothing more intimate, nothing more domestic and ordinary, than the goodness of God. Whereas others present this idea as extraordinary and so foreign to the domestic routines of life, Julian says that on the contrary God's goodness is entirely ordinary. Thus, because we should expect and accept grace as routine, without, of course, taking it for granted, she implicitly criticizes all of us who are startled, even astounded, by grace.

This same sense of ordinariness is inherent in her metaphor of ground. Thanks to Paul Tillich the idea of "ground" may have lost its fresh, metaphorical power; yet it could well be that Julian originated the idea, which in the fourteenth century, especially coupled with the metaphor of clothing, would have been much more striking. Also, "ground" would have meant far more to people who walked everywhere and had an agrarian economy. She uses the metaphor repeatedly, from the beginning, as we have seen, to the end: "God," she writes, "is the ground of our kindly reason" (173). And God "says full merrily, 'I am the ground of you [sic] beseeking'" (181).

Metaphor is a fitting trope to explain the visions she has received and is central to her rhetorical style—if only because God himself instructs her through metaphor and analogy: "I could not rid myself of these three homely images—pellets . . . herring scales . . . raindrops"; and "he showed me a simple example" of "a solemn king" revealing his true feelings in private and in public (15). Or in a startling mathematical metaphor, "I saw God in a point" (178). But she is just as comfortable with syllogistic discourse, with antithesis, and with climax, arguing from the smallest to the greatest. All these give a systematic quality to her writing (not to be confused with systematic theology). Each idea builds on the one before and leads to the one that follows, so her paragraphs begin with such words as "it follows," "for," "so," and "and," which reinforce her rigorous, and syllogistic-like, causal linkings. She uses antithesis frequently in describing Christ, for instance, as "highest and mightiest" and simultaneously "so lowly, meek, and most homely and most courteous" (15–16). In her experience (and in our own) high and mighty people are not meek, much less courteous; the expression "high and mighty," in fact, means quite the opposite. By juxtaposing the two here and throughout her discourse, she draws our attention to how antithetical Christ's character is from the normal expectations we have of rulers or of anyone in power. By yoking these two biblical principles, she throws into relief the full nature of Christ; often in the Bible, one or the other is highlighted, but Julian balances them.

One of the best examples of her use of climax comes in chapter 48: "For mercy works in keeping us. Mercy works by turning all things to good. Mercy, for love, suffers us to fail by measure and design. . . . Our failing is dreadful, our falling is shameful, our dying is sorrowful" (and then she returns to the idea of mercy, 95). In the first half, the climax occurs in the verb phrases—"works in keeping," "works by turning," "suffers us to fail." Then she turns the final verb into a noun, which begins another sequence of three, each becoming stronger or more significant—"failing," "falling," "dying," though the complete sentences of all three move climactically. Julian cannot explain the greatness of mercy without moving through the sequence of failing, falling, and dying, the ultimate terror; but through even that anguish God's mercy shines.

As I read Julian, one thing becomes vividly clear: I am in the presence of a deeply educated, highly sophisticated, and richly subtle mind. Remember that she was illiterate until her mid-thirties. Remember that she learned to read and write on her own and did not have the advantage of an education emphasizing grammar and rhetoric. Yet somehow she mastered both. Not only that, but it appears from a manuscript uncovered early in the twentieth century that she wrote a draft of her book (could she have written others that have not survived?) and then rewrote it, the mark of a writer. And she emphasizes words, or language, as one of the three ways God taught her and so by extension teaches us.

I am reminded yet again of the low expectations I have brought to each woman I have encountered on my trip backward in time, from Mrs. Cowman to Mary Wilder Tileston, from Adelaide Procter to Madame Guyon, and now to Julian. The explanations of her visions remind me of the implicit arguments Tileston's individual devotionals make through their often jarring juxtapositions. I cannot ignore how domesticity finds a central place in the devotional work of women, whether in the fourteenth or in the twentieth century. However, nothing prepared me for the response I received as I was reading the book.

I decided to take Julian with me to the doctor and then to a salon—a day of waiting for appointments, away from my computer. I took the book so that I could keep working. Everyone wanted to know what I was reading, which happens to me fairly often because I carry books everywhere. But in the salon two of the stylists pressed me for details. Who was Julian? What's the book about? Is it easy to read? Yes, I said, it is easy to read; in fact I read it today sitting in various waiting rooms. It's the first book written in English by a woman. Julian was a hermit and lived in the fourteenth century. It's about the spiritual visions she received from God.

I figured that my final statement would end the conversation. But I was as wrong about that as I was about what Julian's writing would be like. The women wanted to see the book, know where they could buy it or what library stocked it, and they wrote down the title, Julian's name, and the name of the translator. I have no idea whether either picked up *Revelation of Love* or what they made of it if they did. But one thing is certain: The *idea* of this book by a fourteenth-century, self-taught recluse has immediate and enormous appeal to ordinary women.

Catherine of Siena

Catherine of Siena stands somewhere between Margery Kempe and Julian of Norwich in her appeal and in her life. She did not travel extensively like Kempe, but she was not a recluse like Julian. Like Kempe and Julian, she lacked formal education; unlike Kempe but like Julian, however, she eventually did learn to read and much later to write, nevertheless dictating her work. She did not marry, nor did she become a nun but a member of the Mantellate, a group of laywomen affiliated with the Dominican order. After joining the group, she served a kind of spiritual apprenticeship by remaining at home for three years and learning how to pray.

Of the three kinds of spiritual discourse she composed—letters, *The Dialogue*, and prayers—her prayers are the most moving. According to scholar Mary O'Driscoll, O.P., during the three-year period of intense prayer and solitude Catherine received her theological insight

169

that "love of God and the love of neighbor are inseparable in the Christian life, to such an extent that not only can one not exist without the other, but that they increase and decrease in like proportion."[5] Whereas Kempe emphasized God's grace in ordinary life and Julian focused on the many ways God sends his love and the many ways for us to receive it, Catherine emphasized the dual nature of Christianity—concern for this world and concern for the next.

Of all the devotional writers, early or late, Catherine attended to the small and large events of life. Like Margery and Julian, she worked and thought domestically—doing household chores in her home, caring for the sick and the poor in Siena, such work acceptable and expected of women. As the twenty-third child of her parents (her twin sister died in infancy, as did many of her siblings), she would have been an expert in household chores. But her tact, sensitivity, and compassion brought her a different ministry: She became a peace broker for fighting families and then for cities like Florence and Pisa; in short, she became politically active. She combined the modern roles of family therapist, intervention counselor, and conflict negotiator. One of her greatest efforts occurred in 1376 when the rulers of Florence asked her to intervene on their behalf with Pope Gregory XI, then living in Avignon, rather than Rome. Not only did she work for the Florentines but also pled with the Pope to return to Rome, which he did later that year, shortly before he died. Because the new pope, Urban VI, angered the cardinals with his reforms, they invalidated his election and put Clement VII in his place. Schism resulted. Although Catherine had only eighteen months to live, she spent that time working for restoration and healing; she died in Rome where she had gone at Pope Urban's request.

Let me pause in this brief recounting of Catherine's place in European history to explain that I initially encountered Catherine during my first trip to Tuscany, several years before I read the four excerpts in Tileston's *Joy and Strength*. My husband and I were staying southeast of Florence and planning a visit to Siena, about an hour south. As I was studying the guidebooks I'd brought with us, I discovered Catherine. It was clear that we could spend all our time in Siena just on Catherine herself. Later when I learned how significant her role in the politics of the day, I thought about the many courses in European history I had taken over the years and of all the books I had read. Where was Catherine? Just as John Tebbell is silent about the influence of women on American postbellum publishing, so were the courses in European history silent about Catherine of Siena, despite the emphasis on the split in the Roman Catholic Church. (There is now a National Center of Catherinian Studies in Rome.) Yet Catherine's role in state and church matters had to be so unusual for a woman in the fourteenth century as to merit some mention. But perhaps having a ministry of prayer automatically disqualified her for inclusion in political history (as it still would today).

Even so, however significant was Catherine's dedication to peace, she is not remembered as a politician but as a theologian, one of two women to have been officially designated as "doctor of the church," both she and Teresa of Avila (whom I discuss below) so named by Pope Paul VI on October 15, 1970. "The significance of this declaration is immense," writes O'Driscoll, "for it places this unschooled woman among the major Church theologians, thereby recognizing her ecclesial role as a teacher whose doctrine is relevant for the whole Church and for all time."[6] It is all the more remarkable since, as O'Driscoll points out, Catherine did not write "a logically developed doctrinal system,"[7] any more than Julian did. Rather, like Julian—and Margery Kempe—Catherine emphasizes how ordinary Christians can live extraordinary lives.

No matter what she wrote, Catherine repeats this assurance: God comes to us in the midst of our day-to-day lives and wants us to live through everyday events for him. We see this, for instance, in her letter to the wife of a Florentine tailor. Unlike what we might expect from a mystic, Catherine urges Monna Agnese to be prudent in such spiritual practices as prayer and fasting, her advice demonstrating that she knows the demands of a housewife and therefore refuses to burden Agnese with unnecessary demands or guilt. "When you can find the time for prayer, I beg you to use it," she writes.[8] She tells her to fast only on the days specified by the Church and then only if she feels strong enough. Should she fast on Saturday (standard practice)? Again, only if you can, writes Catherine. And since she writes during the summer, she urges Agnese to "drink something besides water every day" and "when this intense heat is over, fast on the feasts of holy Mary, if you can."[9] Here is sensible advice, which puts spiritual practice into Agnese's own hands. Catherine is thereby recognizing that God is not a one-size-fits-all deity but a person who deals individually with his creatures. Catherine's advice reminds me of nineteenth-century devotionals because, despite their sometimes formulaic structure—and Catherine's letters are highly formulaic in their openings and closings—they nevertheless manage to allow for a wide variety of religious experience and need.

In her prayers, Catherine demonstrates a command of language that is reminiscent of Julian. For example, she too uses antithesis and metaphor, and if her metaphors are not as unusual as Julian's, they are nevertheless appropriate and rooted in the metaphors of Scripture: fire, sheep, citadel, light, gardens. Often she combines metaphor and antithesis, as in this prayer:

> O immeasurable love!
> O gentle love!
> Eternal fire!
> You are that fire ever blazing,
> O high eternal Trinity!
> You are direct
> without any twisting,
> genuine without any duplicity,
> open
> without any pretense.[10]

This prayer of praise and adulation has a twofold purpose, of course, as is often true of the work of the women mystics. Catherine describes God's attributes to him in thankfulness at the same time that she has her eyes and ears on an audience of people like herself. She implies that we are to imitate God in our behavior; we are to be direct, genuine, open. She also implies, through her antithesis, that we are twisting, duplicitous, pretentious creatures. Toward the end of the prayer—which reads more like a poem—she makes the point explicit: "Our sin lies in nothing else/ but in loving what you hate/ and hating what you love," thus giving the reason why she begins the prayer as she does, exploring God's attributes and thus what he loves and simultaneously hates. And her use of chiasmus (or verbal crossing, like a mirror image)—"loving what you hate and hating what you love"—reinforces the earlier antithesis. Catherine, like Julian, is as much a master rhetorician as theologian. Or to put it another way, her theology is masterly if not least in part because her rhetoric is masterly.

In a prayer for Passion Sunday, the second Sunday before Easter, composed the year before her death, we find further examples of chiasmus, as well as anaphora, or repetition at the beginning of consecutive sentences. I read the prayer, too, on Passion Sunday:

> You have shown us love
> in your blood,
> and in your blood
> you have shown us your mercy
> and generosity.[11]

The effect of this crossing heightens and extends our understanding of the atonement; the blood is more than just an example of love but also of mercy and generosity. Or we could say that mercy and generosity define God's love. Catherine elaborates further what God has shown "in this blood," which is that our sins weigh God down, a striking theological conceit. Our sins do not weigh us down, though they should, but first and foremost they have a dramatic effect on God himself, which is another way of saying that human beings are important, far more important than even we think ourselves to be. So our sin is not in thinking ourselves significant but in thinking of ourselves as significant *in the wrong way.* Catherine repeats the phrase "in this blood" in anticipation of Good Friday and to teach us what the atonement means for both God and humankind. The face of the soul—a metaphor—has been washed in the blood and clothed by the blood. This reminds us of Julian's metaphor about God's love being the clothes we wear. Catherine develops the metaphor even more intimately, for blood is so personal, so significant, so fundamental to life and at the same time almost abhorrent because so intimate—witness the emphasis in Judaism—that God cannot touch us more deeply or closely than by cleaning us and clothing us with his blood.

Two-thirds of the way through the prayer Catherine's point of view changes; the second person pronoun now refers not to God but to someone else. O'Driscoll claims that Catherine is speaking of and to herself, but I disagree, except perhaps that she makes herself representative of the whole human race. Rather, when she says, "Rouse yourself;/ open the eye of your understanding"[12] she is talking to us, to those who would read or hear her prayer later. Not until the final three lines, with the use of the first person singular, is she clearly addressing herself, having implicated herself in her own exhortations to her audience. Such a structure is in keeping with all the daily devotional writing we have looked at. Even though the writer or compiler, for example Mrs. Cowman, may be addressing an audience outside herself, yet at the same time the address rings true because it has come from an unspoken but nevertheless perceptible need of the author.

This prayer also demonstrates a distinguishing characteristic of Catherine's metaphors: how she often anthropomorphizes not only the soul (female; she uses the female pronoun) but also God, for instance in *The Dialogue*, which is her culminating work: "O eternal, infinite Good! O mad lover! . . . Why then are you so mad? Because you have fallen in love with what you have made!"[13] The extreme image of a Creator frenzied with love for his creatures anticipates poets like John Donne and George Herbert. This may not be an image that we find palatable today because of its very intimacy and our equation of sex and love, but Catherine would not have made such an equation.

Shortly after finishing this section on Catherine of Siena, I read the *New York Times Magazine* special issue on "Women: The Shadow Story of the Millennium" (May 16, 1999). The last person I expected to encounter was Catherine of Siena—not exactly a household name, not exactly someone general readers would be interested in. And yet there she was, in an article by Jennifer Egan (a novelist), titled "Power Suffering." Naturally, just as feminist scholars have done, Egan focuses on Catherine's eating disorder, or, as Egan puts it, Catherine's "appetite for self-mortification," "one of the saint's most enduring traits" that led "to her death, at 33, of starvation."[14] Egan presents Catherine as an emblem for all female icons, religious and secular, even including Diana, the late Princess of Wales.

Despite the typical emphasis on the sensational aspects of Catherine's life, Egan does admit that Catherine eventually rejected her self-mortification and in her letters warned other women not to follow that path.[15] And, more significantly, Egan emphasizes Catherine's public role, thus no doubt changing readers' perceptions of a fourteenth-century woman, whose voice in the letters Egan describes as "emphatic, even imperious."[16] But should we accept Egan's claim that "such a public life was extraordinary to the point of being freakish"?[17] Extraordinary, certainly—but freakish? Many readers today already think of anyone with a deep religious commitment as medieval and those women mystics as decidedly unusual without adding the idea that a woman with public power was "freakish"; were she so perceived, she would not have been so frequently asked to intervene in difficult political disputes. Nevertheless, Egan's article is evidence that Catherine, along with Julian and other women mystics, are being taken seriously and given the credit due them as influential women of the last millennium.

With this, let's look at one of the passages selected by Tileston before turning to the other Catherine, Catherine of Genoa. The April 30 devotional in *Joy and Strength* has only two entries, a verse from Psalms and the selection from Catherine. Not only does it talk about power—a subject at the heart of Egan's article—but it does so from God's perspective. That is, Catherine writes as if she were God speaking to his followers. The passage does several things: explains why God created human beings, explains his nature, and explains the relationship of God and his people. Therefore, briefly and concisely Catherine provides her readers with an immense theological lesson, which makes it worth quoting in full (I have changed the language from sixteenth-century to twenty-first-century English):

> I desire that you should consider with firm faith that I, your most glorious God, who have created you for eternal blessedness, am eternal, sovereign, omnipotent. I will that you should seriously meditate that in Me, your God, dwell the most perfect knowledge and infinite wisdom; so that in My government of you, the heavens, and the earth, and the entire universe, I cannot be deceived in any way, or misled by any error. Were it otherwise, I should neither be all wise, nor should I be God. Also consider attentively that, as I am your God, so am I infinitely good, yea, love itself is My essence; that, therefore, I cannot will anything but that which is useful and salutary to you and to all men; nor can I wish any evil to My creatures. Thus illuminated by the living light of faith, you will perceive that I, your God, have infinitely more knowledge, power, and will to advance your happiness than you have. Therefore seek with all diligence to submit yourself totally to My will; so shall you abide in continual tranquility of spirit, and shall have Me forever with you.

The opening lines anticipate the Westminster Confession that the purpose of life is to love God and enjoy him forever—a subject worthy, says Catherine, of frequent and intensive meditation. Then comes God's definition of himself—the reason, Catherine implies, that we can trust the promise of eternal blessedness: He himself is eternal, sovereign, omnipotent. The remainder of this passage simply expands on these three characteristics of God, demonstrating that each is part and parcel of the other. For example, because God is omnipotent, he is therefore sovereign. His omnipotent wisdom allows him to govern with full knowledge of all events and personalities. There is an implied contrast here with human government and governors, secular and religious, who cannot govern as God can and reminds us of Catherine's concern for human government, of her pleas with secular and religious leaders to govern rightly and mercifully. In fact a subtext of this passage surely is her own work as mediator and her own meditative practices, which gave her the insight and wisdom to mediate political disputes wisely and justly. It is almost as if Catherine writes this for herself, first and foremost, particularly the following: "I, your God, have infinitely more knowledge, power, and will to advance . . . happiness than you have." Knowledge, power, and will were necessary for Catherine's work, which she grounded in the knowledge, power, and will of God. And this passage is a striking contrast to the kind of power that, according to Egan, Catherine's life evidenced: power of or over the body, the only power available to women (then and now).

Catherine of Genoa

With Catherine of Genoa, also called Adorna, we reach the fifteenth century. Catherine was born in 1447 and died sixty-three years later in 1510. Although she was married, she shares with the other Catherine a work among the sick and destitute—Adelaide Procter also comes to mind immediately as another woman devotional writer who did not spare herself in this regard—and a passion for the contemplative life. The list of those whom she influenced within Catholicism reads like a who's who: Francis de Sales, François Fénelon, Cardinal John Henry Newman. More than any other medieval woman mystic Catherine of Genoa had the largest and most direct influence on American Protestants of the nineteenth century. Benedict J. Groeschel, drawing on an unpublished manuscript by John Farino on the nineteenth-century interest in Catherine, discusses her wide-ranging influence. Thomas C. Upham, who taught moral philosophy at Bowdoin College, published a biography of Catherine in 1845. He emphasized Catherine's belief in a second conversion, which was close to the Congregationalist and Methodist doctrine of perfectionism. On the other hand, such evangelical writers as John Morgan, who taught at Oberlin College, interpreted her doctrine as the baptism of the Holy Spirit. Various Protestant magazines like the *Methodist Quarterly Review* or the popular *Hours at Home*, carried articles on Catherine and the work Upham had done on the mystic. Her particular appeal appeared to be her lay status and her dedication to the poor. Catherine apparently also influenced the nascent women's rights movements through Phoebe Palmer.

Although Upham published his study in 1845, a translation of *Life and Doctrine of Catherine of Genoa*, one of three primary sources about Catherine, did not appear until 1896, largely done by the wife of the founder of Brook Farm, Mrs. George Ripley. (The *Life* has long been out of print.) Mary Wilder Tileston could not have read Ripley's translation before publishing *Daily Strength* in 1884; nor would she have been reading a Methodist publication. However, given the numerous excerpts from Upham in both *Daily Strength* and *Joy and Strength*, she knew Upham's work well, and, in fact, the December 15 entry in *Daily Strength* includes a passage about Catherine written by Upham: "The inner life of Catherine of Genoa was characterized, in a remarkable degree, by what may be termed rest, or quietude; which is only another form of expression for true interior peace" (the passage continues for several more lines). So from Upham to Tileston to Cowman—who also cites Upham—such is the devotional genealogy we can trace.

When I read Catherine's words in the October 11 entry in *Daily Strength*, I consider this genealogy, how a fifteenth-century laywoman, mystic, and humanitarian influenced nineteenth-century women and then through them reached out to twentieth-century Lettie Cowman, who desperately needed "true interior peace" while she nursed her dying husband. Recall Mrs. Cowman's reference to reading *Joy and Strength*. She was struggling hard against her own complaining and despairing spirit, something Catherine had no patience with: "He who complains, or thinks he has a right to complain, because he is called in God's Providence to suffer, has something within him which needs to be taken away" (*Daily Strength*, 285). These words could have been written just for Lettie Cowman; she was convinced that God had called her to suffer, convinced that such suffering put her in a place of spiritual privilege and so gave her a right, as we've seen, to complain to God. On the other hand, and perhaps because of Catherine's influence, she recognized her complaints as sinful, which resulted in the paradoxical or contradictory diaries she kept. Catherine wrote

177

for Mrs. Cowman and for all of us who have that same penchant for self-pity and complaint. Catherine had it herself.

Catherine knew privilege and wealth; she was a member of the influential Guelph family, the youngest of five children. Her father, Giacomo Fieschi, had been Viceroy of Naples, and her mother came from another important Genovese family. Through her father she was an indirect descendant of Pope Innocent IV (her ancestor Roberto Fieschi was the pope's brother). Had her father not died when Catherine was fourteen, she might never have written the words about complaint, might never have known how destructive was self-pity. She might have continued happy and pampered and wealthy, and we would have been the poorer. But from pain and disappointment came the great spiritual insights Catherine received when she was twenty-six and that formed the basis of her two great works, *Purgation and Purgatory* and *The Spiritual Dialogue*, neither of which she wrote but were compiled from her teachings.

What happened after her father died? As was customary, Catherine's eldest brother Giacomo became her guardian and for political and financial reasons decided to marry her to a member of one of the Fieschi family's bitterest enemies, the Adorno family. On January 14, 1463, at the age of sixteen, Catherine married Guiliano Adorno; her uncle, a bishop, performed the ceremony. For the next ten years, Catherine's fate follows closely that of so many other privileged women of that time and later; in fact her story resembles that of Madame Guyon and her own unhappy marriage, at least at the beginning. (It is also interesting that Catherine, too, has been linked with the quietist movement.) Catherine suffered from severe depression, possibly triggered by neglect and the dissipated behavior of her husband, who was destroying his fortune on the proverbial three pleasures of all wealthy playboys: wine, women, and song. Despite the social prominence of both the Fieschi and Adorno families, for the first five years of her marriage Catherine refused to take her expected place in Genovese society (thanks largely to her husband's behavior). Only the pleadings of her family caused her to return to a modest and moderate social life for the next five years. However, during Christmas of 1472 she again became acutely depressed and once more retired from social intercourse. It is not hard to imagine the gossip her behavior caused, no doubt far worse than that caused by her husband, his mistress, and his illegitimate child. Husbands, after all, were expected to behave thus; wives were expected to accept such behavior and live as if their husbands were solely devoted to their wives. Today we might admire Catherine's refusal to play aristocratic social games, but her family, clearly, was of another mind.

A few months later, when Catherine visited a priest to make the required Lenten confession, so acute was her depression that she found herself unable to do anything other than kneel and ask for a blessing. It was then that she finally understood how boundless is God's love and how great her misery. We could say that as deep as she knew her misery to be she suddenly knew that God's love was infinitely deeper—and this knowledge led her to renounce the world and sin. This understanding did not come from a vision, at first, like Julian's, but nevertheless had as profound and lasting an effect on Catherine's life and on those around her as had Julian's vision.

Catherine spent the next several days in prayer and contemplation, meditating on her own unworthiness and on the gracious goodness of God to love her regardless of her sin. Then, during her meditations, she saw Christ carrying the cross—what Ettore Vernazza who wrote the *Life* called a vision—and the sight of Christ with the cross moved her to do what she could not do a few days before: confess her sins. Vernazza's description of her conversion, writes Groeschel, "is one of the classic descriptions of an adult conversion"[18] In *The Spiritual Dialogue* Catherine explains that she heard Christ tell her that he had shed his blood to atone for *her* sins: the atonement, a cornerstone of the Protestant Reformation, understood and accepted by Catherine and a reason for her profound influence among Protestants.

She was not, however, a "Protestant," for despite her vision of the atonement she spent the next four years in self-imposed penance and physical mortification, for the first fourteen months wearing a hair shirt, sleeping with thorns in her bed, keeping her eyes on the ground when she walked, spending at least six hours a day in prayer, and refusing her favorite foods. For instance, she loved fruit but refused it, and meat also; she seasoned any tantalizing dish with hepatic oil and a bitter herb to keep her from eating (part two of *The Spiritual Dialogue*, 120). Was she attempting to atone for her sins by exacting such extreme physical hardships from herself? Protestant commentators argue that she wanted only to share Christ's suffering and to recognize in a bodily way the gap between her unworthiness and God's grace, though she herself says that no one can share in Christ's suffering. Perhaps, though, the argument in the face of the severity of her penance remains unconvincing. Her penance had a distinguishing characteristic, however, in that she did not withdraw from the world, as she had before; her conversion, on the contrary, propelled her into the world, for during this period she began what became her lifelong ministry of work with the poor in the slums of Genoa—a work in which her profligate husband eventually joined her.

Guiliano's profligacy led to bankruptcy, a great disgrace in Genoa, but his bankruptcy was soon followed by his conversion, perhaps the result of his failed finances. Catherine and her husband were reconciled, he agreeing to live celibately with her, which they did for the twenty years remaining of his life. The two moved into a small house near the Panmmatone hospital for the sick and indigent of Genoa, where they worked, Guiliano becoming a Franciscan tertiary. Catherine not only worked in the hospital but also in the homes of the poor, cleaning and doing laundry. She became director of the hospital in 1490 and for the next six years she had numerous mystical visions that formed the basis for the teachings published as her books twelve years after she died. Much of what we know about her life comes from *The Spiritual Dialogue;* part two describes her early work with the poor and dying, part three her own final illness and death. It also records the words and commands she believed God gave her. God told her that she would work among the poor and the filthy and that when called to someone's aid, even though she was in prayer, she should immediately leave her room. Yet she was not naturally drawn to the sick, in fact quite the opposite. She found the stench and dirt and oozing sores of the poor so repugnant that she became physically ill. Because dealing with lice, for instance, made her nearly retch, she made herself eat them. To overcome her repulsion of open sores, she sucked the pus from them and rubbed her nose in it to accustom herself to the stench. Such discipline allowed her to work tirelessly when the black plague arrived in Genoa in 1493. Although anyone with means fled the city, she remained behind, and of those who did remain four-fifths died. Clearly she was needed to bring comfort to the dying.

The allegorical debate between Body and Soul in *The Spiritual Dialogue*, though moving at times and sharing themes that we have found in other devotional writers, is also disturbing and uncomfortable and not because of the messy physical descriptions of parts two and three. Rather, Catherine appears to make Body the enemy of Soul, makes Body the location of sin and temptation, Soul the seeker of God's love. Body, however, presents a case to Soul as to why Soul and not Body should bear the responsibility for sin; in this Catherine is perhaps rejecting the prevailing view of the body as inherently tainted. If so, then this, like her understanding of the atonement, is in advance of her time.

A year after her conversion, Catherine started to receive communion every day, an unusual practice in the fifteenth century, and two years later, in 1476, she began to fast during Advent and Lent, a practice she continued until 1499, when Don Cattaneo Marabotto, who became hospital director after her, became her first spiritual advisor. Are her fasts evidence of an eating disorder, as so many feminist scholars like to claim? According to the evidence, Catherine had no trouble eating at other times of the year, nor was she debilitated by her fasts. Not until her final illness did she find it painful to eat; she was, however, able to take communion, provided her lips were first wet with water. Doctors called her illness supernatural but, given the symptoms, it was probably kidney disease (witnesses called her "yellow as saffron," emphasized her extreme thirst, cited her words about feeling on fire, within and without; 143).

The third part of *The Spiritual Dialogue* graphically describes the suffering of the last four months of her life and makes uncomfortable reading for us in the twenty-first century who have sanitized death. Not for us the following words: "At night, at the tenth hour, she complained of the fire and vomited some black clotted blood. There were also black blotches all over her body and in her weakness and suffering she could not recognize any of those who stood around her.

"On the thirteenth, at the twenty-third hour, she vomited a great deal of blood, and that continued all night, so that she was extremely weak" (147). Although the descriptions of illness are dissimilar, the dialogue is reminiscent of the diaries Mrs. Cowman kept as her husband slowly died: the repetitions, the slow passing of time. Catherine's words as reported by the writer strike the same alternation between acute, almost unbearable physical and spiritual suffering, and ecstatic joy. For instance, in a long speech following a particularly difficult night, Catherine talks about her suffering as coming from God, but in the same spirit as the passage used by Tileston,

Catherine refuses to complain, complaining being a sin of the body. Rather, she says:

> All those things that I have undergone
> that seemed intense suffering
> were, because of your will, sweet and consoling. . . .
> in the midst of the pain my body endures,
> without comfort of any kind,
> I still cannot say that I am suffering.
> You make all things bearable,
> and my joy is such that it cannot be imagined or expressed.
>
> Pages 144–45

The writer (scholars do not know and can only speculate about his identity) depicts Catherine during this speech as having her arms stretched out, looking like someone nailed to a cross.

Recall the entries from Mrs. Cowman's journals about the sleepless nights, the despair, the spiritual respite and refreshment, the movement from anguish to joy, the testimony that, like Catherine, Lettie and Charlie Cowman knew that God made "all things bearable." Recall, too, the almost moment-by-moment witness—the dates, the times, the physical and emotional extremity they were in. Even the records of the deaths of Catherine and of Charlie sound remarkably similar—a genre of its own for those considered saints? "Thus in that very hour, in all peace and tranquillity, she gently left this life and went to her sweet love. . . . Until the very last she was clear in mind . . ." (148). Catherine's "happy death" is not unlike Charlie's own, yet Mrs. Cowman could not have read these words as we can and compared them to those she wrote in private to remain private. In the story of death, public and private discourse merge, at least in these two texts, perhaps because the writer, like Mrs. Cowman, did not intend it as a public document but for "some illuminated people" and his "most beloved daughter," the immediate audience (150).

Both Catherine and Mrs. Cowman admit that they have much to complain about and even at one level appear to indulge themselves in complaining, despite their rejection of it as appropriate for creatures living by God's grace. However, Catherine transcends bitterness through daily communion, meditation, and prayer as she focuses on the atonement; Lettie Cowman transcends bitterness in much the same way (excepting communion). Lettie clings to the image of God's stream through arid land, Catherine to the spiritual conversation between body, soul, and God and the belief that "God's grace has allowed the soul/ to participate in His life,/ to become one with Him,/ in the sharing of His goodness" (86).

Teresa of Avila

Her religious name was Teresa of Jesus, though she is generally known by the city she lived in all her life. A participant of the Counter-Reformation, she founded seventeen religious houses (Barefoot Carmelites), the first in San José, during the last twenty years of her life, partly to counteract the growing influence of Calvinism, which she considered detestable if not evil, and partly to return the Carmelite order to its original impulse of poverty and service; the order, as she well knew, had strayed far from its mission and theology. She wrote several books, among them an autobiography, *Book of Her Life;* a handbook for her nuns, *The Way of Perfection;* and her best-known work, *Interior Castle*, an allegorical book of mystical theology. According to Carole Slade in a study of the autobiography, the officers of the Inquisition were Teresa's primary audience for all her work, and her work cannot be understood apart from her confrontations with the Inquisitors.[19] Like Madame Guyon, she lived under suspicion of heresy, in her case because she founded a reformed Carmelite order that rejected standards of social class, privilege, and wealth of the contemporary Carmelites and Castilian society. Taking inspiration from the Franciscans, she insisted on a rejection of the world and a commitment to poverty (she also read Catherine of Siena).

Teresa de Ahumada y Cepeda was born on March 28, 1515, her parents the wealthy Alonso Sánchez de Cepeda and his second wife, Beatriz de Ahumeda (Teresa chose to use her mother's rather than her father's name). Her paternal ancestors were Jews who had converted to Catholicism some time during the late 1470s or 1480s, when persecution of the Jewish population in Castile and Aragon began and culminated in the Edict of Expulsion issued around 1492. The Edict offered Jews a choice: convert or leave. However, no one ever fully trusted those who converted, called *conversos* or new Christians, no matter how long ago or recent their conversion, in part because the Jewish converts lived and worked just as they had before their conversion. This suspicion fell on Teresa's grandfather, Juan Sánchez, who in 1485 was accused by the Inquisitors of Toledo of secretly practicing Judaism. Having been found guilty, Teresa's grandfather and his children were ordered to process to Toledo's churches seven Fridays in a row. Honor was everything in Castilian society, and Sánchez had been humiliated; he therefore left Toledo for Avila, where he became a wealthy merchant of wools and silks. Despite his success both financially and socially, despite his winning a *pleito de hidalguía*, which gave him official status as a gentleman and the privilege not to pay taxes, he and his descendants, including Teresa, could not overcome the stigma of Judaism.[20]

Nevertheless, Don Alfonso and Doña Beatriz, herself from an Old Christian Avilan family of great esteem, raised Teresa and her eleven full and half sisters and brothers as strict, orthodox Catholics. "My father," writes Teresa, "was a man of the most rigid chastity. My mother, too, was a very virtuous woman . . . , she was also particularly chaste" (*The Life of Saint Teresa of Avila*, 66). Her mother, though, had one bad habit, at least according to her husband: She read chivalric romances. Following her mother's example, Teresa became a lifelong reader, first passionate too about chivalric romances, which she criticized in herself, later reading widely in devotional and mystical literature. Her mother died when Teresa was thirteen, but her greatest legacy to her daughter had already been given, even if Teresa had to hide her reading habit from her father, who detested it: "So excessively was I absorbed in it that I believe, unless I had a new book, I was never happy" (69).

Throughout her autobiography we find numerous references to reading, so unusual in the still largely oral culture of the fifteenth century; people didn't begin to read as we think of it until well into the eighteenth century, and certainly few women of her time would have been readers. She uses the book as an image of her own life: "From this point onward, I am speaking of another and a new book—I mean, of another and a new life" (219). Her conversion was in part influenced by reading *The Confessions of St. Augustine:* "It was at this time that I was given the *Confessions* . . . , and I think the Lord must have ordained this, for I did not ask for the book nor had I ever seen it. . . . I used to find a great deal of comfort in reading about the lives of saints who had been sinners before the Lord brought them back to Himself. . . . When I started to read the *Confessions*, I seemed to see myself in them" (117). Teresa discovered what countless other women have discovered—the providential book—and her statement reflects the experience of Tileston and Cowman and their readers. In fact Teresa's words could serve as emblem for all readers of devotional literature, whether daily devotionals or otherwise, and the comfort they bring. But Teresa attests to something else: the very act of composition comforts, which means that the devotional writer receives at least as much comfort as, if not more than, her readers.

Despite her passion for reading, Teresa did not have a passion for writing or think that she had anything worth writing about; in *Book of Her Life* and in *Interior Castle*, she asserts that she was ordered or instructed to write (Slade claims that the Inquisitors issued the orders), much against her own wishes: "I have no learning, nor have I led a good life. . . . I am almost stealing the time for writing, and that with great difficulty, for it hinders me from spinning and I am living in a poor house and have numerous things to do" (123) and later "I myself am fit only to talk" (205). Teresa, particularly concerned that her work remain anonymous, begged her superiors to keep her authorship a secret, and because she trusted that they would do so wrote "quite freely. In any other case, I should have great scruples about writing at all, except to confess my sins. . . . The very thought that I am a woman is enough to make my wings droop" (123). But is this merely an expected disclaimer or an attempt by a skillful rhetorician to win over her audience? Her tone is not droopy-winged, nor her persistence in founding convents despite disapproval the action of a woman with droopy wings. Yet, genuine or disingenuous, who of the women in this study speaks so movingly of her ambivalence toward writing or about the benefits—and the hazards—of reading?

Even though Teresa came to see her early reading as worthless, her habit of reading helped the process of her conversion, and reading continued to be her great solace and guide, as well as the heart of her writing:

> I stopped at the house of this uncle of mine, which, as I have said was on the road, and he gave me a book called *Third Alphabet* which treats of the Prayer of Recollection. During this first year I had been reading good books (I no longer wanted to read any others, for I now realized what harm they had done me) but I did not know how to practise prayer, or how to recollect myself, and so I was delighted with the book and determined to follow that way of prayer with all my might. As by now the Lord had granted me the gift of tears, and I liked reading, I

began to spend periods in solitude, to go frequently to confession and to start upon the way of prayer with this book for my guide.

Page 80

For someone who had not wanted to be a writer, she was a remarkable one—indeed, a remarkably literate woman, which distinguishes her from the other women considered above.

As strongly as she did not want to write, just as strongly did she resist becoming a nun. Because her mother had died and her elder sister had married, her father decided to board his daughter in the local Augustinian convent of our Lady of Grace, where she lived for eighteen months. Although she came to enjoy her life in the convent, she says that "I was still anxious not to be a nun. . . . By the end of my time there I was much more reconciled to being a nun—though not in that house, because of the very virtuous practices which I had come to hear that they observed and which seemed to me altogether excessive" (74). The convent was known as the most rigorous in the city and with only fourteen nuns was the smallest. But even after that admission, she still resisted. Her arguments for the nunnery sound as much like foot-dragging as Jonah's response to God giving him a ticket to Nineveh. "The trials and distresses of being a nun," she writes, "could not be greater than those of purgatory. . . . This decision, then, to enter the religious life seems to have been inspired by servile fear more than by love" (75). Contrast this with what she writes in chapter 11: "I shall now speak of those who are beginning to be the servants of love—for this, I think, is what we become when we resolve to follow in this way of prayer Him Who so greatly loved us" (125). Teresa, though, had a long way to go before love motivated her life.

If the nunnery was to be her fate, let it be a well-heeled and -cared for fate; let it be a mirror of Castilian upper-crust society; let it have none of the disciplinary demands of the Augustinians. She loved the world—and her honor, that unspoken Castilian code—too much. And for wealthy, privileged doñas like herself, there was a convent ready-made to answer.

La Encarnación, one of the largest convents in Avila, served upper-class women, who descended from the "best" men of the city. Many novitiates arrived with servants, even slaves, and kept them after taking orders. They had their own apartments, unlike women without much money, who lived in dormitories. The women, like American Southerners, knew who was who—kin, lineage, social class, and distinction—and they made those distinctions part of their daily society, just as they would have done outside the convent. They called each by her family name (not her religious name), even using the honorific Doña, if applicable. And it was applicable for Teresa, who fully participated in the privileges, the gossip, the cliques, and the intrigues of this oh-so-worldly otherworld, for as I said Castilian honor, not prayer, remained uppermost in Teresa's mind. Honor had two essential ingredients: sexual purity or virginity for unmarried women and ethnic purity, specifically no Jewish or Moorish blood. Unfortunately and much to Teresa's shame, she knew, if others did not, that she failed on both counts; she certainly did not want anyone to find out. According to recent scholars, she was not a virgin when she entered the convent—and she had "tainted" blood.

Jodi Bilinkoff in her fascinating study *The Avila of Saint Teresa* cites a Spanish history of Teresa's convent that provides details of Teresa's "dowry," status, and living conditions.[21] She entered the convent with a bed, mattress, pillows, sheets, blankets, bedspreads, cushions, and a rug—rather like a well-to-do college student of today—plus numerous cloaks, habits, and mantles made of the best wool (her father's wealth was largely based on the wool trade). From her father she received an annual income of about twenty-five fanegas of grain or two hundred gold ducats, enough to live well, enough to pay for Masses to be said for her, enough for a yearly feast to celebrate her patron saint, Joseph: "I used to try to keep his feast with the greatest possible solemnity; but, though my intentions were good, I would observe it with more vanity than spirituality, for I always wanted things to be done very meticulously and well" (*Book of Her Life*, 94). Only rich nuns could afford to sponsor such a yearly feast.

Bilinkoff also describes Teresa's living quarters: two floors, a staircase, a kitchen, an eating area. Only the wealthiest nuns were given two-floor apartments. Hers was large enough to accommodate her youngest sister and other relatives who lived with Teresa. Because of her wit and beauty—she was known as the convent beauty—and her wealth, she attracted a large following; the description of her apartment sounds like that of a Parisian or Spanish salon. Eventually, after Teresa's conversion, she used the meetings to plan her own convent at San José.

Unlike other convents, La Encarnación had no rule about remaining within its walls (a rule of enclosure), and indeed Teresa was as often absent as present—yet another privilege of her wealth and social class. However, her initial absence brought no joy, for, having become seriously ill with a paralyzing disease shortly after taking her vows, she had to leave the convent for two years:

> All my bones seemed to be out of joint and there was a terrible confusion in my head. . . . I was all doubled up, like a ball, and no more able to move arm, foot, hand or head. . . . I could hardly endure the terrible cold fits of quartan ague, from which I suffered and which were very severe. I still had a dreadful distaste for food.
>
> Pages 90–91

Her family and fellow nuns believed that she would die, and once when she went into a coma, her family, thinking she had died, began preparing her for burial by dropping wax on her eyelids. Her illness began in 1538 and continued until 1554, the years during which she slowly moved from a frivolous, insincere nun to a dedicated Christian in full service to God—the years in which she read her uncle's book, Augustine's book, and Catherine of Siena's book. During these years she established her habit of prayer and developed her systematic theology on prayer, which her superiors so wanted her to explain.

When she came to write *Interior Castle*, she approached the task with as much trepidation as any writer—fear that she was inadequate, fear that she would repeat herself, fear that her audience would misunderstand, themes sounded in her other writing but intensified here. Had it not been for her vow of obedience, she would not have written her most complete examination of prayer. Although today the idea of obedience has gone much out of favor, Teresa and the other women considered here as the foremothers of nineteenth- and twentieth-century devotional writers share this value. Each wrote (or dictated) out of obedience, either directly at the command of a religious superior, or at the impulse of God, as she perceived that impulse. They needed to explain and defend their visions, exhort their followers, comfort their friends and family, persuade those in power to repent and reform. Their work is both pastoral and prophetic, both Old Testament and New. It melds domestic and private concerns with public matters. It indeed established the spiritual concerns that later women would explore.

Epilogue

I began with a confession, that I did not read devotional books because I had an innate suspicion of them as being sloppy, anti-intellectual, patronizing to the reader. More than that I mentally accused devotional compilers of theft, of using or misusing the work of other, often great, writers for purposes those writers never intended; of twisting words out of context; of bad reading for nonreaders. I even pitied people who were addicted to these books and who would no more think of starting their day without a page from at least one than they would start their day without a pot of coffee. Daily devotionals, I believed, exert a pernicious, even poisonous influence (some readers of this study may still think this, though I hope I have offered reasons to reconsider). They teach readers to accept what should be resisted, to be satisfied when they should be restless, to practice false serenity in the face of turbulence. I had all these beliefs, as I said, without having myself read any devotionals, without knowing a thing about the compilers.

Did I say beliefs? Better to call them prejudices, and it was because I had these deeply held prejudices that I could not understand how devotionals had attracted so many readers or how two devotionals in particular had had such a long life and such far-reaching influence. I certainly could not understand how women whom I respected read and were inspired by devotionals. But as C. S. Lewis said in what should be a better-known book, *An Experiment in Criticism*, critics should examine how readers read texts before shunting them off to the Salvation Army bin like so many used T-shirts and sweaters. Loyalty to a book looms large in Lewis's theory and rereading a book even larger. On both counts daily devotionals get the gold. There are no more loyal readers than those of daily devotionals, as the publishing records and the testimonies of readers attest. To take but one example: The elderly mother of a friend has for most of her adult life started her day with Mrs. Cowman—fifty or so years of familiarity that has yet to breed contempt.

Once I began to read these devotionals, and read them daily, I realized that I was the anti-intellectual, I the sloppy, patronizing person. I had judged too quickly, leapt to too many conclusions. Now after more than two years with this genre I have some tentative answers to my initial questions: What attracts readers to daily devotionals? What attracts readers to *these* devotionals—the ones by Tileston and Cowman first off but also Julian of Norwich or Catherine of Siena? What kind of genre is this? Throughout this study I have suggested what these answers might be. Here in the final chapter I want to summarize these, make explicit the parallels and similarities among the women discovered, and talk briefly about two contemporary versions of the devotional reader, one secular, one religious—books I found during a search for new devotionals at a local branch of a bookstore chain. The genre is as strong as ever.

What started as suspicion and doubt has ended in admiration, and not grudging admiration, either. When Mary Wilder Tileston and Mrs. Charles E. (Lettie) Cowman sat down to compile their devotionals, they faced a formidable task, one I certainly did not appreciate. The paperwork alone is daunting, the need for a crackerjack memory prodigious, the organizational requirements more complex than making croissants or opening a restaurant. And think of the questions to answer before beginning.

Whom to choose? What to focus on? Which Scripture passages match or complement or gloss which writers? Or the other way around? Should one begin with a passage from Job or 1 Peter or with a poem by Lucy Larcom, a prayer by Catherine of Siena, a piece of theological wisdom from Mother Julian? What should be the balance between familiar and less or unfamiliar authors? Contemporary authors and ancient? Or the balance between prose and poetry? Shorter and longer entries? Then there are the questions about theme(s) and the movement from one theme to the next or between recurring themes. What might readers need or expect for September 11 or February 23? During the winter months should entries focus on themes to lighten the darkness or to emphasize the need for hibernation, rest, separation? Choosing entries for major religious holidays like Christmas might seem easy, but offering fresh thoughts for well-trod holidays is not.

And always a compiler needs to keep her readers in mind, to read for them, to in some ways become the readers the compiler wants or expects and may already be herself. This might mean no more than that a compiler must find her own work a comfort or a challenge before another reader will do so. This too may seem like a simple task, but I am no longer certain it is so because it requires a dual perspective, simultaneously subjective and objective, experiencing the work from within and from without: to say to oneself, "Today I need to read *this*"; to say for one's readers, "Here is what they need to read today." Writing any book now seems a much simpler task than compiling a daily devotional, and to compile one to last more than a hundred years nearly unimaginable, if only because our reading tastes today are so different from those of Tileston's time, or because all reading tastes change with time. I imagine trying to update *Daily Strength*, keeping the same daily Bible passages, but using a contemporary translation like the New Revised Standard or the New International Version and modernizing the other readings. Right away I am stuck, for though I can think of some obvious choices—Henri Nouwen, Flannery O'Connor, C. S. Lewis, Wendell Berry, Gerard Manley Hopkins, Madeleine L'Engle—I wonder whether they are too obvious. I wonder whether they are aphoristic enough for snippets, for sound bites. And how easy to think of men, how hard to think of women, unless I go to the sources of the great devotional literature from the middle of the millennium.

Today I would be able to go all the way back to Hildegard of Bingen, who wrote early in our millennial history, something Mary Wilder Tileston and Lettie Cowman could not do because Hildegard's work has only recently become available. I would also be able to pick choice passages from Margery Kempe, whose work connects so intrinsically with that of Julian of Norwich and the other medievalists I discussed in chapter 6. I doubt that Tileston or Cowman was directly influenced by medieval women and their devotional literature. Certainly the form—the daybook—did not come from them. Nevertheless, they knew and used the most important of them, and they sound the same themes as do women like Julian, Catherine, or Teresa: obedience, humility, submission, serenity, prayer and meditation, joy, worship, transformation of the ordinary into the extraordinary, perseverance, passion, and compassion—all in the midst of suffering. If there is a single thread that connects every woman, from Margery Kempe, Madame Guyon, Adelaide Procter, to Tileston and Cowman, it is suffering—the ordinary, mundane, and uneventful suffering shared by us all. These women had a way of taking seriously the common experiences of suffering so that readers know that their lives have meaning, purpose, and value. All this with few specifics.

We don't hear Cowman give five steps to overcoming grief. We don't hear Tileston advise women about colicky babies or burned vegetables, but when she cites Catherine Adorna on complaining or Madame Guyon on resigning oneself to God, readers supply their own details. It may be one of the most remarkable aspects of this genre that it has the effect of specificity within (or despite) the universality or generality of its language, not unlike the Bible itself, and could well be a central reason for the longevity of the best examples of its kind.

Devotional writers also saw their own work, despite its flaws, as anointed. The work came from God—a compulsion or command he had given them, a service that they and no others could perform. They also made reading a fundamental of the spiritual life, and not just for those in a cloister or working for God full-time. Reading matters for women with jobs and husbands and children. As I said above, writer-compilers work as intermediaries. Passionate about reading, they preserve their reading—and so preserve in particular now-discarded women writers—by casting their reading in the form of a daily collection of meditations. Devotional compilers could thus help others establish the discipline of daily study and meditation that they themselves had learned was so essential for a content-led and contented, and so Christian, life. Accept what comes as sent from God; accept the wisdom of others as gifts from the Spirit.

~

Open any recently published book to the copyright page and read the Library of Congress Cataloging-in-Publication Data for a brief description of the book. It is often better than the summaries the publisher provides either on the dust jacket or on the back of the book. Someone at the Library of Congress has skimmed (or read) the book and decided on its categories—what the book is about—and so how the book should be cataloged and thus where it should be shelved in a library or in a bookstore. Here are the descriptions of the two books I found on my devotional hunt. The first book, in fact, appeared in no less than four bookstores, including my college bookstore, where I bought it, and on all on-line stores. The author has even registered the title as her trademark.

1. Women—Religious life—Meditation.
2. Women—Conduct of life—Meditations.
3. Simplicity.
4. Self-actualization (Psychology).
5. Devotional calendars.

Here is the second:

1. Christian life—Presbyterian authors.
2. Christianity—Terminology.

As we take a closer look at each book, it is important to keep these descriptions and their obvious differences in mind.

On the copyright page of the first book, I note that the initial printing occurred in November 1995; my copy is the fortieth printing. I recall reading somewhere that this book has more than 400,000 copies in print; if so, and in only three to four years, that makes *Simple Abundance: A Daybook of Comfort and Joy* by Sarah Ban Breathnach[1] more astonishingly successful than Tileston's *Daily Strength;* whether it will stay in print as long I cannot predict.

The Library of Congress reader calls the book religious and devotional, a collection of meditations, and so it is, if we secularize the definition of religious and devotional, if we accept the self as the basis of a "religious" view of life, as Breathnach does. *Simple Abundance* is a daily devotional, the meditations written by Breathnach, the citations collected by her. But instead of a passage of Scripture at the head of each devotional we find quotations from a Pond's Cold Cream advertisement that appeared in *Good Housekeeping* in December 1947 (March 11 entry titled "Sending and Receiving Personal Signals"); from Judy Garland (March 23 entry titled "Always Be a First-Rate Version of Yourself"); from Coco Chanel and Geoffrey Beene (April 6 and April 9, "Classic Chic 101: The Color Story" and "Affordable Luxury," respectively); Julia Child (September 11, "Having Your Cake and Eating It, Too"). Breathnach, it appears, has solved the problem I posed for myself—which writers would I include in an up-to-date devotional—but solved it far differently. However, she also includes a few writers favored by Tileston, DeRose, and Cowman, such as Longfellow, Emerson, Thoreau, Ruskin, Elizabeth Barrett and Robert Browning—but no Catherine of Siena, no Julian of Norwich. I don't know that Rosalind Russell or even Anne Tyler or Annie Dillard is sufficient substitute.

Breathnach's quotations and themes indicate the shift in focus from medieval women writers of devotional literature, nineteenth- and early twentieth-century compilers, and today. However, the purpose of the devotional remains the same: to offer advice, hope, support to women who are overwhelmed or despairing. As Breathnach tells readers in her foreword, she

> wanted to write . . . a book that would show me how to reconcile my deepest spiritual, authentic, and creative longings with often-overwhelming and conflicting commitments—to my husband and daughter, invalid mother, work at home, work in the world, siblings, friends, and community. . . . I knew I wasn't the only woman frazzled, depressed, worn to a raveling.

Notice how Breathnach makes herself the first reader of her own work, a characteristic I have suggested all devotionalists share. Notice too that she connects her own experience with that of her audience and that it is specifically female. She goes on a search for what she calls "simple abundance," as if she were an adventurer clearing new territory for those who would follow. And follow they apparently do. *"Simple Abundance,"* she claims, "has enabled me to encounter everyday epiphanies, find the Sacred in the Ordinary, the Mystical in the mundane, fully enter into the sacrament of the present moment." Again, these are the same characteristics I have noted throughout this study about each of the women I've considered and even in the same vocabulary (I wrote most of this before reading Breathnach)—and a mark of what makes a devotional succeed. But Breathnach, unlike the other writers, provides the details of the ordinary. If, as I said, Tileston fails to mention colicky babies, Breathnach is not so reticent:

> . . . everything in my life is significant enough to be a continuous source of reflection, revelation, and reconnection: bad hair, mood swings, car

pools, excruciating deadlines, overdrawn bank accounts, dirty floors, grocery shopping, exhaustion, illness, nothing to wear, unexpected company, even the final twenty-five pounds.

This may be narcissistic, as I think it is, but it nevertheless completely captures the experience of contemporary women, who do not need to supply their own lived details, as with Cowman or Tileston, but who need merely nod in resigned agreement with Breathnach's list.

There are two other striking similarities. Breathnach tells her audience that "reading books changes lives. So does writing them." As I have argued throughout, devotionals succeed only when the writers or compilers have first found comfort in their own work—when writing the work has changed them, just as reading the work will change their audience. This is Breathnach's admission too. The other similarity is the emphasis on reading itself. Read, read, read, she advises, and includes a bibliography of books she has read (not necessarily authors she has cited), and an eclectic bibliography it is, everyone from Christians C. S. Lewis, Madeleine L'Engle, and Brother Lawrence to mystery (food) writer Diane Mott Davis, Margaret Sangster, and Gilda Radner, many of the women little known. She prefaces the bibliography with a quote by John Kieran, "I am a part of all I have read," and then lists the sources for the quotes she uses: "Collecting the pithy and the profound has been an absorbing pastime for over twenty years, and I gather them from . . . books, magazine articles, reviews, newspaper features, radio interviews, television broadcasts, plays, and films." Breathnach makes me wonder how many years Tileston or Cowman spent collecting their "pithy and profound" sayings.

Lest her audience miss the point about reading she includes an entry specifically on that subject, December 15, "Meditation for Women Who Read Too Much," which begins with a quote from Louisa May Alcott and then Virginia Woolf on women who are too fond of books, an impossibility according to Breathnach. No woman, she says, can read too much: "Any time of the day is perfect for reading. Any place. Any excuse. . . . There are no bad side effects from reading too much." If only that were true. Recollect Teresa's words on reading: She knew that some books could be or were bad for readers; she knew that some books were better than others.

Breathnach has provided a twist to the form of the devotional beyond that I've already mentioned. At the end of each month, she gives a list of suggestions for readers to practice the advice the entries offer. What is striking about them—what makes her emphasis so clear—is their focus. For example, every suggestion for February but one focuses on oneself: Write yourself a love letter about yourself, buy yourself a rose, wear perfume, red lipstick, bake yourself some fudge. These are Breathnach's practical suggestions for learning to live with simple abundance; these are the comforts and joys she offers. But by far the most extreme example of self on self must be that in March: "Collect your favorite affirmations," she orders, "and then record them on your tape recorder in your own voice. After you've recorded your tape, lie down on your bed, close your eyes, and play it back using headphones. Do this several times a week. This is a *very* powerful tool for transformation." From what to what she does not say. Imagine it. Listening to your own voice reading your favorite affirmations, which in some sense become affirmations you yourself have composed—and doing so several times a week—thus shutting out everything but the sound of your own voice by using headphones. What, I wonder, happened to husband, ailing mother, children, siblings, community? The Library of Congress reader put it mildly when she noted "self-actualization" as subject of the book.

Nevertheless, there is no doubt that Breathnach has written and compiled a devotional, nor that she follows in the long tradition I have traced; she is interested in preserving what women have said or written. And it cannot be coincidence that previous to writing *Simple Abundance* she wrote two books on Victoriana, or, in her words, books "celebrating nineteenth-century domestic life." She even shares the same motivations, to help readers find comfort and joy. But the source of that comfort and joy—what a difference. The source of Breathnach's rest is the Self, herself, yourself, myself. The source of comfort for Tileston, Cowman, Dyer, DeRose, Margery Kempe, and Teresa is God. They believed that the self was the source of the problem, not the place to look for the solution.

I may have found my first pernicious devotional.

To turn to the other book that I cite above with its Library of Congress description is to return to tradition, medieval tradition, in thought and in form. Kathleen Norris's new book, *Amazing Grace: A Vocabulary of Faith*,[2] is not a daily devotional, though many of the eighty entries begin with a quote; nor were her two previous books *The Cloister Walk* and *Dakota: A Spiritual Geography* daily devotionals, both minor best sellers and critically acclaimed. But devotionals they are.

Norris, an award-winning poet, writes in the spirit and shape of Teresa or the two Catherines—meditations on the language of faith, focusing on those words that before her conversion repelled, confused, or dismayed her, hard words like Christ, salvation, repentance, heresy. Hers is a theology that any woman devotional writer from the middle ages would have recognized, for not only does Norris share the shape and form but also the humility of those writers, asking readers to forgive her shortcomings while entering into the process of faith: "I hope that the reader will indulge me as I try on my scary words for size, as I wiggle them around on my tongue, as I play with them, and let their odd stories unfold."[3] In the first metaphor the words of faith are the clothes Norris wears, in the second the bread or host of communion, in the third a holy toy. Two of the metaphors may be contemporary, but the idea of faith and metaphor hearkens back to the first women who composed devotionals.

Several other characteristics are reminiscent of the medievalists: Norris's adult conversion—she calls her new book "my 'coming out' as a Christian"[4]—and her emphasis on salvation, a subject that merits a brief pause, for it is not a subject that has come up in my discussion, which now surprises me. I do not find it in the list of the themes of women devotionalists; rather my emphasis has been on comfort in the midst of suffering, an emphasis I have supported through examples of the devotionals themselves. However, Norris brings me up short as she describes an encounter with a woman hostile to Christianity: "I realized what troubled me most was her use of the word 'comfort.' . . . I said that I didn't think that it was comfort I was seeking, or comfort that I'd found . . . but salvation."[5] In my search for parallels, I wonder whether I was blind to this theme among the older writers because it so clearly was not a theme of the Victorians—or whether the Victorian devotionals were simply reflecting their own culture. Victorians certainly put comfort high on their list of values, whereas comfort was not something a woman in the twelfth or fourteenth century cared about. Rather, as Norris forces me to reconsider writers like Teresa or Catherine of Siena, I realize that underlying the emphasis on prayer, meditation, and worship is salvation. I also realize that the stories of their vision are salvation stories, just as much as Paul's on the road to Damascus. Because of their salvation, they comforted others, which is a far different thing than seeking comfort for oneself. Nevertheless, I also wonder whether Norris has quite expressed the whole truth—that salvation, once it comes, offers the only comfort possible. As I read and studied Mrs. Cowman, Mary Wilder Tileston, and their foremothers I (perhaps naively) assumed that for them salvation was the prerequisite for the comfort they offered their readers.

If I categorize Norris as medieval—in this study always a positive attribute—how might Norris characterize herself? Would she be comfortable (to use that word again) with my calling her medieval? Given one of her devotional entries, "Medieval," I think she would approve. For Norris, because ours is the narrow age, the medieval period "elastic by comparison,"[6] it annoys her when people use "medieval" as an insult, rather than as a compliment. But she goes further:

> I think we could use more medieval thinking these days, and not less. We might come to value the mindset that could conceive of poetry, religion, medicine, and the natural sciences as discipline having more in common than not, employing much of the same language, metaphor, and imagery.[7]

If she is right, then *Amazing Grace* is a contribution to contemporary medieval thinking, just as it is a contribution to and a continuation of the venerable tradition of women writing devotional literature.

Before I end, I want to take a closer look at just one of Norris's devotionals, as I have looked at each writer, and because each emphasizes prayer I have chosen one of Norris's own devotionals, "Prayer as Mystery" (in which there are three prayers). Not only does this meditation almost more than any other in *Amazing Grace* show her as heir of the earlier medieval writers, it also shows her as heir to the Victorian devotionalists. Prayer, she writes, "is an invitation to recognize holiness, and to utter simple words—'Holy, Holy, Holy'—in response. Attentiveness is all."[8] That is Norris's medieval side, as is her becoming "a prayer partner with a prostitute this year."[9] How like the Catherines. And here is the first link with Tileston and Cowman: "Prayer . . . is ordinary experience lived with gratitude and wonder, a wonder that makes us know the smallness of oneself in an enormous and various universe." And here is a second: She is just as likely to quote a Buddhist as a Benedictine monk, contemporary novelist Andrea Dworkin as medieval writers Margery Kempe or Mechtild of Magdeburg; it is not the *exact* theology that matters.

The worlds of Kathleen Norris and Sarah Ban Breathnach are worlds apart, yet both contribute to the world of devotional literature. Norris stands solidly within the circle of women discussed in these pages; Breathnach stands outside, a secular devotionalist, if that phrase is not contradictory but only oxymoronic. Both writers show that women readers today are no less hungry for daily sustenance and spiritual nurturance than women early in this century, in the mid-nineteenth century, in the sixteenth century, and so on back to the first woman who entered the eclectic, all-encompassing, this- and other-worldly form of literature. Almost the only genre open to women at first, the devotional has become quintessentially women's own. Each woman who enters it reflects those who have written or compiled before her as she shapes and reshapes it for her own vision and time. Thus the devotional, whether in daybook form or following the form of short undated meditations to be read daily, is both timely and timeless, both particular and circumstantial and universal. Above all, as I said in the introduction to chapter 3, the devotional is democratic, by which I mean that it turns no one away. It reflects Christ's words, inviting everyone who is weary to come. All are welcome. None is excluded.

Scholars have ignored this genre, perhaps because of its embarrassing inclusivity. If anyone can read a devotional, if anyone can compose one, wherein lies the skill, even the art? I view this attitude as similar to that which long devalued quilt-making, a domestic and not a fine or high art. And so just as with quilt-making, the devotional is a domestic art. At its best, it lies close to home, indeed even becoming home, a place for pilgrims to rest, recuperate, and then return to the daily demands life makes.

NOTES

Prologue

1. See, for instance, the December 6, 1998, list that includes *Amazing Grace.*

2. *Spiritual Moments with the Great Hymns* (Grand Rapids: Zondervan, 1997), 49.

Chapter 1 Mrs. Charles E. (Lettie) Cowman

1. *God's Revivalist and Bible Advocate* (1 November 1923): 13.

2. Mikiso Hane, *Modern Japan: A Historical Survey* (Boulder, Colo.: Westview Press, 1986), 109.

3. Not only is *Streams* translated into Chinese and more than a dozen other languages, but also Russian. The publishing history of the book and its sequels is striking. P. J. Zondervan purchased the rights from the OMS International in 1965 (Zondervan is now part of HarperCollins). The book had some two million copies in print. In the early 1980s the book was redesigned and a few years later had sold another half million copies. Then in 1997 Zondervan issued an updated edition in contemporary language—gone are the King James and the Revised Standard versions of Scripture, the archaic language. For instance, the publisher also issued a *Streams in the Desert Journal* and two *Streams in the Desert* calendars—an engagement calendar and a wall calendar.

This remarkable publishing history is ignored by the definitive, four-volume *History of Book Publishing in the United States*, written by John Tebbell.

4. On the other side of the world, Krakatau Island in the Malay Archipelago explodes; according to scientists who visit the island nine months later, the only surviving life-form is a spider. Thirty-six thousand people are killed by the resulting tidal waves that browbeat Sumatra and Java. The explosion affects tides and weather as far away as Alaska, and in New Haven and Poughkeepsie fire trucks are called out on false alarms. For five years afterward, the dust veil from the explosion causes lower than normal temperatures worldwide. Iowa no doubt experienced heavier, deeper snowfalls as a result. Yet Lettie Cowman never mentions any of this in her diary; even then she was immune to monumental events of the world, perhaps a reaction to her father's inordinate interest in political and social events.

5. Robert D. Wood, *In These Mortal Hands: The Story of the Oriental Missionary Society, the First Fifty Years* (Greenwood, Ind.: OMS, 1983).

6. Much the same impetus appears to motivate Mrs. Cowman's devotional selections; her books become a story of her own religious, epiclike journey.

7. In this correspondence we find the topical details Mrs. Cowman's publications lack, for instance frequent comments about the great flu epidemic and her hiding out from it.

8. See George W. Marsden's discussion of Brooks in *The Soul of the American University: From Protestant Establishment to Established Nonbelief* (New York: Oxford University Press, 1994), chapter 11, 118–95.

9. Richard Hooker (1554–1600), English writer and theologian, is best known for his *Laws of Ecclesiastical Polity* (1594), which helped determine Anglican theology.

10. Jonathan Edwards (1703–1758), American preacher, theologian, and writer, helped precipitate the Great Awakening.

11. Matthew Henry (1662–1714), an English nonconformist minister, is best known today for his elegantly written devotional commentary, originally called *Exposition of the Old and New Testaments* (1708–1710). Because of his sudden death, his commentary ends with the Book of Acts but was later finished by numerous other ministers and the whole edited by G. Burder and John Hughes in 1811.

12. Theodore Parker (1810–1860), Unitarian minister and lecturer, is best known for his work as an abolitionist. Strongly influenced by Ralph Waldo Emerson's transcendentalism, while in seminary Parker came to doubt the infallibility of the Bible and the exclusive claims of Christianity, which caused him to be shunned by other Unitarians.

13. John R. Stilgoe, *Alongshore* (New Haven: Yale University Press, 1994), 348.

14. David D. Hall, *Worlds of Wonder, Days of Judgment* (New York: Knopf, 1989), 27–28.

15. Lettie B. Cowman (Mrs. Charles E. Cowman), *Charles E. Cowman, Missionary Warrior* (1928; reprint, Grand Rapids: Zondervan, 1967), 376, 412.

16. Wood, *In These Mortal Hands*, 17.

17. Even in this theme Mrs. Cowman contradicts herself. In a later entry based on Exodus 3:1–2, the meditation reads in part that "the vision came in the midst of common toil, and that is where the Lord delights to give His revelations. He seeks a man who is on the ordinary road. . . ." (325). "Common toil" and "the ordinary road" presuppose society.

18. Hall, *Worlds of Wonder, Days of Judgment*, 118.

19. Ibid. Nevertheless, it is true that the Reformation directed Christians toward intense individual piety.

20. Ted Leeson, *The Habit of Rivers: Reflections on Trout Streams and Fly Fishing* (New York: Lyons and Burford, 1994), 25.

21. Marsden, *The Soul of the American University*, 161.

22. Ibid., 79.

Chapter 2 Mary Wilder Tileston

1. *Publishers Weekly* (21 July 1934): 205.

2. Could this have been Tileston's own alma mater? Since her schools are not named, we can only speculate.

3. For the list and the idea about the impact of educational "compilations," I am indebted to Cynthia Ozick's "The Question of Our Speech: The Return to Aural Culture," in *Metaphor and Memory* (New York: Vintage 1991), 146–72.

4. Ibid., 163.

5. Ibid., 164.

6. Ibid., 165.

7. D. J. Enright, *Collected Poems*, as cited in A. S. Byatt, "A Sense of Religion: Enright's God," in *Passions of the Mind* (New York: Vintage, 1993), 175–76.

8. A. S. Byatt, "George Eliot's Essays," in *Passions of the Mind*, 85.

9. Ibid.

10. I have chosen the passages simply by opening the book. I defend this nonscholarly approach because isn't this the way we assume a scrapbook daily devotional comes into being in the first place? A game of darts, a throw of the dice, blindman's buff?

Chapter 3 From Mrs. Cowman's Library

1. *God's Revivalist and Bible Advocate* (1 November 1923): 13.

2. Apologetically, Boston officials eventually erected a statue in M. E. Dyer's honor.

3. Although I am not dismissing the devotionals by men, which she read and were important to her, I am more interested in Mrs. Cowman's matriarchal, not patriarchal, lineage. We already know enough about the men in her

spiritual life, who for the most part are not anonymous or unknown, as is Dyer.

4. After my failed attempt to find information on Dyer through her publisher—not even the Harper archives at Columbia University had any record of Dyer or her book, much to the surprise and chagrin of the librarians—I did not hold out much hope that I would be more successful stalking DeRose, particularly since Stokes had long been out of business. Because I knew that J. B. Lippincott had bought Stokes, and it was still going strong, I called the publishing house to learn that Lippincott was now a publisher of only health and related books. Its trade or popular book division had been sold and all correspondence related to same shipped off. When I found out that Harper now owned Lippincott's né Stokes's stock, I knew nothing would come from a phone call to those same librarians.

Chapter 4 The Company of British Women

1. Most of these efforts have proved short-lived, the books coming into print and just as quickly going out of print, demonstrating how hard it was to be a nineteenth-century woman writer in the late-twentieth century.

2. There are biographies now available for many of these hitherto "unknown" women, and interlibrary loan is an invaluable resource.

3. I would certainly make this claim for shorter works but also for a novel, such as that by Helen Hunt Jackson. Cowman quotes Jackson, whose novel *Ramona* was a best-seller; it is still possible to find a copy or two in many public libraries.

4. John Tebbell, *A History of Book Publishing in the United States*, vol. 2, 271.

5. *Littell's* (27 January 1866): 265.

6. This appears to be the logic John Tebbell used in his *History of Book Publishing in the United States;* excepting Stowe, only Jackson and Tileston merit brief mention, although now-obscure male writers are ubiquitous.

7. Tileston spells her name Adelaide Anne Procter; Cowman, Adelaide Proctor. Tileston is correct.

8. Peter Ackroyd, *Dickens* (New York: Harper Perennial, 1992), 1040.

9. Gill Gregory has recently published *The Life and Poetry of Adelaide Anne Procter: Poetry, Feminism and Fathers* (Brookfield, Vt.: Ashgate Publishing), 1998, evidence of new interest in this little-known woman.

10. According to Charles Dickens, ten years before she assumed the pen name Mary Berwick, a few poems had been included in *The Book of Beauty*.

11. Ackroyd, *Dickens*, 579.

12. Ibid., 590.

13. Ibid.

14. Ibid., 591.

15. Ibid., 739.

16. Ibid.

17. Quoted by Alice C. Kellogg in *Catholic World* 63 (July 1896): 522.

18. Ackroyd, *Dickens*, 743.

19. David Quammen, *The Song of the Dodo: Island Biogeography in an Age of Extinction* (New York: Touchstone, 1996), 248.

20. Wislawa Szymborska, "Conversation with a Stone."

21. In Showalter's volume, I finally find a reference to Rossetti's devotional *Time Flies*, which in the selected bibliography Showalter lists as having been published in London by S.P.C.K., a well-known religious publisher.

22. Elaine Showalter, *Maude/ On Sisterhoods and a Woman's Thoughts about Women* (New York: New York University, 1993).

23. Bob and Shelley Hudson, comps., *Companions for the Soul* (Grand Rapids: Zondervan, 1995).

24. Showalter, *Maude*, xxiv.

25. Ibid.

26. "Miss Muloch," *Littell's Living Age* (12 May 1877): 371.

27. Ibid., 372

28. Ibid., 370.

29. The volume was published in 1860, 1861, 1864, 1866, 1867, 1868, and 1870.

30. *Christian Remembrancer*, vol. 2, 11.

31. *Christian Remembrancer* (spring 1859): 150.

32. *Examiner* (September 1858): 32; reprinted in *Littell's Living Age* (4 September): 735.

33. Ibid. Charles inherited his grandfather's keen eye but also his penchant for regular, good food, as we learn in *Voyage of the Beagle*.

34. *Christian Remembrancer*, 162.

Chapter 5 In American and French Company

1. Lucy Larcom, "A Strip of Blue," *Atlantic Monthly* (1870); subsequently published in *Wild Roses of Cape Ann* (Houghton Mifflin, 1881).

2. Reading the review of her first memoir in *Atlantic Monthly* cited above (that same issue reviews a new collection of poems by Tennyson) and a review in *Outlook* of the sequel triggers so many associations that I must repeat how at home Larcom would have been at the end of the twentieth century (she was born in 1826 and died in 1893). I think of contemporary theories of teaching composition because Larcom had something to say about how to teach writing. I think of the debates about children's reading; she held strong opinions on this issue. I think of Polartec, the success story today of Malden Mills in her hometown of Lowell, and wonder what Larcom would have thought of new man-made fibers. I think of Katherine Paterson's children's novel about the Lowell mill girls of the late nineteenth century. How close did Paterson come to getting it right? Larcom would know. I imagine her satisfaction, know-

ing that her town is still a literary subject, whether in the catalogues of Land's End or in local libraries.

3. *Outlook* (16 February 1895): 270.

4. Quoted in *Outlook*, 270.

5. *Atlantic Monthly* (March 1890): 419.

6. *Outlook*, 270.

7 Shirley Marchalonis, *The Worlds of Lucy Larcom: 1824–1893* (Athens, Ga.: University of Georgia, 1989), 6.

8. Marchalonis, *The Worlds of Lucy Larcom*, 254–55.

9. Ibid., 233.

10. *North American Review* (July 1833): 141.

11. The title comes from a story Child told about Madame de Staël, who, apparently, was called "the first woman in the republic" by Napoleon. When I take the latter volume off the shelf of my college library, I note that I am the first person to check it out. Yet four books down the shelf there is a well-worn volume. Curious, I pull it from the shelf too: Charlotte Perkins Gilman. I wonder, *Why Gilman and not Child?* Could it be, as Shirley Marchalonis speculates about Lucy Larcom, that twentieth-century attitudes toward people of faith had all but "annihilated the men and women who wrote based on belief in a personal God" (*The World of Lucy Larcom*, 6)? Gilman doesn't have that handicap or the handicap of having written from a traditional view of women's roles. Despite the highly nontraditional and unconventional careers of such women as Larcom, Child, Craik, Tileston, Cowman, they wrote for a living, writing under their own names, supporting husbands and other relatives with their poetry and prose. Gilman, therefore, has fit well with the feminist scholarly agenda of dismissing domesticity, the traditional space women occupied. Child, on the other hand, has not.

12. I am also the first person to take the book out of the SUNY (State University of New York) Brockport campus, another small indication of how difficult to change scholarly and literary judgments of nineteenth-century women writers and the habits and tastes of late-twentieth-century readers.

13. *Atlantic Monthly* (December 1882): 841.

14. Carolyn L. Karcher, *The First Woman in the Republic: A Cultural Biography of Lydia Maria Child* (Duke University Press, 1994), 58.

15. Ibid.

16. *North American Review* (July 1833): 844.

17. John Tebbell.

18. See Milton Meltzer's *Tongue of Flame: The Life of Lydia Maria Child*, Bruce Mills's *Cultural Reformations: Lydia Maria Child and the Literature of Reform*, and *Letters from New York: Lydia Maria Francis Child*, edited by Mills.

19. *North American Review*, 142.

20. Applewood Press is bringing some of Child's self-help books back into print.

21. It came out in 1832 and was part of a three-volume work, *The Ladies' Family Library:* volume one on Madame de Staël and Madame Roland and volume two on Lady Russell and Madame Guyon. Volume three is *Biographies of Good Wives*, a provocative title. Madame de Staël was another favorite of devotional compilers.

22. *Atlantic Monthly*, 844.

23. Their names form a lovely litany of married and single women: Mrs. Mary Lowe Dickinson, Miss Hamersley, Mrs. Theodore Irving, Mrs. F. Payson, Mrs. C. D. P. Field, Mrs. J. F. Ruggles, Mrs. I. C. Davis, Miss S. B. Schenck, and Miss G. H. Libby.

24. H. O. McCrillis, *New England Magazine* (January 1907): 550.

25. Ibid.

26. Ibid., 555.

27. Ibid., 563.

28 Ibid.

29. Max O'Rell, "Petticoat Government," *North American Review* (1896): 101.

30. Ibid., 102.

31. Ibid., 103.

32. Ibid.

33. Ibid., 114.

34. Tileston no doubt knew Thomas C. Upham's *Life and Religious Experience of Madame de la Mothe Guyon: Together with Some Account of the Personal History and Religious Opinions of Fénelon, Archbishop of Cambray.* Anne Tavis in *Fits, Trances, and Visions: Experiencing Religion and Explaining Experience from Wesley to James* (Princeton University Press, 1999) describes Upham as an "academic mental philosopher" (122). A Congregational minister, Upham taught at Bowdoin College in Maine. Thanks to Tavis for pointing out Patricia Ward's article "Madame Guyon and Experiential Theology in America" (*Church History* 67, no. 3 [September 1998]: 489–91, 495). Reading it and Tavis's own work has provided yet another view of daily devotionals, which could also be considered an aspect of the "experiential" approach to religion; in fact, I might argue that these daily devotionals can be read as, or constitute, an informal history of the religious practices of American women.

35. Christian Literature Crusade has published a biography, *Madame Jeanne Guyon: Child of Another World*, by Dorothy Gawne Coslet, 1984; and Bethany House has recently released *Madame Guyon* by Jan Johnson (1999) in its Women of Faith series.

36. Jeanne Marie Bouvier de la Motte Guyon, *The Autobiography of Madame Guyon*, trans. Thomas Taylor Allen (New Canaan, Conn.: Keats, 1980). The introduction is by Ruth Bell Graham.

37. Marie-Florine Bruneau, *Women Mystics Confront the Modern World: Marie de l'Incarnation (1599–1672) and Madame Guyon (1648–1717)*, SUNY series in Western Esoteric Traditions (Albany, N.Y.: State University of New York, 1998), 125.

38. Bruneau, *Women Mystics Confront the Modern World*, 129.

39. Ibid., 143.

Chapter 6 A Venerable Devotional Tradition

1. Cathleen Medwick, *Teresa of Avila: The Progress of a Soul* (New York: Knopf, 1999).

2. John Skinner, trans., *The Book of Margery Kempe* (New York: Image Books, Doubleday, 1998), 4.

3. Sheila Upjohn, *All Shall Be Well: Daily Readings from Julian of Norwich* (Harrisburg, Pa.: Morehouse, 1992).

4. Julian of Norwich, *Revelation of Love*, trans. John Skinner (New York: Image Books, Doubleday, 1996).

5. Mary O'Driscoll, *Catherine of Siena: Passion for the Truth, Compassion for Humanity: Selected Spiritual Writings* (New Rochelle, N.Y.: New City Press, 1993), 10. This is one of the best introductions to Catherine and her work; I am indebted to the author for the historical information.

6. Ibid., 11.

7. Ibid., 13.

8. Ibid., 35.

9. Ibid.

10. Ibid, 61–62.

11. Ibid., 82.

12. Ibid., 83.

13. Ibid., 89.

14. Jennifer Egan, "Power Suffering," *New York Times Magazine* (16 May 1999): 108.

15. Sister Suzanne Noffke is preparing a new edition of Catherine's letters in multiple volumes to be published by Cornell University Press.

16. Egan, "Power Suffering," 111.

17. Ibid., 110.

18. *Catherine of Genoa: Purgation and Purgatory the Spiritual Dialogue*, trans. and notes by Serge Hughes, introduction by Benedict J. Groeschel, O.F.M.C.A.P. (Manwah, N.J.: Paulist Press, 1979), 4.

19. Carole Slade, *St. Teresa of Avila: Author of a Heroic Life* (Berkeley: University of California Press, 1995).

20. Until the 1940s Teresa's biographers and scholars suppressed the knowledge of her ancestry, which offers evidence of how long a reach this stigma—and antisemitism—had.

21. Jodi Bilinkoff, *The Avila of Saint Teresa: Religious Reform in a Six-teenth-Century City* (Ithaca: Cornell University Press, 1989).

Epilogue

1. Sarah Ban Breathnach, *Simple Abundance: A Daybook of Comfort and Joy* (New York: Warner Books, 1995).

2. Kathleen Norris, *Amazing Grace: A Vocabulary of Faith* (New York: Riverhead Books, 1998).

3. Ibid., 9.

4. Ibid., 6.

5. Ibid., 4.

6. Ibid., 234.

7. Ibid., 235.

8. Ibid., 350.

9. Ibid., 351.